Sams **Teach Yourself**

Java™

in **24** **Hours**

Sixth Edition

SAMS   800 East 96th Street, Indianapolis, Indiana, 46240 USA

Sams Teach Yourself Java™ in 24 Hours, Sixth Edition

Copyright © 2012 by Sams Publishing

ISBN-13: 978-0-672-33575-4
ISBN-10: 0-672-33575-1

Library of Congress Cataloging-in-Publication Data:

Cadenhead, Rogers.

  Sams teach yourself Java in 24 hours / Rogers Cadenhead.

    p. cm.

  ISBN-13: 978-0-672-33575-4 (pbk.)

  ISBN-10: 0-672-33575-1 (pbk.)

  1. Java (Computer program language) I. Title.

  QA76.73.J38C335 2012

  005.13'3—dc23

                            2011038994

Printed in the United States of America

Third Printing: February 2013

Trademarks

All terms mentioned in this book that are known to be trademarks or service marks have been appropriately capitalized. Sams Publishing cannot attest to the accuracy of this information. Use of a term in this book should not be regarded as affecting the validity of any trademark or service mark.

Warning and Disclaimer

Every effort has been made to make this book as complete and as accurate as possible, but no warranty or fitness is implied. The information provided is on an "as is" basis. The author and the publisher shall have neither liability nor responsibility to any person or entity with respect to any loss or damages arising from the information contained in this book.

Bulk Sales

Sams Publishing offers excellent discounts on this book when ordered in quantity for bulk purchases or special sales. For more information, please contact

  U.S. Corporate and Government Sales
  1-800-382-3419
  corpsales@pearsontechgroup.com

For sales outside the United States, please contact

  International Sales
  international@pearson.com

Acquisitions Editor
Mark Taber

Development Editor
Songlin Qiu

Managing Editor
Sandra Schroeder

Senior Project Editor
Tonya Simpson

Copy Editor
Charlotte Kughen,
The Wordsmithery LLC

Indexer
Larry Sweazy

Proofreader
Apostrophe Editing
Services

Technical Editor
Boris Minkin

Publishing Coordinator
Vanessa Evans

Book Designer
Gary Adair

Compositor
TnT Design, Inc

Contents at a Glance

Table of Contents

About the Author

Rogers Cadenhead is a writer, computer programmer, and web developer who has written more than 20 books on Internet-related topics, including *Sams Teach Yourself Java in 21 Days.* He maintains the Drudge Retort and other websites that receive more than 20 million visits a year. This book's official website is at www.java24hours.com.

Dedication

With this edition of the book, I'd like to break from tradition and cheat my family and friends out of praise, because frankly it's going to their heads. I dedicate this book to James Gosling, Mike Sheridan, Kim Polese, Bill Joy, and the others who launched the first version of this amazing programming language back in 1995. A language I was once surprised to see running on a web page is now running apps on millions of Android phones around the world—a testimonial to the visionary work you did at the late Sun Microsystems. Long may the purple reign!

Acknowledgments

To the folks at Sams—especially Mark Taber, Songlin Qiu, Tonya Simpson, Charlotte Kughen, and Boris Minkin. No author can produce a book like this on his own. Their excellent work will give me plenty to take credit for later.

To my wife, Mary, and my sons, Max, Eli, and Sam. Although our family has not fulfilled my dream of becoming death-defying high-wire trapeze acrobats, I'm the world's proudest husband and father in a household of acrophobics.

Reader Acknowledgments

I'd also like to thank readers who have sent helpful comments about corrections, typos, and suggested improvements to the book. The list includes Brian Converse, Philip B. Copp III, Wallace Edwards, M.B. Ellis, Kevin Foad, Adam Grigsby, Mark Hardy, Kelly Hoke, Donovan Kelorii, Russel Loski, Jason Saredy, Mike Savage, Peter Schrier, Gene Wines, Jim Yates, and others who shall remain nameless because they helped me improve the book before I started this list.

We Want to Hear from You!

As the reader of this book, *you* are our most important critic and commentator. We value your opinion and want to know what we're doing right, what we could do better, what areas you'd like to see us publish in, and any other words of wisdom you're willing to pass our way.

You can email or write me directly to let me know what you did or didn't like about this book—as well as what we can do to make our books stronger.

Please note that I cannot help you with technical problems related to the topic of this book, and that due to the high volume of mail I receive, I might not be able to reply to every message.

When you write, please be sure to include this book's title and author as well as your name and phone or email address. I will carefully review your comments and share them with the author and editors who worked on the book.

E-mail: feedback@samspublishing.com

Mail: Mark Taber
            Executive Editor
            Sams Publishing
            800 East 96th Street
            Indianapolis, IN 46240 USA

Reader Services

Visit our website and register this book at informit.com/register for convenient access to any updates, downloads, or errata that might be available for this book.

Introduction

As the author of computer books, I spend a lot of time lurking in the computer section of bookstores, observing the behavior of readers while I'm pretending to read the latest issue of *In Touch Weekly* magazine.

Because of my research, I've learned that if you have picked up this book and turned to the introduction, I have only 12 more seconds before you put it down and head to the coffee bar for a double-tall-decaf-skim-with-two-shots-of-vanilla-hold-the-whip latte.

So I'll keep this brief: Computer programming with Java is easier than it looks. I'm not supposed to tell you that because thousands of programmers have used their Java skills to get high-paying jobs in software development, web application programming, and mobile app creation. The last thing any programmer wants is for the boss to know that anyone who has persistence and a little free time can learn this language, the most popular programming language in use today. By working your way through each of the one-hour tutorials in *Sams Teach Yourself Java in 24 Hours*, you'll be able to learn Java programming quickly.

Anyone can learn how to write computer programs—even if they can't program a DVR. Java is one of the best programming languages to learn because it's a useful, powerful, modern technology that's embraced by thousands of programmers around the world.

This book is aimed at nonprogrammers, new programmers who hated learning the subject, and experienced programmers who want to quickly get up to speed with Java. It uses Java 7, the version of the language just released.

Java is an enormously popular programming language because of the things it makes possible. You can create programs that feature a graphical user interface, design software that makes the most of the Internet, read XML data, create a game that runs on an Android cell phone, and more.

This book teaches Java programming from the ground up. It introduces the concepts in English instead of jargon with step-by-step examples of working programs you will create. Spend 24 hours with this book and you'll be writing your own Java programs, confident in your ability to use the language and learn more about it. You also will have skills that are becoming increasingly important—such as network computing, graphical user interface design, and object-oriented programming.

These terms might not mean much to you now. In fact, they're probably the kind of thing that makes programming seem intimidating and difficult. However, if you can use a computer to balance your checkbook, or create a photo album on Facebook, you can write computer programs by reading *Sams Teach Yourself Java in 24 Hours*.

At this point, if you would rather have coffee than Java, please reshelve this book with the front cover facing outward on an endcap near a lot of the store's foot traffic.

HOUR 1
Becoming a Programmer

You've probably heard that computer programming is insanely difficult. It requires a degree in computer science, thousands of dollars in computer hardware and software, a keen analytical mind, the patience of Job, and a strong liking for caffeinated drinks.

Aside from the part about caffeine, you heard wrong. Programming is easier than you might think, despite what programmers have been telling people for years to make it easier for us to get high-paying jobs.

This is a great time to learn programming. Countless programming tools are being made available as free downloads from the Web, and thousands of programmers distribute their work under open-source licenses so people can examine how programs are written, correct errors, and contribute improvements. Even in a down economy, many companies are hiring programmers.

Millions of mobile devices use Android, an operating system whose apps are all written in Java. If you have an Android phone, you've been enjoying the work of Java programmers every time you look up a movie, get driving directions, or fire an antagonistic avian at a poorly built fortress of swine.

This book aims to teach Java programming to two kinds of people: the ones who never tried to program before and the ones who tried programming but hated it like Lord Voldemort hates orphaned British schoolchildren. The English language is used as much as possible instead of jargon and obscure acronyms, and all new programming terms are thoroughly explained as they are introduced.

If I've succeeded, you will finish this book with enough programming skills to be a danger to yourself and others. You'll be able to write programs, dive into other programming books with more confidence, and learn new languages more easily. (Programming languages, I mean. This book won't help you master Spanish, French, or Klingon.) You also will have skills with Java, the most widely used programming language on the planet.

WHAT YOU'LL LEARN IN THIS HOUR:

▶ Choosing which programming language to learn first

▶ Using programs to boss your computer around

▶ Discovering how programs work

▶ Fixing program errors

▶ Selecting a Java development tool

▶ Getting ready to write programs

The first hour of this book provides an introduction to programming followed by instructions on how to set up your computer so you can write Java programs.

Choosing a Language

If you're comfortable enough with a computer to prepare a nice-looking résumé, balance a checkbook, or share your vacation photos on Facebook, you can write computer programs.

The key to learning how to program is to start with the right language. The programming language you choose often depends on the tasks you want to accomplish. Each language has strengths and weaknesses. For many years, people learned to program with some form of the BASIC language because the language was created with beginners in mind.

NOTE

The BASIC language was invented in the 1960s to be easy for students and beginners to learn (the B in BASIC stands for *Beginner's*). The downside to using some form of BASIC is that it's easy to fall into sloppy programming habits with the language.

Microsoft Visual Basic has been used to write thousands of sophisticated programs for commercial, business, and personal use. However, programs created with some versions of Visual Basic can be slower than programs written in other languages such as C# and Visual C++. This difference is especially noticeable in programs that use a lot of graphics, such as games.

This book covers the Java programming language, which is offered by Oracle Corporation. Though Java is more difficult to learn than a language such as Visual Basic, it's a good starting place for several reasons. One advantage of learning Java is that you can use it on the Web and mobile phones. Java programs can be used to create Android phone apps, browser games, and other hot areas of software development.

Another important advantage is that Java requires an organized approach for getting programs to work. You must be particular about how you write programs; Java balks when you don't follow its rules.

When you start writing Java programs, you might not see the language's persnickety behavior as an advantage. You might tire of writing a program and having several errors to fix before the program is finished.

In the coming hours, though, you learn about Java's rules and the pitfalls to avoid. The benefit of this extra effort is that the programs you create are more reliable, useful, and error-free.

Java was invented by developer James Gosling as a better way to create computer programs. While working at Sun Microsystems, Gosling was unhappy with the way the C++ programming language was performing on a project, so he created a new language that did the job better. It's a matter of contentious debate whether Java is superior to other programming languages, of course, but the success of the language over the past decade demonstrates the strength of his design. Three billion devices across the world are running Java. More than 1,000 books have been published about the language since its introduction. (This is my sixteenth!)

Regardless of whether Java is the best language, it definitely is a great language to learn. You'll get your first chance to try out Java during Hour 2, "Writing Your First Program."

Learning any programming language makes it much easier to learn subsequent languages. Many languages are similar to each other, so you aren't starting from scratch when you dive into a new one. For instance, many C++ and Smalltalk programmers find it fairly easy to learn Java because Java borrows a lot of ideas from those languages. Similarly, C# adopts many ideas from Java, so it's easier to pick up for Java programmers.

Telling the Computer What to Do

A computer program, also called *software*, is a way to tell a computer what to do. Everything that the computer does, from booting up to shutting down, is done by a program. *Windows 7* is a program; *Call of Duty* is a program; the driver software you installed with your printer is a program; even an email virus is a program.

Computer programs are made up of a list of commands the computer handles in a specific order when the program is run. Each command is called a *statement*.

If your house had its own butler, and you were a high-strung Type-A personality, you could give your servant a detailed set of instructions to follow:

> Dear Mr. Jeeves,
>
> Please take care of these errands for me while I'm out asking Congress for a bailout:
>
> Item 1: Vacuum the living room.
>
> Item 2: Go to the store.
>
> Item 3: Pick up soy sauce, wasabi, and as many California sushi rolls as you can carry.
>
> Item 4: Return home.
>
> Thanks,
>
> Bertie Wooster

NOTE

C++ is mentioned several times this hour, so you might be tripping over the term wondering what it means—and how it's pronounced. C++ is pronounced *C-Plus-Plus*, and it's a programming language developed by Bjarne Stroustrop at Bell Laboratories. C++ is an enhancement of the C programming language, hence the *Plus-Plus* part of the name. Why not just call it C+? The Plus-Plus part is a computer programming joke you'll understand later in this book.

If you tell a butler what to do, there's a certain amount of leeway in how your requests are fulfilled. If California rolls aren't available, Jeeves could bring Boston rolls home instead.

Computers don't do leeway. They follow instructions literally. The programs that you write are followed precisely, one statement at a time.

The following is one of the simplest examples of a computer program, written in BASIC. Take a look at it, but don't worry yet about what each line is supposed to mean.

```
1 PRINT "Shall we play a game?"
2 INPUT A$
```

Translated into English, this program is equivalent to giving a computer the following to-do list:

> Dear personal computer,
>
> Item 1: Display the question, "Shall we play a game?"
>
> Item 2: Give the user a chance to answer the question.
>
> Love,
>
> Snookie Lumps

Each of the lines in the computer program is a statement. A computer handles each statement in a program in a specific order, in the same way that a cook follows a recipe or Mr. Jeeves the butler follows the orders of Bertie Wooster. In BASIC, the line numbers are used to put the statements in the correct order. Other languages such as Java do not use line numbers, favoring different ways to tell the computer how to run a program.

Figure 1.1 shows the sample BASIC program running Joshua Bell's AppleSoft BASIC interpreter. The interpreter runs in a web browser, and you can find it at www.calormen.com/Applesoft.

Because of the way programs operate, it's hard to blame the computer when something goes wrong while your program runs. The computer is just doing exactly what you told it to do. The blame for program errors lies with the programmer. That's the bad news.

The good news is you can't do any permanent harm. No one was harmed during the making of this book, and no computers will be injured as you learn how to program in Java.

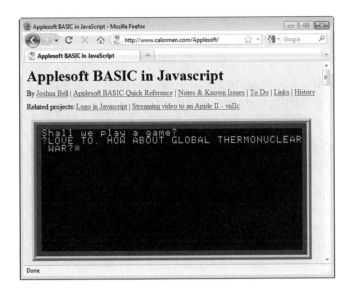

FIGURE 1.1
An example of a BASIC program.

NOTE

The quote "Shall we play a game?" is from the 1983 movie *WarGames*, in which a young computer programmer (Matthew Broderick) saves the world after nearly causing global thermonuclear war. You learn how to do that in *Sams Teach Yourself to Endanger Humankind with Java in 24 Hours*.

How Programs Work

Most computer programs are written in the same way that you write a letter—by typing each statement into a text editor. Some programming tools come with their own editor, and others can be used with any text-editing software.

When you have finished writing a computer program, you save the file to disk. Computer programs often have their own filename extension to indicate what type of file they are. Java programs must have the extension `.java`, as in `Calculator.java`.

To run a program you have saved as a file, you need some help. The kind of help that's needed depends on the programming language you're using. Some languages require an *interpreter* to run their programs. The interpreter is a program that interprets each line of a computer program and tells the computer what to do. Most versions of BASIC are interpreted languages. The advantage of interpreted languages is that they are faster to test. When you are writing a BASIC program, you can try it out immediately, fix errors, and try again. The primary disadvantage is that interpreted languages run slower than other programs.

Other programming languages require a *compiler*. The compiler takes a computer program and translates it into a form that the computer can understand. It also makes the program run as efficiently as possible. The compiled program can be run directly without the need for an interpreter. Compiled

NOTE

If your text editor is a word processing program that has features such as boldface text, font sizes, and other stylistic touches, do not use those features while writing a computer program. Programs should be prepared as text files with no special formatting. Notepad, a word processor that comes with Windows, saves all files as unformatted text. You also can use the vi editor on Linux systems to create text files without formatting.

programs run more quickly than interpreted programs but take more time to test. You have to write your program and compile it before trying it out. If you find an error and fix it, you must compile the program again.

Java is unusual because it requires both a compiler and an interpreter. You learn more about this later as you write Java programs.

When Programs Don't Work

Many new programmers become discouraged when they start to test their programs. Errors appear everywhere. Some of these are *syntax errors*, which are identified by the computer as it looks at the program and becomes confused by what you wrote. Other errors are *logic errors*, which are noticed only by the programmer as the program is being tested (and might be overlooked entirely). Logic errors sneak by the computer unnoticed, but they often cause it to do something unintended.

As you begin writing your own programs, you become well acquainted with errors. They're a natural part of the process. Programming errors are called *bugs*, a term that dates back a century or more to describe errors in technical devices. The process of fixing errors has its own term also: *debugging*. It's no coincidence that so many ways exist to describe programming errors. You get a lot of debugging experience as you learn programming—whether you want it or not.

Choosing a Java Programming Tool

Before you can start writing Java programs, you need Java programming software. Several programs are available for Java, including the Java Development Kit, Eclipse, IntelliJ IDEA, and NetBeans. Whenever Oracle releases a new version of Java, the first tool that supports it is the Java Development Kit (JDK).

To create the programs in this book, you must use version 7 of the JDK or another programming tool that can work in conjunction with it. The JDK is a set of free command-line tools for creating Java software. The JDK lacks a graphical user interface, so if you have never worked in a nongraphical environment such as DOS or Linux, you're going to be shocked—and not in a good way—when you start using the JDK.

Oracle offers another free tool, the NetBeans integrated development environment, that's a much better way to write Java code. NetBeans offers a graphical user interface, source code editor, user interface designer, and project manager. It works in complement to the JDK, running it behind the scenes, so you must have both tools on your system when you begin developing Java programs.

The programs in this book were created with NetBeans, which you can download and install in a bundle with the JDK. You can use other Java tools as long as they support JDK 7.

Installing a Java Development Tool

Every hour of this book ends with a Java programming project you can undertake to enhance your knowledge of the subject matter while it percolates in your brain.

You can't do any of that Java programming if you lack a Java programming tool on your computer.

If you have a programming tool such as NetBeans or the JDK, you can use it to develop the tutorial programs in the next 23 hours. However, you already should have some familiarity with how to use the tool. Learning Java and a complex development tool at the same time can be daunting.

If you don't have a Java development tool, you ought to consider using NetBeans 7, which is freely available from Oracle's website: www.netbeans.org.

To find out how to download and install NetBeans, read Appendix A, "Using the NetBeans Integrated Development Environment."

Summary

During this hour, you were introduced to the concept of programming a computer—giving it a set of instructions that tell it what to do. You also might have downloaded and installed a Java development tool that you will use as you write sample programs throughout the book.

If you are still confused about programs, programming languages, or Java in general, don't sweat. Everything will begin to make sense in the next hour, "Writing Your First Program," which gingerly steps through the process of creating a Java program.

NOTE

Oracle offers comprehensive documentation for the Java language in web page format. You don't need this information to use this book because each topic is discussed fully as it is introduced, but these pages come in handy when you write your own programs.

You can download the entire documentation, but it might be more convenient to browse it as needed from Oracle's website. The most up-to-date Java documentation is available at http://download.oracle.com/javase/7/docs/api.

Q&A

Q. **BASIC? C++? Smalltalk? Java? What are the names of these languages supposed to mean?**

A. BASIC gets its name from an acronym that describes what it is: Beginner's All Symbolic Instruction Code. C++ is a programming language that was created to be an improvement on the C language, which itself was an improvement of the B programming language. Smalltalk is an innovative object-oriented language developed in the 1970s that had numerous ideas adopted by Java.

Java goes against the tradition of naming a language with an acronym or other meaningful term. It's just the name that Java's developers liked the best, beating out WebRunner, Silk, Ruby, and others. When I create my own programming language, it will be named Salsa. Everybody loves salsa.

Q. **Why are interpreted languages slower than compiled ones?**

A. They're slower for the same reason that a person interpreting a live speech in a foreign language is slower than a translator interpreting a printed speech. The live interpreter has to think about each statement that's being made as it happens, while the other interpreter can work on the speech as a whole and take shortcuts to speed up the process. Compiled languages can be much faster than interpreted languages because they do things to make the program run more efficiently.

Q. **Do you answer questions only about Java?**

A. Not at all. Ask me anything.

Q. **Okay, what is the lowest score ever given on *Dancing with the Stars*?**

A. The worst dance by a celebrity contestant on the hit ABC show was performed by the rapper Master P during the second season in 2006. His Paso Doble with professional dancer Ashly DelGrosso scored a lowest-ever 8. Judges Len Goodman and Bruno Tonioli scored it a 2 and judge Carrie Ann Inaba a 4.

Tonioli's take: "It was a nightmare. ... It looked like a child on the mall lost looking for his mother."

Goodman: "I know viewers think they're being kind by bringing you back. They're not. They're being cruel—to Ashly, to the judges."

Inaba: "I actually thought that that was your best dancing."

Master P trained only 20 hours for the show, compared to 130 for the other contestants at that point in the season. He also refused to wear dancing shoes and performed in basketball sneakers. The dance was his last before being voted off.

The dance can be seen on YouTube, where one commenter writes, "Thumbs up if you're watching this just to see the 2 paddle."

Workshop

Quiz

Test your knowledge of the material covered in this hour by answering the following questions.

1. Which of the following is not a reason that people think computer programming is painfully difficult?

    A. Programmers spread that rumor to improve their employment prospects.

    B. Jargon and acronyms are all over the place.

    C. People who find programming too difficult are eligible for a government bailout.

2. What kind of tool runs a computer program by figuring out one line at a time?

    A. A slow tool

    B. An interpreter

    C. A compiler

3. Why did James Gosling hole up in his office and create Java?

    A. He was unhappy with the language he was using on a project.

    B. His rock band wasn't getting any gigs.

    C. When you can't visit YouTube at work, the Internet is pretty dull.

Answers

1. **C.** Computer book authors didn't get a bailout either.

2. **B.** Compilers figure out the instructions beforehand so that the program can run faster.

3. **A.** He was frustrated with C++. Back in 1991 when Gosling created Java, people thought that YouTube was the place that held YouToothpaste.

Activities

If you'd like to better introduce yourself to the subjects of Java and computer programming, do the following activities:

- ▶ Visit Oracle's Java site at www.oracle.com/technetwork/topics/ newtojava, and read some of the Get Started with Java Technology pages.

- ▶ Using English sentences instead of a programming language, write a set of instructions to add 10 to a number selected by a user, and then multiply the result by 5. Break the instructions into as many short one-sentence lines as you can.

To see solutions to the activities at the end of each hour, visit the book's website at www.java24hours.com.

HOUR 2
Writing Your First Program

As you learned during Hour 1, "Becoming a Programmer," a computer program is a set of instructions that tells a computer what to do. These instructions are given to a computer using a programming language.

During this hour, you create your first Java program by entering it into a text editor. When that's done, you save the program, compile it, and test it out.

What You Need to Write Programs

As explained in Hour 1, to create Java programs you must have a development tool that supports the Java Development Kit (JDK) such as the NetBeans integrated development environment (IDE). You need a tool that can compile and run Java programs and a text editor to write those programs.

With most programming languages, computer programs are written by entering text into a text editor (also called a *source code editor*). Some programming languages come with their own editor. Oracle's development tool NetBeans includes its own editor for writing Java programs.

Java programs are simple text files without any special formatting such as centered text or boldface text. The NetBeans source code editor functions like a simple text editor with an extremely useful enhancement. Color text highlights identify different elements of the language as you type. NetBeans also indents lines properly and provides helpful programming documentation.

Because Java programs are text files, you can open and edit them with any text editor. You could write a Java program with NetBeans, open it in Windows Notepad and make changes, and open it again later in NetBeans without any problems.

WHAT YOU'LL LEARN IN THIS HOUR:

▶ Entering a program into a text editor

▶ Naming a Java program with the class statement

▶ Organizing a program with bracket marks

▶ Storing information in a variable

▶ Displaying the information stored in a variable

▶ Saving, compiling, and running a program

▶ Fixing errors

Creating the Saluton Program

The first Java program that you create is an application that displays a traditional greeting from the world of computer science: "Saluton mondo!"

To prepare for the first programming project in NetBeans, if you haven't already done so, create a new project called Java24 by following these steps:

1. Choose the menu command File, New Project.

2. Choose the project category Java and the project type Java Application, and then click Next.

3. Enter Java24 as the project's name. You see the error message "Project folder already exists and is not empty" if you created this project already.

4. Deselect the Create Main Class checkbox.

5. Click Finish.

The Java24 project is created in its own folder. You can use this project for all Java programs you write as you progress through this book.

Beginning the Program

NetBeans groups related programs together into a project. If you don't have the Java24 project open, here's how to retrieve it:

▶ Choose File, Open Project.

▶ Find and select the NetBeansProjects folder (if necessary).

▶ Choose Java24 and click Open Project.

The Java24 project appears in the Projects Pane.

To add a new Java program to the current project, choose File, New File. The New File Wizard opens, as shown in Figure 2.1.

The Categories pane lists the different kinds of Java programs you can create. Click the Java folder in this pane to see the file types that belong to this category. For this first project, choose the Empty Java File type, and click Next.

In the Class Name field, enter Saluton and click Finish to create the new Java program. An empty file named Saluton.java opens in the source code editor.

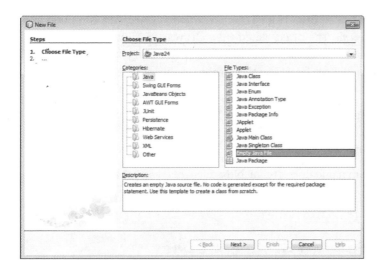

FIGURE 2.1
The New File Wizard.

Using the source editor, begin your Java programming career by entering each line from Listing 2.1. These statements are called the program's source code.

LISTING 2.1   The Saluton Program

main command of program

```
1: public class Saluton {
2:     public static void main(String[] arguments) {
3:         // My first Java program goes here
4:     }
5: }
```

CAUTION

Don't enter the line number and colon at the beginning of each line—these are used in this book to reference specific line numbers.

Make sure to capitalize everything exactly as shown, and use your spacebar or Tab key to insert the blank spaces in front of Lines 2–4. When you're done, choose File, Save or click the Save All Files button to save the file.

At this point, Saluton.java contains the bare-bones form of a Java program. You will create several programs that start exactly like this one, except for the word Saluton on Line 1. This word represents the name of your program and changes with each program you write. Line 3 also should make sense—it's a sentence in actual English. The rest is probably new to you.

The class Statement

The first line of the program is the following:

writing a class

```
class Saluton {
```

Translated into English, this line means, "Computer, give my Java program the name Saluton."

As you might recall from Hour 1, each instruction you give a computer is called a *statement*. The `class` statement is the way you give your computer program a name. It's also used to determine other things about the program, as you will see later. The significance of the term `class` is that Java programs also are called *classes*.

In this example, the program name `Saluton` matches the document's file name, `Saluton.java`. A Java program must have a name that matches the first part of its filename and should be capitalized the same way.

If the program name doesn't match the filename, you get an error when you try to compile some Java programs, depending on how the `class` statement is being used to configure the program.

What the `main` Statement Does

The next line of the program is the following:

```
public static void main(String[] arguments) {
```

This line tells the computer, "The main part of the program begins here." Java programs are organized into different sections, so there needs to be a way to identify the part of a program that is handled first.

The `main` statement is the entry point to most Java programs. The most common exceptions are *applets*, programs that are run as part of a web page, and *servlets*, programs run by a web server. Most programs you write during upcoming hours use `main` as their starting point.

ending commands

Those Squiggly Bracket Marks

In the `Saluton` program, every line except Line 3 contains a squiggly bracket mark of some kind—either a { or a }. These brackets are a way to group parts of your program (in the same way that parentheses are used in a sentence to group words). Everything between the opening bracket { and the closing bracket } is part of the same group.

These groupings are called *blocks*. In Listing 2.1, the opening bracket on Line 1 is associated with the closing bracket on Line 5, which makes your entire program a block. You use brackets in this way to show the beginning and end of your programs.

Blocks can be located inside other blocks (just as parentheses are used in this sentence (and a second set is used here)). The `Saluton` program has brackets on Line 2 and Line 4 that establish another block. This block begins with the main statement. Everything inside the main statement's block is a command for the computer to handle when the program is run.

The following statement is the only thing located inside the block:

```
// My first Java program goes here
```

comments

This line is a placeholder. The `//` at the beginning of the line tells the computer to ignore this line because it was put in the program solely for the benefit of humans who are looking at the source code. Lines that serve this purpose are called *comments*.

Right now, you have written a complete Java program. It can be compiled, but if you run it nothing happens. The reason why is that you haven't told the computer to do anything yet. The main statement block contains only a single comment, which is ignored. You must add some statements inside the opening and closing brackets of the main block.

NOTE

NetBeans can help you figure out where a block begins and ends. Click one of the brackets in the source code of the Saluton program. The bracket you clicked turns yellow along with its corresponding bracket. The Java statements enclosed within these yellow brackets comprise a block.

Storing Information in a Variable

In the programs you write, you need a place to store information for a brief period of time. You can do this by using a *variable*, a storage place that can hold information such as integers, floating-point numbers, true-false values, characters, and lines of text. The information stored in a variable can change, which is how it gets the name variable.

In Saluton.java file, replace Line 3 with the following:

```
String greeting = "Saluton mondo!";
```

variable name   *how to write text*

used for text variables

This statement tells the computer to store the line of text "Saluton mondo!" in a variable called greeting.

In a Java program, you must tell the computer what type of information a variable will hold. In this program, greeting is a *string*—a line of text that can include letters, numbers, punctuation, and other characters. Putting String in the statement sets up the variable to hold string values.

When you enter this statement into the program, a semicolon must be included at the end of the line. Semicolons end each statement in your Java programs. They're like periods at the end of a sentence. The computer uses them to determine when one statement ends and the next one begins.

Putting only one statement on each line makes a program more understandable (for us humans).

Displaying the Contents of a Variable

If you run the program at this point, it wouldn't display anything. The command to store a line of text in the greeting variable occurs behind the scenes. To make the computer show that it is doing something, you can display the contents of that variable.

Insert another blank line in the Saluton program after the String greeting = "Saluton mondo!" statement. Use that empty space to enter the following statement:

```
System.out.println(greeting);
```

printing variables to console

way to print things to console

This statement tells the computer to display the value stored in the greet-ing variable. The System.out.println statement tells the computer to display a line on the system output device—your monitor.

Saving the Finished Product

Your program should now resemble Listing 2.2, although you might have used slightly different spacing in Lines 3–4. Make any corrections that are needed and save the file (by choosing File, Save or the Save All Files button).

LISTING 2.2   The Finished Version of the Saluton Program

```
1: class Saluton {
2:     public static void main(String[] args) {
3:         String greeting = "Saluton mondo!";
4:         System.out.println(greeting);
5:     }
6: }
```

way to end lines

When the computer runs this program, it runs each of the statements in the main statement block on Lines 3 and 4. Listing 2.3 shows what the program would look like if it were written in the English language instead of Java.

LISTING 2.3   A Line-by-Line Breakdown of the Saluton Program

```
1: The Saluton program begins here:
2:     The main part of the program begins here:
3:         Store the text "Saluton mondo!" in a String variable named
greeting
4:         Display the contents of the variable greeting
5:     The main part of the program ends here.
6: The Saluton program ends here.
```

Compiling the Program into a Class File

Before you can run a Java program, you must compile it. When you compile a program, the instructions given to the computer in the program are converted into a form the computer can better understand.

NetBeans compiles programs automatically as they are saved. If you typed everything as shown in Listing 2.2, the program compiles successfully.

A compiled version of the program, a new file called `Saluton.class`, is created. All Java programs are compiled into class files, which are given the `.class` file extension. A Java program can be made up of several classes that work together, but in a simple program such as `Saluton` only one class is needed.

Fixing Errors

As you compose a program .in the NetBeans source editor, errors are flagged with a red alert icon to the left of the editor pane, as shown in Figure 2.2.

Error Icon

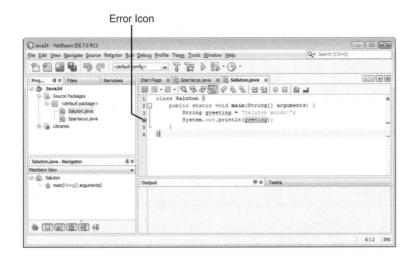

NOTE
The Java compiler speaks up only when there's an error to complain about. If you compile a program successfully without any errors, nothing happens in response. This is a little anticlimactic. When I was starting out as a Java programmer, I was hoping successful compilation would be met with a grand flourish of celebratory horns.

FIGURE 2.2
Spotting errors in the Source Editor.

The icon appears on the line that triggered the error. You can click this icon to display an error message that explains the compiler error with these details:

▶ The name of the Java program

▶ The type of error

▶ The line where the error was found

TIP

This book's official website www.java24hours.com includes source files for all programs you create. If you can't find any typos or other reasons for errors in the Saluton program but there are still errors, go to the book's website and download Saluton.java from the Hour 2 page. Try to run that file instead.

Here's an example of an error message you might see when compiling the Saluton program:

```
cannot find symbol.
symbol  : variable greeting
location: class Saluton
```

The error is the first line of the message: "cannot find symbol." These messages often can be confusing to new programmers. When the error message doesn't make sense to you, don't spend much time trying to figure it out. Instead, take a look at the line where the error occurred and look for the most obvious causes.

For instance, can you determine what's wrong with the following statement?

```
System.out.println(greeting);
```

The error is a typo in the variable name, which should be greeting instead of greting. (Add this typo in NetBeans to see what happens.)

If you get error messages when creating the Saluton program, double-check that your program matches Listing 2.2, and correct any differences you find. Make sure that everything is capitalized correctly and all punctuation marks such as {, }, and ; are included.

Often, a close look at the line identified by the error message is enough to reveal the error (or errors) that need to be fixed.

Running a Java Program

NOTE

You might be asking yourself why "Saluton mondo!" is a traditional greeting. The phrase means "Hello world!" in Esperanto, an artificial language created by Ludwig Zamenhof in 1887 to facilitate international communication. It's only a traditional greeting in the sense that I'm trying to start that tradition.

To see whether the Saluton program. does what you want, run the class with the Java Virtual Machine (JVM), the interpreter that runs all Java code. In NetBeans, choose the menu command Run, Run File. An output pane opens below the source editor. In this pane, if there were no errors, the program displays the output, as shown in Figure 2.3.

If you see the text "Saluton Mondo!" you have just written your first working Java program! Your computer has just greeted the world—a tradition in the computer programming field that's as important to many of us as caffeine, short-sleeved dress shirts, and *Call of Duty*.

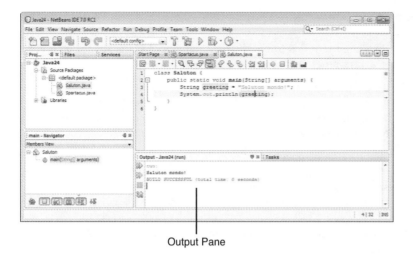

FIGURE 2.3
Running your first Java program.

Output Pane

Summary

During this hour, you got your first chance to create a Java program using the NetBeans IDE. You learned that to develop a Java program you need to complete these four basic steps:

1. Write the program with a text editor.

2. Compile the program into a class file.

3. Tell the Java Virtual Machine to run the class.

4. Call your mother.

Along the way, you were introduced to some basic computer programming concepts such as compilers, interpreters, blocks, statements, and variables. These will become clearer to you in successive hours. As long as you got the Saluton program to work during this hour, you're ready to proceed.

(The fourth step has nothing to do with Java programming. It's just something my mother suggested I put in the book.)

Q&A

Q. **How important is it to put the right number of blank spaces on a line in a Java program?**

A. It's completely unimportant. Spacing is strictly for the benefit of people looking at a computer program—the Java compiler couldn't care less. You could have written the `Saluton` program without using blank spaces or used the Tab key to indent lines, and it would compile successfully.

Although the number of spaces in front of lines isn't important, you should use consistent spacing in your Java programs. Why? Because spacing makes it easier for you to see how a program is organized and to which programming block a statement belongs.

Q. **A Java program has been described as a class and as a group of classes. Which is it?**

A. Both. The simple Java programs you create during the next few hours are compiled into a single file with the extension `.class`. You can run these with the Java Virtual Machine. Java programs also can be made up of a set of classes that work together. This topic is fully explored during Hour 10, "Creating Your First Object."

Q. **If semicolons are needed at the end of each statement, why does the comment line** `// My first Java program goes here` **not end with a semicolon?**

A. Comments are completely ignored by the compiler. If you put `//` on a line in your program, this tells the Java compiler to ignore everything to the right of the `//` on that line. The following example shows a comment on the same line as a statement:

```
System.out.println(greeting); // hello, world!
```

Q. **I couldn't find any errors in the line where the compiler noted an error. What can I do?**

A. The line number displayed with the error message isn't always the place where an error needs to be fixed. Examine the statements that are directly above the error message to see whether you can spot any typos or other bugs. The error usually is within the same programming block.

Q. **How can I visit Antarctica?**

A. If you're not willing to become a scientific researcher or a support staffer such as a cook, an electrician, or a doctor, you can become one of the 10,000 people who visit the frozen continent annually as tourists.

Flyovers are available from Australia, New Zealand, and South America and cost around $1,000 per person.

Several cruise ships visit for a trip lasting from 10 days to three weeks, the most expensive of which is around $25,000. Some cruises offer a chance to kayak or hike among penguins, visit icebergs, and even camp overnight.

The Polar Cruises website at www.polarcruises.com provides more information for prospective Antarctica visitors.

The British Antarctic Survey offers a piece of advice for visitors: "Do not walk onto glaciers or large snowfields unless properly trained."

Workshop

Test your knowledge of the material covered in this hour by answering the following questions.

Quiz

1. When you compile a Java program, what are you doing?

    A. Saving it to a disk

    B. Converting it into a form the computer can better understand

    C. Adding it to your program collection

2. What is a variable?

    A. Something that wobbles but doesn't fall down

    B. Text in a program that the compiler ignores

    C. A place to store information in a program

3. What is the process of fixing errors called?

    A. Defrosting

    B. Debugging

    C. Decomposing

Answers

1. **B.** Compiling a program converts a `.java` file into a `.class` file or a set of `.class` files.

2. **C.** Variables are one place to store information; later you learn about others such as arrays and constants. Weebles wobble but they don't fall down, and comments are text in a program that the compiler ignores.

3. **B.** Because errors in a computer program are called *bugs*, fixing those errors is called *debugging*. Some programming tools come with a tool called a debugger that helps you fix errors.

Activities

If you'd like to explore the topics covered in this hour a little more fully, try the following activities:

▶ You can translate the English phrase "Hello world!" into other languages using Yahoo's Babelfish at http://babelfish.yahoo.com. Write a program that enables your computer to greet the world in a language such as French, Italian, or Portuguese.

▶ Go back to the `Saluton` program and add one or two errors. For example, take a semicolon off the end of a line or change the text `println` on one line to `print1n` (with a number 1 instead of the letter L). Save the program and try to compile it. Compare the error messages you get to the errors you caused.

To see solutions to these activities, visit the book's website at www.java24hours.com.

HOUR 3
Vacationing in Java

Before you venture further into Java programming, it's worthwhile to learn more about the language and see what programmers are doing with it today. Though Java has outgrown its origins as a language focused on web browser programs, you can still find some interesting examples of how Java is used on the Web.

During this hour, we take a look at sites that feature Java programs and talk about the history and development of the language.

To go on this vacation, you need a web browser that has been set up to run Java programs.

Load your browser of choice, put on your best batik shirt, and get ready to take a vacation. You won't be leaving your house, and you won't experience the simpler pleasures of tourism, such as reckless cab drivers, exotic food, exotic locals, exotic locals with food, and so on. Look on the bright side though: no traveler's check hassles, no passports, and no Montezuma's revenge.

First Stop: Oracle

The Java vacation begins at www.java.com, a site created by Oracle, the company that owns the Java language.

A Java program that runs as part of a web page is called an *applet*. Applets are placed on pages like other elements of a page. A markup language called HTML defines where the program should be displayed, how big it is, and what the program does when it runs. Java also enhances the Web in two other ways: Desktop programs written in Java can be launched from a web browser, and Java servlets are run by web servers to deliver web applications.

Oracle's Java division leads the development of the Java language and related software. The Java in Action section of Java.com showcases how Java is being used on websites, Android phones, and other platforms. Millions of devices run programs written with Java. Figure 3.1 shows RuneScape, a massively multiplayer online game powered by Java. You can play the game for free by using any web browser to visit www.runescape.com.

FIGURE 3.1
The Java-powered online game
RuneScape.

Java.com provides a place to learn about how Java is being used. Oracle also offers a more technically oriented website for Java programmers at http://www.oracle.com/technetwork/java. This site is the place to find the latest released versions of NetBeans and the Java Development Kit along with other programming resources.

A Brief History of Java

Bill Joy, one of the executives at Sun Microsystems when the company created Java, called the language "the end result of 15 years of work to produce a better, more reliable way to write computer programs." Java's creation was a little more complicated than that.

Java was developed in 1990 by James Gosling as a language that would serve as the brains for smart appliances (interactive TVs, omniscient ovens, SkyNet military satellites that enslave mankind, and so on). Gosling was unhappy with the results he was getting by writing programs with a programming language called C++. In a burst of inspiration, he holed up in his office and wrote a new language to better suit his needs.

Gosling named his new language Oak after a tree he could see from his office window. The language was part of his company's strategy to make a fortune when interactive TV became a multimillion-dollar industry. That still hasn't happened today (though Netflix, TiVo, and others are making a game attempt), but something completely different took place for Gosling's new language. Just as Oak was about to be scrapped, the Web became popular.

In a fortuitous circumstance, many qualities that made Gosling's language good on its appliance project made it suitable for adaptation to the Web. His team devised a way for programs to be run safely from web pages and a catchy new name was chosen to accompany the language's new purpose: Java.

Although Java can be used for many other things, the Web provided the showcase it needed. When the language rose to prominence, you had to be in solitary confinement or a long-term orbital mission to avoid hearing about it.

There have been eight major releases of the Java language:

> ▶ **Fall 1995:** Java 1.0—The original release

> ▶ **Spring 1997:** Java 1.1—An upgrade that improved support for graphical user interfaces

> ▶ **Summer 1998:** Java 2 version 1.2—A huge expansion, making the language a general-purpose programming language

> ▶ **Fall 2000:** Java 2 version 1.3—A release for enhanced multimedia

> ▶ **Spring 2002:** Java 2 version 1.4—An upgrade of Internet support, XML capabilities, and text processing

> ▶ **Spring 2004:** Java 2 version 5—A release offering greater reliability and automatic data conversion

> ▶ **Winter 2006:** Java 6—A upgrade with a built-in database and web services support

> ▶ **Summer 2011:** Java 7—The current release, which adds new core language improvements, memory management improvements, and the Nimbus graphical user interface

NOTE

You might have heard that Java is an acronym that stands for Just Another Vague Acronym. You also might have heard that it was named for the Gosling's love of coffee. The story behind Java's naming contains no secret messages or declarations of liquid love. Java was chosen as the name for the same reason that comedian Jerry Seinfeld likes to say the word salsa: It sounds cool.

Going to School with Java

The Web includes numerous resources for educators and schoolchildren. Because Java programs can offer a more interactive experience than standard web pages, some programmers have used the language to write learning programs for the Internet.

For one such example, visit http://www.cs.ubc.ca/~van/sssjava to access a ski jump simulator created by Michiel van de Panne, a computer science professor at the University of British Columbia. The program uses Java to demonstrate physics-based animation as a skier tries several different slopes and jumps. The motion of the skier is controlled by moving a mouse one of eight directions, each of which affects the success of a jump. Figure 3.2 shows one run of the program right before my virtual skier met a gruesome end.

FIGURE 3.2
A ski-jump simulator can be experienced interactively on the Web using a Java program.

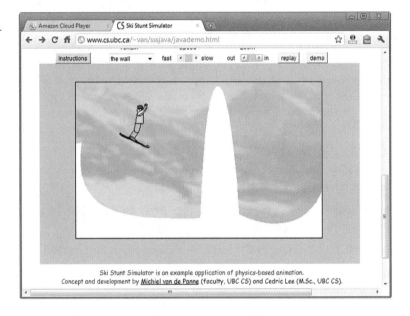

Numerous educational programs are available for many different operating systems, but one thing that makes this program stand out is its availability. The simulator is run directly from a web page. No special installation is needed, and, unlike most desktop software, it isn't limited to a particular operating system. You can run Java programs on any computer that has a Java Virtual Machine (JVM).

The JVM loaded by a browser is the same one used to run the `Saluton` program during Hour 2, "Writing Your First Program." A browser's JVM only can run Java programs that are set up to run on web pages and cannot handle programs set up to run elsewhere, such as in a file folder.

The first browsers to support Java included a built-in JVM. Today, browsers support Java by relying on the Java Plug-in, a JVM that works as a browser enhancement.

TIP
Oracle includes the Java Plug-in with the JDK and other products, so it might already be installed on your computer. To check if Java is installed, visit the www.java.com website. The "Do I Have Java?" link can detect the presence of Java.

A Java program, such as the ski-jump simulator, does not have to be written for a specific operating system. Because operating systems like Windows also are called platforms, this advantage is called *platform independence*. Java was created to work on multiple systems. Originally, Java's developers believed it needed to be multiplatform because it would be used on a variety of appliances and other electronic devices.

Users can run the programs you write with Java on a variety of systems without requiring any extra work from you. Under the right circumstances, Java can remove the need to create specific versions of a program for different operating systems and devices.

Lunch in JavaWorld

After working up an appetite on the slopes, take a lunch break with *JavaWorld*, an online magazine for Java programmers. Visit www.javaworld.com.

JavaWorld offers how-to articles, news stories, and research centers on hot areas of Java development. One of the advantages of the publication's web format is that it can display functional Java programs in conjunction with articles. Figure 3.3 shows a Java poetry magnet board that accompanies a tutorial explaining how it is written.

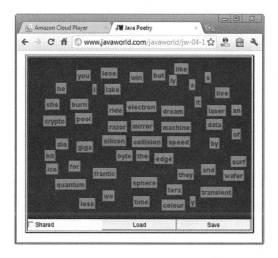

FIGURE 3.3
A *JavaWorld* how-to article on how to create a poetry magnet board includes a working example of the program.

NOTE

JavaWorld occasionally moves things around, but at the time of this writing, you can go directly to the poetry magnet board tutorial at www.cadenhead.org/poetry. If that page is unavailable, use the site's search engine to look for the word "poetry."

JavaWorld publishes articles and commentary about the language and its development. One issue that has been hotly debated since Java's introduction is whether the language is secure.

Security is important because of the way Java programs work when they are placed on a web page. The Java programs you have tried during this hour were downloaded to your computer. When the program was finished downloading, it ran on your computer.

Unless you know a whole lot of people, most web pages you visit are published by strangers. In terms of security, running their programs isn't a lot different than letting the general public come over and borrow your computer. If the Java language did not have safeguards to prevent abuse, its programs could introduce viruses onto your system, delete files, play the collected works of Justin Bieber, and do other unspeakable things. Java includes several different kinds of security to make sure that its programs are safe when run from web pages.

The main security is provided by restrictions on Java programs running over the Web:

▶ No program can open, read, write, or delete files on the user's system.

▶ No program can run other programs on the user's system.

▶ All windows created by the program are identified clearly as Java windows.

▶ Programs cannot make connections to websites other than the one from which they came.

▶ All programs are verified to make sure that nothing was modified after they were compiled.

Although there are no guarantees, the language has been proven to have enough safeguards to be usable over the Web.

The Java language also offers a more flexible security policy for programs that run in a browser. You can designate some companies and programmers as trusted developers, which enables their Java programs to run in your browser without the restrictions that normally would be in place.

This system of trust is established through the use of signed applets that have *digital signatures*, files that clearly identify the author of a Java program. These signatures are created in collaboration with independent verification groups such as VeriSign.

If you ever have authorized a program to run in a browser such as Internet Explorer or Google Chrome, you have worked with a similar system of trust and identity verification.

Applets can still be useful today, but over the years other technology, such as Flash, Silverlight, and HTML5, have been employed for web page–based programs. Java is more commonly encountered on mobile apps, server programs, and desktop software.

Watching the Skies at NASA

The first afternoon stop on the Java tour is a trip to NASA, a U.S. government agency that makes extensive use of Java. One of the most popular examples is SkyWatch, an applet that helps stargazers keep an eye out for orbiting satellites. Load it in your browser by visiting www.cadenhead. org/nasa; you are forwarded automatically to NASA's SkyWatch site.

SkyWatch superimposes the current location and path of eight different satellites—which you can add or drop from view—over a globe of the world. The applet running in Figure 3.4 shows the SEASAT-1 satellite making a patch from the Bootes constellation to the Hercules constellation.

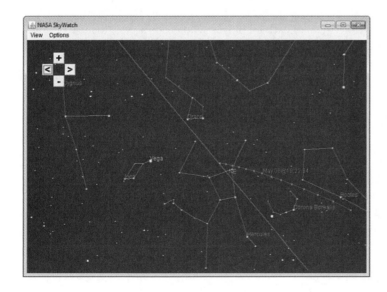

FIGURE 3.4
NASA's SkyWatch applet monitors the location and path of orbiting satellites, a boon to metal bird-watchers.

The applet redraws the position of each tracked satellite as it runs. This kind of real-time update is possible because the Java language is multi-threaded. *Multithreading* is a way for the computer to do more than one thing at the same time. One part of a program takes care of one task, another part takes care of a different task, and the two parts can pay no attention to each other. Each part of a program in this example is called a *thread*.

In a program such as SkyWatch, each satellite could run in its own thread. If you use an operating system such as Windows 7, you're using a type of this behavior when you run more than one program at the same time. If you're at work playing Desktop Tower Defense in one window while running a company sales report in another window and making a long-distance call to a friend, congratulate yourself—you're multithreading!

Getting Down to Business

At this point in your travels, you might have the impression that Java is primarily of use to space buffs, atrocious poets, and terrible skiers. The next stop on our trip shows an example of Java getting down to business.

Direct your web browser to the JTicker website at www.jticker.com.

The publisher of JTicker, a company called Stock Applets, develops Java programs that display business news headlines and stock quotes for use on other websites. Figure 3.5 shows a demo of its scrolling stock ticker.

Unlike other stock analysis programs that require the installation of software on the computers of each employee who needs access, the use of Java enables customers of Stock Applets to make the programs available to anyone with a web browser. All employees have to do is access the company's website.

FIGURE 3.5
Java programs from Stock Applets report stock market prices.

You can think of a program like this stock ticker applet in several different ways. One is to think of a program as an object—something that exists in the world, takes up space, and has certain things it can do. *Object-oriented programming* (OOP), which Java uses (read more in Hour 10, "Creating Your First Object"), is a way of creating computer programs as a group of objects. Each object handles a specific job and knows how to speak to other objects. For example, a stock ticker program could be set up as the following group of objects:

- ▶ A quote object, which represents an individual stock quote

- ▶ A portfolio object, which holds a set of quotes for specific stocks

- ▶ A ticker object, which displays a portfolio

- ▶ An Internet object, a user object, and many others

Under that model, the stock ticker software is a collection of all the objects necessary to get work done.

OOP is a powerful way to create programs, and it makes the programs you write more useful. Consider the stock software. If the programmer wants to use the quote capabilities of that program in some other software, the quote object can be used with the new program. No changes need to be made.

Stopping by Java Boutique for Directions

This world tour of Java programs is being led by a professional who is well-versed in the hazards and highlights of web-based travel. You'll be venturing out on your own trips soon, so it's worthwhile to stop at one of the best guides for the tourist who wants to see Java: Java Boutique at http://javaboutique.internet.com.

Java Boutique features a directory of Java programs and programming resources related to the language. One of the best uses of the site for programmers is to see what programs are available that offer source code. In case you're unfamiliar with the term, *source code* is another name for the text files that are used to create computer programs. The Saluton.java file you developed during Hour 2 is an example of source code.

The Source Code link on the Java Boutique's home page lists the programs in the site's directory that include their source code.

One of the programs whose source code is available is Aleksey Udovydchenko's Absolute, a space videogame in which you control a ship and blast your way through an asteroid field (see Figure 3.6). The game features scrolling animation, graphics, keyboard control, and sound. To learn more and play the game, visit http://javaboutique.internet.com/Absolute.

FIGURE 3.6
Source code for Java programs such as Aleksey Udovydchenko's space shoot-'em-up Absolute can be found using Java Boutique.

NOTE

Gamelan's Java Applet Ratings Service (JARS), a directory of browser-based Java programs and other resources available at www.jars.com, often includes programs that are accompanied by the source code used to create them. The language has been adopted by thousands of programmers around the world, partially because of the simplicity of the language.

The entire Absolute program was written in just more than 700 lines of code. That's an extremely small number, considering everything the program does. Java includes an extensive library of classes you can use in your own programs. Udovydchenko employs a class called Image to display graphics such as asteroids and an AudioClip class to play sounds such as laser fire and explosions.

One goal of Java's design was to make it easier to learn than C++, the language Gosling was having fits with on his smart-appliance project. Much of Java is based on C++, so programmers who have learned to use that language find it easier to learn Java. However, some of the elements of C++ that are the hardest to learn and use correctly are not present in Java.

For people learning programming for the first time, Java is easier to learn than C++. Some languages are created to make it easier for experienced programmers to harness the capabilities of the computer in their programs.

These languages include shortcuts and other features that programming veterans easily understand.

Java does not use some of these features, preferring to make the language as simple as an object-oriented programming language can be. Java was created to be easy to learn, easy to debug, and easy to use Java includes numerous enhancements that make it a worthy competitor to other languages.

Running Java on Your Phone

The last stop on your whirlwind tour of Java is the nearest Google Android cell phone. Every single program that runs on Android has been programmed with Java. These mobile programs, which extend the functionality of the phones, are called apps. One of the most popular apps is a game called Angry Birds, shown in Figure 3.7.

FIGURE 3.7
Angry Birds and all other Android apps were created with the Java language.

You can learn more about this game, if you're not already familiar with it, by visiting www.angrybirds.com. (But don't do it! The game will obliterate any hope you had of being productive for the rest of the day, week, or even month—depending on how much you hate fortified pigs.)

Android ends the trip around Java because it's becoming an incredibly popular place for the language to be used. After you learn Java, you can apply your skills developing your own apps using the Android Software Development Kit (SDK), a free programming toolkit that runs on Windows, MacOS, and Linux.

More than 250,000 apps have been created for Android phones and other devices that run the mobile operating system. You learn more about it in Hour 24, "Writing Android Apps."

Summary

Now that the hour-long vacation is over, it's time to put away your luggage and get ready for a return to actual Java programming.

During the next 21 hours, you will master the basic building blocks of the Java language, learn how to create your own objects to accomplish tasks in object-oriented programming, design graphical user interfaces, and much more.

Unless you've stopped reading this book to play Angry Birds.

Q&A

Q. Why are Java applets no longer popular?

A. When the Java language was introduced in the mid-'90s, most people were learning the language to write applets. Java was the only way to create interactive programs that ran in a web browser.

Over the years, alternatives emerged. Macromedia Flash, Microsoft Silverlight, and the new web publishing HTML5 standard all offer ways to put programs on web pages.

Applets were hampered by poor loading time and slow support for new versions of Java by browser developers. A Java plug-in was introduced that could run the current version of Java in browsers, but by that time Java had outgrown its origins and was a sophisticated general-purpose programming language.

Q. What's a Chris Steak House, and why does Ruth have one?

A. Ruth's Chris Steak House, the chain of more than 120 upscale steak restaurants across the United States and a handful of other countries, has an odd two-first-name name that reveals its humble origins and the stubborn streak of its founder.

The chain was founded in 1965 as a solitary New Orleans restaurant owned by Ruth Fertel, a single mother of two sons. Fertel saw a classified ad offering a restaurant for sale and took out a $22,000 home mortgage to buy it (equivalent to around $150,000 in present dollars).

She reached a deal to keep the name Chris Steak House with original owner Chris Matulich, but later had to relocate after a kitchen fire.

Fertel's contract did not permit her to use the Chris Steak House name anywhere but the original location, so she renamed it Ruth's Chris Steak House. Though she had no restaurant or culinary expertise, the business was so successful that she began offering it as a franchise within 12 years. She disregarded several suggestions over the years to change the name to broaden its appeal.

"I've always hated the name," she once told a reporter for *Fortune* magazine, "but we've always managed to work around it."

Fertel, who died in 2002, was born on Feb. 5, 1927—the same day that Matulich opened the steakhouse.

Workshop

If your mind hasn't taken a vacation by this point, test your knowledge of this hour with the following questions.

Quiz

1. How did object-oriented programming get its name?

   A. Programs are considered to be a group of objects working together.

   B. People often object because it's hard to master.

   C. Its parents named it.

2. Which of the following isn't a part of Java's security?

   A. Web programs cannot run programs on the user's computer.

   B. The identity of a program's author is always verified.

   C. Java windows are labeled as Java windows.

3. What is a program's capability to handle more than one task called?

   A. Schizophrenia

   B. Multiculturalism

   C. Multithreading

Answers

1. **A.** It's also abbreviated as OOP.

2. **B.** Programmers can use digital signatures and an identity-verification company such as VeriSign in Java, but it isn't required.

3. **C.** This also is called multitasking, but the term *multithreading* is used in conjunction with Java because a separately running part of a program is called a thread.

Activities

Before unpacking your luggage, you can explore the topics of this hour more fully with the following activities:

▶ Use the Java Boutique site at http://javaboutique.internet.com to find out what card games have been developed using the language.

▶ Visit Oracle's website for Java users, www.java.com, and click the "Do I Have Java?" link. Follow the instructions to see whether Java's present on your computer. Download and install the most up-to-date version, if prompted to do so.

Solutions for the activities in this book are presented on the book's website at www.java24hours.com.

HOUR 4
Understanding How Java Programs Work

An important distinction to make in Java programming is where your program is supposed to be running. Some programs are intended to work on your computer. Other programs are intended to run as part of a web page.

Java programs that run locally on your own computer are called *applications*. Programs that run on web pages are called *applets*. During this hour, you learn why that distinction is important.

Creating an Application

The Saluton program you wrote during Hour 2, "Writing Your First Program," is an example of a Java application. The next application you create calculates the square root of a number and displays the value.

With the Java24 project open in NetBeans, begin a new application:

1. Choose File, New File. The New File Wizard opens.

2. Choose the category Java and the file type Empty Java File, and then click Next.

3. Enter the class name **Root** and click Finish.

NetBeans creates Root.java and opens the empty file in the source editor so you can begin working on it. Enter everything from Listing 4.1, remembering not to enter the line numbers and colons along the left side of the listing. The numbers are used to make parts of programs easier to describe in the book. When you're done, save the file by clicking the Save All button on the toolbar.

WHAT YOU'LL LEARN IN THIS HOUR:

▶ How applications work
▶ Organizing an application
▶ Sending arguments to an application
▶ How applets work
▶ Organizing an applet
▶ Putting an applet on a web page

(handwritten margin note: allows you to print other variables/numbers/texts)

LISTING 4.1   The Full Text of Root.java

```
 1: class Root {
 2:     public static void main(String[] arguments) {
 3:         int number = 225;
 4:         System.out.println("The square root of "
 5:             + number
 6:             + " is "
 7:             + Math.sqrt(number)
 8:         );
 9:     }
10: }
```

(handwritten margin notes: "gets square root")

The Root application accomplishes the following tasks:

▶ Line 3: An integer value of 225 is stored in a variable named number.

▶ Lines 4–8: This integer and its square root are displayed. The Math.sqrt(number) statement in Line 7 displays the square root.

If you have entered Listing 4.1 without any typos, including all punctuation and every word capitalized as shown, you can run the file in NetBeans by choosing Run, Run File. The output of the program appears in the output pane, as shown in Figure 4.1.

FIGURE 4.1
The output of the Root application.

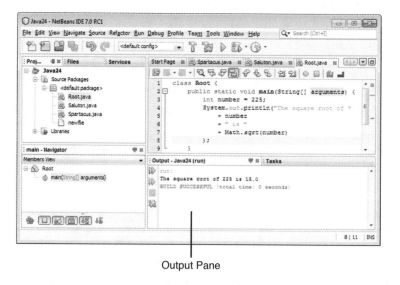

Output Pane

When you run a Java application, the Java Virtual Machine (JVM) looks for a main() block and starts handling Java statements within that block. If your program does not have a main() block, the JVM responds with an error.

Sending Arguments to Applications

You can run Java applications from a command line using `java`, a program that invokes the JVM. NetBeans uses this program behind the scenes when you run programs. When a Java program is run as a command, the JVM loads the application. The command can include extra items of information, as in this example:

```
java TextDisplayer readme.txt /p
```

Extra information sent to a program is called an *argument*. The first argument, if there is one, is provided one space after the name of the application. Each additional argument also is separated by a space. In the preceding example, the arguments are `readme.txt` and `/p`.

If you want to include a space inside an argument, you must put quotation marks around it, as in the following:

```
java TextDisplayer readme.txt /p "Page Title"
```

This example runs the TextDisplayer program with three arguments: `readme.txt`, `/p`, and `"Page Title"`. The quote marks prevent `Page` and `Title` from being treated as separate arguments.

You can send as many arguments as you want to a Java application (within reason). To do something with them, you must write statements in the application to handle them.

To see how arguments work in an application, create a new class in the Java24 project:

1. Choose File, New File.

2. In the New File Wizard, choose the category `Java` and file type `Empty Java File`.

3. Give the class the name **BlankFiller** and click Finish.

Enter the text of Listing 4.2 in the source code editor and save it when you're done. Compile the program, correcting any errors that are flagged by the editor as you type.

LISTING 4.2   The Full Text of `BlankFiller.java`

```
1: class BlankFiller {
2:     public static void main(String[] arguments) {
3:         System.out.println("The " + arguments[0]
4:             + " " + arguments[1] + " fox "
```

LISTING 4.2   Continued

```
5:              + "jumped over the "
6:              + arguments[2] + " dog."
7:        );
8:    }
9: }
```

This application compiles successfully and can be run, but if you try it with the menu command Run, Run File, you get a complicated-looking error:

Output ▼

```
Exception in thread "main" java.lang.ArrayIndexOutOfBoundsException: 0
    at BlankFiller.main(BlankFiller.java:3)
```

This error occurs because the program expects to receive three arguments when it is run. You can specify arguments by customizing the project in NetBeans:

1. Choose the menu command Run, Set Project Configuration, Customize. The Project Properties dialog opens.

2. Enter **BlankFiller** in the Main Class text field.

3. In the Arguments field, enter **retromingent purple lactose-intolerant** and click OK.

Because you've customized the project, you must run it a little differently. Choose the menu command Run, Run Main Project. The application uses the arguments you specified as adjectives to fill out a sentence, as shown in the following output:

Output ▼

```
The retromingent purple fox jumped over the lactose-intolerant dog.
```

Return to the Project Properties dialog and designate three adjectives of your own choosing as arguments, making sure to always include at least three.

Arguments are a simple way to customize the behavior of a program. The arguments are stored in a type of variable called an array. You learn about arrays during Hour 9, "Storing Information with Arrays."

Creating an Applet

When the Java language was introduced, the language feature that got the most attention was applets, Java programs that run on web pages. You can run them in any web browser that handles Java programs and test them with appletviewer, a tool included in the JDK that's supported in NetBeans.

The structure of applets differs from applications. Unlike applications, applets do not have a main() block. Instead, they have several sections that are handled depending on what is happening in the applet. Two sections are the init() block statement and the paint() block. init() is short for initialization, and it is used to take care of anything that needs to be set up as an applet first runs. The paint() block is used to display anything that should be displayed.

To see an applet version of the Root application, create a new empty Java file with the class name RootApplet. Enter the code in Listing 4.3 and make sure to save it when you're done.

LISTING 4.3   The Full Text of RootApplet.java

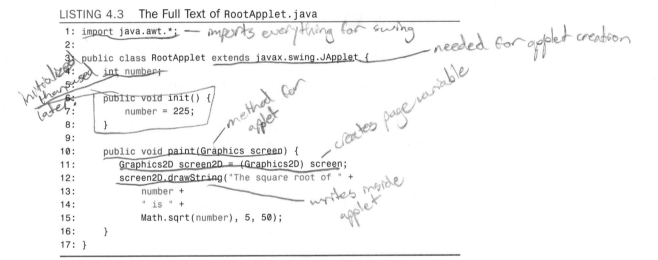

```
 1: import java.awt.*;              — imports everything for swing
 2:
 3: public class RootApplet extends javax.swing.JApplet {      — needed for applet creation
 4:     int number;     — initialized then used later
 5:
 6:     public void init() {        — method for applet
 7:         number = 225;
 8:     }
 9:
10:     public void paint(Graphics screen) {     — creates page variable
11:         Graphics2D screen2D = (Graphics2D) screen;
12:         screen2D.drawString("The square root of " +      — writes inside applet
13:             number +
14:             " is " +
15:             Math.sqrt(number), 5, 50);
16:     }
17: }
```

This program contains many of the same statements as the Root application. The primary difference is in how it is organized. The main() block has been replaced with an init() block and a paint() block.

When you run the program in NetBeans (choose Run, Run File), the applet loads in the appletviewer tool, as shown in Figure 4.2.

Applets are slightly more complicated than applications because they must be able to run on a web page and coexist with other page elements in a browser. You learn how to create them in Hour 17, "Creating Interactive Web Programs."

NOTE

The sample programs in this hour are provided primarily to introduce you to the way Java programs are structured. The main purpose of this hour is to get the programs to compile and see how they function when you run them. Some aspects of the programs will be introduced fully in the hours to come.

FIGURE 4.2
The RootApplet applet running in appletviewer.

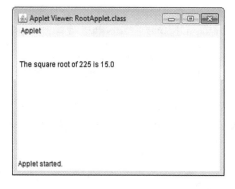

The appletviewer tool is useful for testing, but it gives the wrong impression about applets. They don't run in their own windows as Java applications. Instead, they're placed on web pages as if they are text, photos, or graphics. The applet is presented seamlessly with the rest of the page.

Figure 4.3 shows RootApplet on a web page. The applet window is the white box that displays the program's output: the square root of 225. The heading, paragraphs of text and lightbulb photo are ordinary elements of a web page.

Java applets can be static like the output of this project, but that's a complete waste of the language. Applets usually display dynamic content as in a stock ticker, chat room client, or video games.

FIGURE 4.3
The RootApplet applet on a web page loaded in the Google Chrome browser.

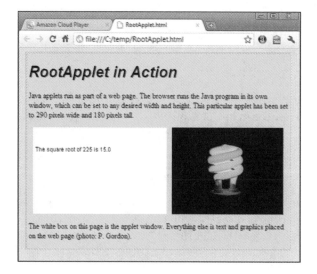

Summary

During this hour, you had a chance to create both a Java application and an applet. These two types of programs have several important differences in the way they function and the way they are created.

The next several hours continue to focus on applications as you become more experienced as a Java programmer. Applications are quicker to test because they don't require you to create a web page to view them; they can be easier to create and more powerful as well.

Q&A

Q. **Do all arguments sent to a Java application have to be strings?**

A. Java stores all arguments as strings when an application runs. When you want to use one of these arguments as an integer or some other non-string type, you have to convert the value. You learn how to do this during Hour 11, "Describing What Your Object Is Like."

Q. **If applets run on web pages and applications run everywhere else, what are Java programs launched by Java Web Start?**

A. Java Web Start is a way to launch Java applications from a web browser. A user clicks a link on a web page to run the program, which is easier than downloading it, running an installation wizard, and starting it like any other desktop software.

Although they're run from a browser, Java Web Start programs are applications instead of applets. The application's always up-to-date because it's retrieved over the web from the program's provider every time it is run.

Google Web Toolkit (GWT), a set of opensource tools for web programming, can convert a Java program into JavaScript, making it run faster and more reliably in web browsers without requiring a Java virtual machine.

Q. **Does the line of succession to the British throne run out at some point?**

A. Under Parliamentary law that has been in place since 1701, the British monarch must be a Protestant descendant of Sophia of Hanover, a German princess who was the heiress to the crown when the law was passed.

There are a finite number of people who are descendants of Sophia, so there's always somebody last in the regal line. The British government only lists the first 38, so genealogists have attempted to fill out the rest of the list themselves.

The last person in the line of succession is Karin Vogel, a German pain therapist in her thirties. She was 4,973rd in line as of 2001, genealogists determined after an exhaustive search that took years. So if all the people ahead of her drop out of the running (to, say, spend more time learning Java programming), Vogel takes over the mortgage of Buckingham Palace and becomes Her Majesty Karin the First.

Vogel is Sophia's great-great-great-great-great-great-great-great-granddaughter. She told the *Wall Street Journal* that becoming monarch would be "too stressful."

If by the time you read this Prince William and Princess Kate have produced a Protestant child, Vogel drops to 4,974.

Workshop

Test your knowledge of the material covered in this hour by answering the following questions.

Quiz

1. Which type of Java program can be run inside a browser?

    A. Applets

    B. Applications

    C. None

2. What does JVM stand for?

    A. Journal of Vacation Marketing

    B. Jacksonville Veterans Memorial

    C. Java Virtual Machine

3. If you get into a fight with someone over the way to send information to a Java application, what are you doing?

    C. Struggling over strings

    B. Arguing about arguments

    C. Feudin' for functionality

Answers

1. **A.** Applets run as part of a web page, whereas applications are run everywhere else.

2. **A, B, or C.** Trick question! The initials stand for all three things, though Java Virtual Machine is the one you need to remember for the next 20 hours.

3. **B.** Applications receive information in the form of arguments. Can't we all just get along?

Activities

If you'd like to apply your acumen of applets and applications, the following activities are suggested:

▶ Using the Root application as a guide, create a NewRoot application that can display the square root of 625.

▶ Using the Root application as a guide, create a NewRoot application that can display the square root of a number submitted as an argument.

To see a Java program that implements each of these activities, visit the book's website at www.java24hours.com.

Storing and Changing Information in a Program

In Hour 2, "Writing Your First Program," you used a *variable*, a special storage place designed to hold information. The information stored in variables can be changed as a program runs. Your first program stored a string of text in a variable. Strings are only one type of information that can be stored in variables. They also can hold characters, integers, floating-point numbers, and objects.

During this hour, you learn more about using variables in your Java programs.

Statements and Expressions

Computer programs are a set of instructions that tell the computer what to do. Each instruction is called a *statement*. The following example from a Java program is a statement:

```
int highScore = 450000;
```

You can use brackets to group a set of statements together in a Java program. These groupings are called *block statements*. Consider the following portion of a program:

```
1: public static void main(String[] args) {
2:     int a = 3;
3:     int b = 4;
4:     int c = 8 * 5;
5: }
```

declaring number variables

Lines 2–4 of this example are a block statement. The opening bracket on Line 1 denotes the beginning of the block, and the closing bracket on Line 5 denotes the end of the block.

WHAT YOU'LL LEARN IN THIS HOUR:

▶ Creating variables

▶ Using the different types of variables

▶ Storing values into variables

▶ Using variables in mathematical expressions

▶ Storing one variable's value into another variable

▶ Increasing and decreasing a variable's value

Some statements are called *expressions* because they involve a mathematical expression and produce a result. Line 4 in the preceding example is an expression because it sets the value of the c variable equal to 8 multiplied by 5. You work with expressions during this hour.

Assigning Variable Types

Variables are the main way that a computer remembers something as it runs a program. The Saluton program in Hour 2 used the greeting variable to hold "Saluton mondo!". The computer needed to remember that text so that the message could be displayed.

In a Java program, variables are created with a statement that must include two things:

> ▶ The name of the variable

> ▶ The type of information the variable will store

Variables also can include the value of the information being stored.

To see the different types of variables and how they are created, run NetBeans and create a new empty Java file with the class name Variable.

Start writing the program by entering the following lines:

```
class Variable {
    public static void main(String[] args) {
        // Coming soon: variables
    }
}
```

Go ahead and save these lines before making any changes.

Integers and Floating-Point Numbers

So far, the Variable program has a main() block with only one statement in it—the comment // Coming soon: variables. Delete the comment and enter the following statement in its place:

```
int tops;
```

This statement creates a variable named tops. It does not specify a value for tops, so for the moment this variable is an empty storage space. The int text at the beginning of the statement designates tops as a variable that is used to store integer numbers. You can use the int type to store most of the nondecimal numbers you need in your computer programs. It can hold any integer ranging from around –2.14 billion to 2.14 billion.

Create a blank line after the int tops statement and add the following statement:

```
float gradePointAverage;
```

This statement creates a variable with the name gradePointAverage. The float text stands for floating-point numbers. Floating-point variables are used to store numbers that might contain a decimal point.

The float variable type holds decimal numbers of up to 38 figures. The larger double type holds decimal numbers up to 300 figures.

Characters and Strings

Because the variables you have dealt with so far are numeric, you might have the impression that all variables are used to store numbers. Think again. You also can use variables to store text. Two types of text can be stored as variables: characters and strings. A _character_ is a single letter, number, punctuation mark, or symbol. A _string_ is a group of characters.

Your next step in creating the Variable program is to create a char variable and a String variable. Add these two statements after the line float gradePointAverage:

```
char key = 'C';
String productName = "Larvets";
```

When you are using character values in your program, you must put single quotation marks on both sides of the character value being assigned to a variable. For string values, you must surround them with double quotation marks.

Quotation marks prevent the character or string from being confused with a variable name or another part of a statement. Take a look at the following statement:

```
String productName = Larvets;
```

This statement might look like one telling the computer to create a string variable called productName and give it the text value of Larvets. However, because there are no quotation marks around the word Larvets,

NOTE

You can use a floating-point variable to store a grade point average such as 2.25 (to pick my own at the University of North Texas—hi, Professor Wells!). You can also use it to store a number such as 0, which is the percentage chance of getting into a good graduate school with my grade point average, which is why I was available in the job market in 1996 when this publisher was looking for computer book authors.

the computer is being told to set the productName value to the same value as a variable named Larvets.

After adding the char and String statements, your program resembles Listing 5.1. Make any necessary changes and be sure to save the file.

LISTING 5.1   The Variable Program

```
1: class Variable {
2:     public static void main(String[] args) {
3:         int tops;
4:         float gradePointAverage;
5:         char key = 'C';
6:         String productName = "Larvets";
7:     }
8: }
```

NOTE

Although the other variable types are all lowercase letters (int, float, and char), the capital letter is required in the word String when creating string variables. A string in a Java program is different than the other types of information you use in variable statements. You learn about this distinction in Hour 6, "Using Strings to Communicate."

The last two variables in the Variable program use the = sign to assign a starting value when the variables are created. You can use this option for any variables you create in a Java program, as you discover later in this hour.

This program can be run but produces no output.

Other Numeric Variable Types

The types of variables you have been introduced to thus far are the main ones you use for most of your Java programming. You can call on a few other types of variables in special circumstances.

You can use the first, byte, for integer numbers that range from –128 to 127. The following statement creates a variable called escapeKey with an initial value of 27:

```
byte escapeKey = 27;
```

The second, short, can be used for integers that are smaller in size than the int type. A short integer can range from –32,768 to 32,767, as in the following example:

```
short roomNumber = 222;
```

useful to make program faster (handwritten note)

The last of the numeric variable types, long, is typically used for integers that are too big for the int type to hold. A long integer can be from –9.22 quintillion to 9.22 quintillion, which is a large enough number to cover everything but government spending.

When working with large numbers in Java, it can be difficult to see at a glance the value of the number, as in this statement:

```
long salary = 264400000;
```
from a .22 quintillion to a .22 quintillion

Unless you count the zeros, you probably can't tell that it's $264.4 million. Java 7 makes it possible to organize large numbers with underscore (_) characters. Here's an example:

```
long salary = 264_400_000;
```
instead of commas

The underscores are ignored, so the variable still equals the same value. They're just a way to make numbers more human readable.

The `boolean` Variable Type

Java has a type of variable called `boolean` that only can be used to store the value `true` or the value `false`. At first glance, a `boolean` variable might not seem particularly useful unless you plan to write a lot of true-or-false quizzes. However, `boolean` variables are used in a variety of situations in your programs. The following are some examples of questions that `boolean` variables can be used to answer:

▶ Has the user pressed a key?

▶ Is the game over?

▶ Is my bank account overdrawn?

▶ Do these pants make my butt look fat?

▶ Can the rabbit eat Trix?

The following statement creates a `boolean` variable called `gameOver`:

```
boolean gameOver = false;
```
true or false

This variable has the starting value of `false`, so a statement like this could indicate in a game program that the game isn't over yet. Later, when something happens to end the game, the `gameOver` variable can be set to `true`.

Although the two possible `boolean` values look like strings in a program, you should not surround them with quotation marks. Hour 7, "Using Conditional Tests to Make Decisions," describes `boolean` variables more fully.

CAUTION

All the improvements offered in Java 7, including underscores in numbers, will be flagged as an error in the NetBeans source code editor unless the IDE has been set up to recognize Java 7. You learn how to do this in Hour 7, "Using Conditional Tests to Make Decisions."

NOTE

Boolean numbers are named for George Boole (1815–1864). Boole, a mathematician who was mostly self-taught until adulthood, invented Boolean algebra, which has become a fundamental part of computer programming, digital electronics, and logic. One imagines that he did pretty well on true-false tests as a child.

Naming Your Variables

Variable names in Java can begin with a letter, underscore character ( ), or a dollar sign ($). The rest of the name can be any letters or numbers. You can give your variables any names you like but should be consistent in how you name variables. This section outlines the generally recommended naming method for variables.

Java is case-sensitive when it comes to variable names, so you must always capitalize variable names the same way. For example, if the `gameOver` variable is referred to as `GameOver` somewhere in the program, an error prevents the program from being compiled.

A variable's name should describe its purpose in some way. The first letter should be lowercase, and if the variable name has more than one word, make the first letter of each subsequent word a capital letter. For instance, if you want to create an integer variable to store the all-time high score in a game program, you can use the following statement:

```
int allTimeHighScore;
```

You can't use punctuation marks or spaces in a variable name, so neither of the following works:

```
int all-TimeHigh Score;
int all Time High Score;
```

If you try these variable names in a program, NetBeans responds by flagging the error with the red alert icon alongside the line in the source editor.

Storing Information in Variables

You can store a value in a variable at the same time that you create the variable in a Java program. You also can put a value in the variable at any time later in the program.

To set a starting value for a variable upon its creation, use the equal sign (=). Here's an example of creating a double floating-point variable called `pi` with the starting value of 3.14:

```
double pi = 3.14;
```

All variables that store numbers can be set up in a similar fashion. If you're setting up a character or a string variable, quotation marks must be placed around the value as described earlier in this hour.

You also can set one variable equal to the value of another variable if they both are of the same type. Consider the following example:

```
int mileage = 300;
int totalMileage = mileage;
```

CAUTION

If you do not give a variable a starting value, you must give it a value before you use it in another statement. If you don't, when your program is compiled, you might get an error stating that the variable "may not have been initialized."

First, an integer variable called `mileage` is created with a starting value of 300. Next, an integer variable called `totalMileage` is created with the same value as `mileage`. Both variables have the starting value of 300. In future hours, you learn how to convert one variable's value to the type of another variable.

As you've learned, Java has similar numeric variables that hold values of different sizes. Both `int` and `long` hold integers, but `long` holds a larger range of possible values. Both `float` and `double` carry floating-point numbers, but `double` is bigger.

You can append a letter to a numeric value to indicate the value's type, as in this statement:

```
float pi = 3.14F;
```
make it float speciﬁc (because it's smaller)

The F after the value 3.14 indicates that it's a `float` value. If the letter is omitted, Java assumes that 3.14 is a `double` value. The letter L is used for `long` integers and D for `double` floating-point values.

Another naming convention in Java is to capitalize the names of variables that do not change in value. These variables are called *constants*. The following creates three constants:

```
final int TOUCHDOWN = 6;
final int FIELDGOAL = 3;
final int PAT = 1;
```
creates constants

Because constants never change in value, you might wonder why one ever should be used—you can just use the value assigned to the constant instead. One advantage of using constants is that they make a program easier to understand.

In the preceding three statements, the name of the constant was capitalized. This is not required in Java, but it has become a standard convention among programmers to distinguish constants from other variables.

All About Operators

Statements can use mathematical expressions by employing the operators +, -, *, /, and %. You use these operators to crunch numbers throughout your Java programs.

An addition expression in Java uses the + operator, as in these statements:

```
double weight = 205;
weight = weight + 10;
```

The second statement uses the + operator to set the `weight` variable equal to its current value plus 10. A subtraction expression uses the - operator:

```
weight = weight - 15;
```

This expression sets the `weight` variable equal to its current value minus 15.

A division expression uses the / sign:

```
weight = weight / 3;
```

This sets the `weight` variable to its current value divided by 3.

To find a remainder from a division expression, use the % operator (also called the modulo operator). The following statement finds the remainder of 245 divided by 3:

```
int remainder = 245 % 3;
```

A multiplication expression uses the * sign. Here's a statement that employs a multiplication expression as part of a more complicated statement:

```
int total = 500 + (score * 12);
```

The `score * 12` part of the expression multiplies `score` by 12. The full statement multiples `score` by 12 and adds 500 to the result. If `score` equals 20, the result is that `total` equals 740: `500 + (20 * 12)`.

[handwritten note: uses order to figure out stuff]

Incrementing and Decrementing a Variable

A common task in programs is changing the value of a variable by one. You can increase the value by one, which is called *incrementing* the variable, or decrease the value by one, which is called *decrementing* the variable. There are operators to accomplish both of these tasks.

To increment the value of a variable by one, use the ++ operator, as in the following statement:

```
x++;
```

This statement adds one to the value stored in the x variable.

To decrement the value of a variable by one, use the - - operator:

```
y--;
```

[handwritten note: postfixing]

This statement reduces y by one.

You also can put the increment and decrement operators in front of the variable name, as in the following statements:

```
++x;
--y;
```

prefixing [handwritten annotation]

NOTE

Confused yet? This is easier than it sounds, if you think back to elementary school when you learned about prefixes. Just as a prefix such as "sub-" or "un-" goes at the start of a word, a prefix operator goes at the start of a variable name. A postfix operator goes at the end.

Putting the operator in front of the variable name is called *prefixing*, and putting it after the name is called *postfixing*.

The difference between prefixed and postfixed operators becomes important when you use the increment and decrement operators inside an expression.

Consider the following statements:

```
int x = 3;
int answer = x++ * 10;
```

What does the answer variable equal after these statements are handled? You might expect it to equal 40—which would be true if 3 was incremented by 1, which equals 4, and then 4 was multiplied by 10.

However, answer ends up with the value 30 because the postfixed operator was used instead of the prefixed operator.

When a postfixed operator is used on a variable inside an expression, the variable's value doesn't change until after the expression has been completely evaluated. The statement int answer = x++ * 10 does the same thing in the same order, as the following two statements:

```
int answer = x * 10;
x++;
```

The opposite is true of prefixed operators. If they are used on a variable inside an expression, the variable's value changes before the expression is evaluated.

Consider the following statements:

```
int x = 3;
int answer = ++x * 10;
```

This does result in the answer variable being equal to 40. The prefixed operator causes the value of the x variable to be changed before the expression is evaluated. The statement int answer = ++x * 10 does the same thing in order, as these statements:

NOTE

Back in Hour 1, "Becoming a Programmer," the name of the C++ programming language was described as a joke you'd understand later. Now that you've been introduced to the increment operator ++, you have all the information you need to figure out why C++ has two plus signs in its name instead of just one. Because C++ adds new features and functionality to the C programming language, it can be considered an incremental increase to C—hence the name C++.

After you work through all 24 hours of this book, you too will be able to tell jokes like this that are incomprehensible to more than 99 percent of the world's population.

```
x++;
int answer = x * 10;
```

It's easy to become exasperated with the ++ and − operators because they're not as straightforward as many of the concepts you encounter in this book.

I hope I'm not breaking some unwritten code of Java programmers by telling you this, but you don't need to use the increment and decrement operators in your own programs. You can achieve the same results by using the + and – operators like this:

```
x = x + 1;
y = y - 1;
```

Incrementing and decrementing are useful shortcuts, but taking the longer route in an expression is fine, too.

Operator Precedence

When you are using an expression with more than one operator, you need to know what order the computer uses as it works out the expression. Consider the following statements:

```
int y = 10;
x = y * 3 + 5;
```

Unless you know what order the computer uses when working out the math in these statements, you cannot be sure what the x variable will be set to. It could be set to either 35 or 80, depending on whether y * 3 is evaluated first or 3 + 5 is evaluated first.

The following order is used when working out an expression:

1. Incrementing and decrementing take place first.

2. Multiplication, division, and modulus division occur next.

3. Addition and subtraction follow.

4. Comparisons take place next.

5. The equal sign (=) is used to set a variable's value.

Because multiplication takes place before addition, you can revisit the previous example and come up with the answer: y is multiplied by 3 first, which equals 30, and then 5 is added. The x variable is set to 35.

Comparisons are discussed during Hour 7. The rest has been described during this hour, so you should be able to figure out the result of the following statements:

```
int x = 5;
int number = x++ * 6 + 4 * 10 / 2;
```

These statements set the `number` variable equal to 50.

How does the computer come up with this total? First, the increment operator is handled, and x++ sets the value of the x variable to 6. However, make note that the ++ operator is postfixed after x in the expression. This means that the expression is evaluated with the original value of x.

Because the original value of x is used before the variable is incremented, the expression becomes the following:

```
int number = 5 * 6 + 4 * 10 / 2;
```

Now, multiplication and division are handled from left to right. First, 5 is multiplied by 6, 4 is multiplied by 10, and that result is divided by 2 (4 * 10 / 2). The expression becomes the following:

```
int number = 30 + 20;
```

This expression results in the `number` variable being set to 50.

If you want an expression to be evaluated in a different order, you can use parentheses to group parts of an expression that should be handled first. For example, the expression x = 5 * 3 + 2; would normally cause x to equal 17 because multiplication is handled before addition. However, look at a modified form of that expression:

```
x = 5 * (3 + 2);
```

In this case, the expression within the parentheses is handled first, so the result equals 25. You can use parentheses as often as needed in a statement.

Using Expressions

When you were in school, as you worked on a particularly unpleasant math problem, did you ever complain to a higher power, protesting that you would never use this knowledge in your life? Sorry to break this to you, but your teachers were right—your math skills come in handy in your computer programming. That's the bad news.

The good news is that the computer does any math you ask it to do. Expressions are used frequently in your computer programs to accomplish tasks such as the following:

▶ Changing the value of a variable

▶ Counting the number of times something has happened in a program

▶ Using a mathematical formula in a program

As you write computer programs, you find yourself drawing on your old math lessons as you use expressions. Expressions can use addition, subtraction, multiplication, division, and modulus division.

To see expressions in action, return to NetBeans and create a new Java file with the class name `PlanetWeight`. This program tracks a person's weight loss and gain as she travels to other bodies in the solar system. Enter the full text of Listing 5.2 in the source editor. Each part of the program is discussed in turn.

LISTING 5.2   The `PlanetWeight` Program

```
 1: class PlanetWeight {
 2:     public static void main(String[] args) {
 3:         System.out.print("Your weight on Earth is ");
 4:         double weight = 205;
 5:         System.out.println(weight);
 6:
 7:         System.out.print("Your weight on Mercury is ");
 8:         double mercury = weight * .378;
 9:         System.out.println(mercury);
10:
11:         System.out.print("Your weight on the Moon is ");
12:         double moon = weight * .166;
13:         System.out.println(moon);
14:
15:         System.out.print("Your weight on Jupiter is ");
16:         double jupiter = weight * 2.364;
17:         System.out.println(jupiter);
18:     }
19: }
```

When you're done, save the file and it should compile automatically. Run the program with the menu command Run, Run File. The output is shown in the output pane in Figure 5.1.

FIGURE 5.1
The output of the PlanetWeight program.

As in other programs you have created, the PlanetWeight program uses a main() block statement for all its work. This statement can be broken into the following four sections:

1. Lines 3–5: The person's weight is set initially to 205.

2. Lines 7–9: Mercury weight loss is calculated.

3. Lines 11–13: Weight loss on the Moon is determined.

4. Lines 15–17: Jupiter weight gain is calculated.

Line 4 creates the weight variable and designates it as a double variable with double. The variable is given the initial value 205 and used throughout the program to monitor the person's weight.

The next line is similar to several other statements in the program:

```
System.out.println(weight);
```

The System.out.println() command displays a string that is contained within its parenthesis marks. On Line 3, the System.out.print() command displays the text "Your weight on Earth is". There are several System.out.print() and System.out.println() statements in the program.

The difference between them is that print() does not start a new line after displaying the text, whereas println() does.

Summary

Now that you have been introduced to variables and expressions, you can give a wide range of instructions to your computer in a program. With the skills you have developed during this hour, you can write programs that accomplish many of the same tasks as a calculator, handling sophisticated mathematical equations with ease. You've also learned that a trip to the Moon is a particularly effective diet plan.

Numbers are only one kind of thing that can be stored in a variable. You also can store characters, strings of characters, and special true or false values called boolean variables. The next hour expands your knowledge of String variables and how they are used.

Q&A

Q. **Is a line in a Java program the same thing as a statement?**

A. No. The programs you create in this book put one statement on each line to make the programs easier to understand; it's not required.

The Java compiler does not consider lines, spacing, or other formatting issues when compiling a program. The compiler just wants to see semicolons at the end of each statement. This line would work just fine in Java:

```
int x = 12; x = x + 1;
```

Putting more than one statement on a line makes a program more difficult for humans to understand when they read its source code. For this reason, it is not recommended.

Q. **Why should the first letter of a variable name be lowercase, as in** gameOver?

A. It's a naming convention that helps your programming in two ways. First, it makes variables easier to spot among the other elements of a Java program. Second, by following a consistent style in the naming of variables, you eliminate errors that can occur when you use a variable in several different places in a program. The style of capitalization used in this book is the one that's been adopted by most Java programmers over the years.

Q. **Can I specify integers as binary values in Java?**

A. You can for the first time in Java 7. Put the characters 0b in front of the number and follow it with the bits in the value. Because 1101 is the binary form for the number 13, the following statement sets an integer to 13:

```
int z = 0b0000_1101;
```

The underscore is just to make the number more readable. It's ignored by the Java compiler.

NetBeans will treat this feature as an error unless your project has been set up to use Java 7. You learn how to do this in Hour 7.

Q. **What the heck are Larvets?**

A. Larvets, the product mentioned in this hour, are snacks made from edible worms that have been killed, dried, and mixed with the same kinds of scrumptious food-like flavoring as Doritos chips. You can order Larvets in three flavors—BBQ, cheddar cheese, and Mexican spice—from the mail-order retailer HotLix at the website www.hotlix.com or by calling 1-800-EAT-WORM.

Workshop

Test your knowledge of variables, expressions, and the rest of the information in this hour by answering the following questions.

Quiz

1. What do you call a group of statements that is contained with an opening bracket and a closing bracket?

    A. A block statement

    B. Groupware

    C. Bracketed statements

2. A `boolean` variable is used to store `true` or `false` values.

    A. True

    B. False

    C. No, thanks. I already ate.

3. What characters cannot be used to start a variable name?

    A. A dollar sign

    B. Two forward slash marks (//)

    C. A letter

Answers

1. **A.** The grouped statements are called a *block statement* or a *block*.

2. **A.** `true` and `false` are the only answers a `boolean` variable can store.

3. **B.** Variables can start with a letter, a dollar sign ($), or an underscore character (_). If you started a variable name with two slash marks, the rest of the line would be ignored because the slash marks are used to start a comment line.

Activities

You can review the topics of this hour more fully with the following activities:

▶ Expand the `PlanetWeight` program to track a person's weight on Venus (90.7% of Earth weight) and his weight on Uranus (88.9% Earth)—and stop snickering because I mentioned Uranus.

▶ Create a short Java program that uses an x integer and a y integer and displays the result of x squared plus y squared.

To see Java programs that implement these activities, visit the book's website at www.java24hours.com.

Using Strings to Communicate

In the film *The Piano*, Holly Hunter portrays Ada, a young Scottish woman who is mute and can express herself only by playing her piano.

Like Ada, your computer programs are capable of quietly doing their work and never stopping for a chat—or piano recital—with humans. But if *The Piano* teaches us anything, it's that communication ranks up there with food, water, and shelter as essential needs. (It also teaches us that the actor Harvey Keitel has a lot of body confidence, but that's a matter for another book.)

Java programs use strings as the primary means to communicate with users. *Strings* are collections of text—letters, numbers, punctuation, and other characters. During this hour, you learn all about working with strings in your Java programs.

Storing Text in Strings

Strings store text and present it to users. The most basic element of a string is a character. A *character* is a single letter, number, punctuation mark, or other symbol.

In Java programs, a character is one of the types of information that can be stored in a variable. Character variables are created with the char type in a statement such as the following:

```
char keyPressed;
```

This statement creates a variable named keyPressed that can store a character. When you create character variables, you can set them up with an initial value, as in the following:

```
char quitKey = '@';
```

The value of the character must be surrounded by single quotation marks.

A string is a collection of characters. You can set up a variable to hold a string value by following `String` with the name of the variable, as in this statement:

```
String fullName = "Ada McGrath Stewart";
```

This statement creates a string variable called `fullName` containing the text "Ada McGrath Stewart" in it, which is the full name of Hunter's pianist. A string is denoted with double quotation marks around the text in a Java statement. These quotation marks are not included in the string itself.

Unlike the other types of variables you have used—`int`, `float`, `char`, `boolean`, and so on—the name of the `String` type is capitalized.

Strings are a special kind of information called objects, and the types of all objects are capitalized in Java. You learn about objects during Hour 10, "Creating Your First Object." The important thing to note during this hour is that strings are different than the other variable types, and because of this difference, `String` is capitalized.

Displaying Strings in Programs

The most basic way to display a string in a Java program is with the `System.out.println()` statement. This statement takes strings and other variables inside the parentheses and displays their values on the system output device, which is the computer's monitor. Here's an example:

```
System.out.println("Silence affects everyone in the end.");
```

This statement causes the following text to be displayed:

```
Silence affects everyone in the end.
```

Displaying text on the screen often is called printing, which is what `println()` stands for—print line. You can use the `System.out.println()` statement to display text within double quotation marks and also to display variables, as you see later. Put all the material you want to be displayed within the parentheses.

Another way to display text is to call `System.out.print()`. This statement displays strings and other variables inside the parentheses, but unlike `System.out.println()`, it enables subsequent statements to display text on the same line.

same line print

You can use `System.out.print()` several times in a row to display several things on the same line, as in this example:

```
System.out.print("She ");
System.out.print("never ");
System.out.print("said ");
System.out.print("another ");
System.out.println("word.");
```

next line print

These statements cause the following text to be displayed:

```
She never said another word.
```

Using Special Characters in Strings

When a string is being created or displayed, its text must be enclosed within double quotation marks. These quotation marks are not displayed, which brings up a good question: What if you want to display double quotation marks?

To display them, Java has created a special code that can be put into a string: \". Whenever this code is encountered in a string, it is replaced with a double quotation mark. For example, examine the following:

```
System.out.println("Jane Campion directed \"The Piano\" in 1993.");
```

This code is displayed as the following:

```
Jane Campion directed "The Piano" in 1993.
```

You can insert several special characters into a string in this manner. The following list shows these special characters; note that each is preceded by a backslash (\).

Special Characters	Display
\'	Single quotation mark
\"	Double quotation mark
\\	Backslash
\t	Tab
\b	Backspace
\r	Carriage return
\f	Formfeed
\n	Newline

ways to display important information

The newline character causes the text following the newline character to be displayed at the beginning of the next line. Look at this example:

```
System.out.println("Music by\nMichael Nyman");
```

This statement would be displayed like this:

```
Music by
Michael Nyman
```

Pasting Strings Together

NOTE

You'll probably see the term concatenation in other books as you build your programming skills, so it's worth knowing. However, pasting is the term used here when one string and another string are joined together. Pasting sounds like fun. Concatenating sounds like something that should never be done in the presence of an open flame.

When you use `System.out.println()` and work with strings in other ways, you can paste two strings together by using +, the same operator that is used to add numbers.

The + operator has a different meaning in relation to strings. Instead of performing some math, it pastes two strings together. This action can cause strings to be displayed together or make one big string out of two smaller ones.

Concatenation is the word used to describe this action because it means to link two things together.

The following statement uses the + operator to display a long string:

```
System.out.println("\"\'The Piano\' is as peculiar and haunting as any" +
    " film I've seen.\"\n\t— Roger Ebert, Chicago Sun-Times");
```

Instead of putting this entire string on a single line, which would make it harder to understand when you look at the program later, the + operator is used to break the text over two lines of the program's Java source code. When this statement is displayed, it appears as the following:

```
"'The Piano' is as peculiar and haunting as any film I've seen."
    — Roger Ebert, Chicago Sun-Times
```

Several special characters are used in the string: \", \', \n, and \t. To better familiarize yourself with these characters, compare the output with the `System.out.println()` statement that produced it.

Using Other Variables with Strings

Although you can use the + operator to paste two strings together, you use it more often to link strings and variables. Take a look at the following:

```
int length = 121;
char rating = 'R';
System.out.println("Running time: " + length + " minutes");
System.out.println("Rated " + rating);
```

This code will be displayed as the following:

```
Running time: 121 minutes
Rated R
```

This example displays a unique facet about how the + operator works with strings. It can cause variables that are not strings to be treated just like strings when they are displayed. The variable length is an integer set to the value 121. It is displayed between the strings Running time: and minutes. The System.out.println() statement is being asked to display a string plus an integer, plus another string. This statement works because at least one part of the group is a string. The Java language offers this functionality to make displaying information easier.

One thing you might want to do with a string is paste something to it several times, as in the following example:

```
String searchKeywords = "";
searchKeywords = searchKeywords + "drama ";
searchKeywords = searchKeywords + "romance ";
searchKeywords = searchKeywords + "New Zealand";
```

adding text to a string

This code would result in the searchKeywords variable being set to "drama romance New Zealand". The first line creates the searchKeywords variable and sets it to be an empty string because there's nothing between the double quotation marks. The second line sets the searchKeywords variable equal to its current string plus the string "drama" added to the end. The next two lines add "romance" and "New Zealand" in the same way.

As you can see, when you are pasting more text at the end of a variable, the name of the variable has to be listed twice. Java offers a shortcut to simplify this process: the += operator. The += operator combines the functions of the = and + operators. With strings, it is used to add something to the end of an existing string. The searchKeywords example can be shortened by using +=, as shown in the following statements:

```
String searchKeywords = "";
searchKeywords += "drama ";
searchKeywords += "romance ";
searchKeywords += "New Zealand";
```

This code produces the same result: searchKeywords is set to "drama romance New Zealand".

Advanced String Handling

There are several other ways you can examine a string variable and change its value. These advanced features are possible because strings are objects in the Java language. Working with strings develops skills you'll use on other objects later.

Comparing Two Strings

One thing you are testing often in your programs is whether one string is equal to another. You do this by using equals() in a statement with both of the strings, as in this example:

```
String favorite = "piano";
String guess = "ukulele";
System.out.println("Is Ada's favorite instrument a " + guess + "?");
System.out.println("Answer: " + favorite.equals(guess));
```

(handwritten margin note: returns boolean value test if string is equal to another)

This example uses two different string variables. One, favorite, stores the name of Ada's favorite instrument: a piano. The other, guess, stores a guess as to what her favorite might be. The guess is that Ada prefers the ukulele.

The third line displays the text "Is Ada's favorite instrument a" followed by the value of the guess variable, and then a question mark. The fourth line displays the text "Answer:" and then contains something new:

```
favorite.equals(guess)
```

This part of the statement makes use of a method. A *method* is a way to accomplish a task in a Java program. This method's task is to determine if one string has the same value as another. If the two string variables have the same value, the text true is displayed. If not, the text false is displayed. The following is the output of this example:

Output ▼

```
Is Ada's favorite instrument a ukulele?
Answer: false
```

Determining the Length of a String

It also can be useful to determine the length of a string in characters. You do this with the length() method. This method works in the same fashion as the equals() method, except that only one string variable is involved. Look at the following example:

```
String cinematographer = "Stuart Dryburgh";
int nameLength = cinematographer.length();
```
— returns length of string (handwritten)

This example sets nameLength, an integer variable, equal to 15. The cine-matographer.length() method counts the number of characters in the string variable called cinematographer and stores this count in the nameLength integer variable.

Changing a String's Case

Because computers take everything literally, it's easy to confuse them. Although a human would recognize that the text *Harvey Keitel* and the text *HARVEY KEITEL* refer to the same thing, most computers would disagree. The equals() method discussed previously in this hour would state authoritatively that *Harvey Keitel* is not equal to *HARVEY KEITEL*.

To get around some of these obstacles, Java has methods that display a string variable as all uppercase letters or all lowercase letters, toUpperCase() and toLowerCase(), respectively. The following example shows the toUpperCase() method in action:

— makes string lowercase (handwritten)

```
String baines = "Harvey Keitel";
String change = baines.toUpperCase();
```
— makes string uppercase (handwritten)

This code sets the string variable change equal to the baines string vari-able converted to all uppercase letters—"HARVEY KEITEL". The toLowerCase() method works in the same fashion but returns an all-lowercase string value.

Note that the toUpperCase() method does not change the case of the string variable it is called on. In the preceding example, the baines vari-able is still equal to "Harvey Keitel".

Looking for a String

Another common task when handling strings is to see whether one string can be found inside another. To look inside a string, use its indexOf() method. Put the string you are looking for inside the parentheses. If the string is not found, indexOf() produces the value –1. If the string is found, indexOf() produces an integer that represents the position where the string begins. Positions in a string are numbered upwards from 0, begin-ning with the first character in the string. In the string "The Piano", the text "Piano" begins at position 4.

The indexOf() method is *case-sensitive*, which means that it only looks for text capitalized exactly like the search string. If the string contains the same text capitalized differently, indexOf() produces the value -1.

One possible use of the indexOf() method would be to search the entire script of *The Piano* for the place where Ada's domineering husband tells her daughter Flora, "You are greatly shamed and you have shamed those trunks."

If the entire script of *The Piano* was stored in a string called script, you could search it for part of that quote with the following statement.

```
int position = script.indexOf("you have shamed those trunks");
```

If that text can be found in the script string, position equals the position at which the text "you have shamed those trunks" begins. Otherwise, it will equal -1.

[handwritten annotation]: returns -1 if it is not in variable, returns whatever line variable B on if true.

Presenting Credits

In *The Piano*, Ada McGrath Stewart was thrown into unfamiliar territory when she moved from Scotland to New Zealand to marry a stranger who didn't appreciate her music. You might have felt lost yourself with some of the topics introduced during this hour.

Next, to reinforce the string-handling features that have been covered, you write a Java program to display credits for a feature film. You can probably guess the movie.

Return to the Java24 project in NetBeans and create a new Java class called Credits. Enter the text of Listing 6.1 into the source editor and save the file when you're done.

LISTING 6.1   The Credits Program

```
 1: class Credits {
 2:     public static void main(String[] args) {
 3:         // set up film information
 4:         String title = "The Piano";
 5:         int year = 1993;
 6:         String director = "Jane Campion";
 7:         String role1 = "Ada";
 8:         String actor1 = "Holly Hunter";
 9:         String role2 = "Baines";
10:         String actor2 = "Harvey Keitel";
11:         String role3 = "Stewart";
12:         String actor3 = "Sam Neill";
13:         String role4 = "Flora";
14:         String actor4 = "Anna Paquin";
15:         // display information
16:         System.out.println(title + " (" + year + ")\n" +
17:             "A " + director + " film.\n\n" +
```

LISTING 6.1   Continued

```
18:                    role1 + "\t" + actor1 + "\n" +
19:                    role2 + "\t" + actor2 + "\n" +
20:                    role3 + "\t" + actor3 + "\n" +
21:                    role4 + "\t" + actor4);
22:        }
23: }
```

Look over the program and see whether you can figure out what it's doing at each stage. Here's a breakdown of what's taking place:

▶ Line 1 gives the Java program the name Credits.

▶ Line 2 begins the main() block statement in which all of the program's work gets done.

▶ Lines 4–14 set up variables to hold information about the film, its director, and its stars. One of the variables, year, is an integer. The rest are string variables.

▶ Lines 16–21 are one long System.out.println() statement. Everything between the first parenthesis on Line 16 and the last parenthesis on Line 21 is displayed onscreen. The newline character (\n) causes the text after it to be displayed at the beginning of a new line. The tab character (\t) inserts tab spacing in the output. The rest are either text or string variables that should be shown.

▶ Line 22 ends the main() block statement.

▶ Line 23 ends the program.

If you do encounter error messages, correct any typos you find in your version of the Credits program and save it again. NetBeans compiles the program automatically. When you run the program, you see an output window like the output pane in Figure 6.1.

FIGURE 6.1
The output of the Credits program.

NOTE

If this hour's trivia related to *The Piano* and the films of director Jane Campion has sparked your curiosity or if you just dig quiet women in braids, visit Magnus Hjelstuen's unofficial *The Piano* website at www.cadenhead.org/piano.

Summary

When your version of `Credits` looks like Figure 6.1, give yourself some credit. Six hours into this book, you're writing longer Java programs and dealing with more sophisticated issues. Strings are something you use every time you sit down to write a program.

At the beginning of *The Piano*, Holly Hunter's character Ada lost her piano when her new husband refused to make his Maori laborers carry it home. Strings cannot be taken away from you. You'll be using strings in many ways to communicate with users.

Q&A

Q. **How can I set the value of a string variable to be blank?**

A. Use an empty string, a pair of double quotation marks without any text between them. The following code creates a new string variable called adaSays and sets it to nothing:

```
String adaSays = "";
```

Q. **I can't seem to get the** `toUpperCase()` **method to change a string so that it's all capital letters. What am I doing wrong?**

A. When you call a String object's toUpperCase() method, it doesn't actually change the String object it is called on. Instead, it creates a new string that is set in all uppercase letters. Consider the following statements:

```
String firstName = "Nessie";
String changeName = firstName.toUpperCase();
System.out.println("First Name: " + firstName);
```

These statements display the text First Name: Nessie because firstName contains the original string. If you switched the last statement to display the changeName variable instead, it would output First Name: NESSIE.

Strings do not change in value in Java after they are created.

Q. **Do all methods in Java display** `true` **or** `false` **in the same way that the** `equals()` **method does in relation to strings?**

A. Methods have different ways of producing a response after they are used. When a method sends back a value, as the equals() method does, it's called returning a value. The equals() method is set to return a Boolean value. Other methods might return a string, an integer, another type of variable, or nothing at all—which is represented by void.

Q. **Why do schools assign grades the letters A, B, C, D and F but not E?**

A. The letter grade E already was being used in an alternative grading system. Until the mid-20th century, in the United States the most popular grading system was to assign E for excellent, S for satisfactory, N for needs improvement or U for the dreaded unsatisfactory. So when the ABCD system came along, giving a failing student an E was considered a not-so-excellent idea.

ESNU grading remains in wide use in elementary schools.

Workshop

The following questions test your knowledge of the care and feeding of a string.

Quiz

1. My friend concatenates. Should I report him to the authorities?

   A. No. It's only illegal during the winter months.

   B. Yes, but not until I sell the story to TMZ.com first.

   C. No. All he's doing is pasting two strings together in a program.

2. Why is the word `String` capitalized, whereas `int` and others are not?

   A. `String` is a full word, but `int` ain't.

   B. Like all objects that are a standard part of Java, `String` has a capitalized name.

   C. Poor quality control at Oracle.

3. Which of the following characters puts a single quote in a string?

   A. `<quote>`

   B. `\'`

   C. `'`

Answers

1. **C.** Concatenation is just another word for pasting, joining, melding, or otherwise connecting two strings together. It uses the + and += operators.

2. **B.** The types of objects available in Java are all capitalized, which is the main reason variable names have a lowercase first letter. It makes it harder to mistake them for objects.

3. **B.** The single backslash is what begins one of the special characters that can be inserted into strings.

Activities

You can review the topics of this hour more fully with the following activities:

▶ Write a short Java program called `Favorite` that puts the code from this hour's "Comparing Two Strings" section into the `main()` block statement. Test it out to make sure it works as described and says that Ada's favorite instrument is not the ukulele. When you're done, change the initial value of the `guess` variable from `ukulele` to `piano`. See what happens.

▶ Modify the `Credits` program so the names of the director and all performers are displayed entirely in uppercase letters.

To see Java programs that implement these activities, visit the book's website at www.java24hours.com.

Using Conditional Tests to Make Decisions

When you write a computer program, you provide the computer with a list of instructions called *statements*, and these instructions are followed to the letter. You can tell the computer to work out some unpleasant mathematical formulas, and it works them out. Tell it to display some information, and it dutifully responds.

There are times when you need the computer to be more selective about what it does. For example, if you have written a program to balance your checkbook, you might want the computer to display a warning message if your account is overdrawn. The computer should display this message only if your account is overdrawn. If it isn't, the message would be inaccurate and emotionally upsetting.

The way to accomplish this task in a Java program is to use a conditional, a statement that causes something to happen in a program only if a specific condition is met. During this hour, you learn how to use the conditionals `if`, `else`, and `switch`.

When a Java program makes a decision, it does so by employing a conditional statement. During this hour, you are checking the condition of several things in your Java programs using the conditional keywords `if`, `else`, `switch`, `case`, and `break`. You also use the conditional operators ==, !=, <, >, <=, >= and ?, along with `boolean` variables.

if Statements

The most basic way to test a condition in Java is by using an `if` statement. The `if` statement tests whether a condition is true or false and takes action only if the condition is true.

WHAT YOU'LL LEARN IN THIS HOUR:

▶ Using the `if` statement for basic conditional tests

▶ Testing whether one value is greater than or less than another

▶ Testing whether two values are equal or unequal

▶ Using `else` statements as the opposite of `if` statements

▶ Chaining several conditional tests together

▶ Using the `switch` statement for complicated conditional tests

▶ Creating complicated tests with the ternary operator

[handwritten annotation: used to test a condition]

[handwritten annotation: condition to test]

You use if along with the condition to test, as in the following statement:

```
if (account < 0) {
    System.out.println("Account overdrawn; you need a bailout");
}
```

[handwritten annotation: what happens if condition is true]

The if statement checks whether the account variable is below 0 by using the less than operator <. If it is, the block within the if statement is run, displaying text.

The block only runs if the condition is true. In the preceding example, if the account variable has a value of 0 or higher, the println statement is ignored. Note that the condition you test must be surrounded by parentheses, as in (account < 0).

The less-than operator < is one of several different operators you can use with conditional statements.

Less Than and Greater Than Comparisons

In the preceding section, the < operator is used the same way as in math class: as a less-than sign. There also is a greater-than conditional operator >, which is used in the following statements:

```
int elephantWeight = 900;
int elephantTotal = 13;
int cleaningExpense = 200;

if (elephantWeight > 780) {
    System.out.println("Elephant too fat for tightrope act");
}

if (elephantTotal > 12) {
    cleaningExpense = cleaningExpense + 150;
}
```

[handwritten annotation: greater than]

The first if statement tests whether the value of the elephantWeight variable is greater than 780. The second if statement tests whether the elephantTotal variable is greater than 12.

If the two preceding statements are used in a program where elephantWeight is equal to 600 and elephantTotal is equal to 10, the statements within each if block are ignored.

You can determine whether something is less than or equal to something else with the <= operator. Here's an example:

less than or equal to

```
if (account <= 0) {
    System.out.println("You are flat broke");
}
```

There's also a >= operator for greater-than-or-equal-to tests.

Equal and Not Equal Comparisons

Another condition to check in a program is equality. Is a variable equal to a specific value? Is one variable equal to the value of another? These questions can be answered with the == operator, as in the following statements:

equal

```
if (answer == rightAnswer) {
    studentGrade = studentGrade + 10;
}

if (studentGrade == 100) {
    System.out.println("Show off!");

}
```

You also can test inequality, whether something is not equal to something else, with the != operator, as follows:

```
if (answer != rightAnswer) {    not equal
    score = score - 5;
}
```

You can use the == and != operators with every type of variable except for strings, because strings are objects.

Organizing a Program with Block Statements

Up to this point, the if statements in this hour have been accompanied by a block contained within the { and } brackets. (I believe the technical term for these characters is "squiggly bracket marks.")

Previously, you have seen how block statements are used to mark the beginning and end of the main() block of a Java program. Each statement within the main() block is handled when the program is run.

An if statement does not require a block statement. It can occupy a single line, as in this example:

```
if (account <= 0) System.out.println("No more money");
```

can be a single line with no blocks({})

CAUTION

The operator used to conduct equality tests has two equal signs: ==. It's easy to confuse this operator with the = operator, which is used to give a value to a variable. Always use two equal signs in a conditional statement.

The statement that follows the `if` conditional only is executed if the conditional is true.

Listing 7.1 is an example of a Java program with a block statement used to denote the `main()` block. The block statement begins with the opening bracket { on Line 2 and ends with the closing bracket } on Line 13. Create a new empty Java file called Game in NetBeans and enter the text in Listing 7.1.

LISTING 7.1   The Game Program

```
 1: class Game {
 2:     public static void main(String[] arguments) {
 3:         int total = 0;
 4:         int score = 7;
 5:         if (score == 7) {
 6:             System.out.println("You score a touchdown!");
 7:         }
 8:         if (score == 3) {
 9:             System.out.println("You kick a field goal!");
10:         }
11:         total = total + score;
12:         System.out.println("Total score: " + total);
13:     }
14: }
```

When you run the program, the output should resemble Figure 7.1.

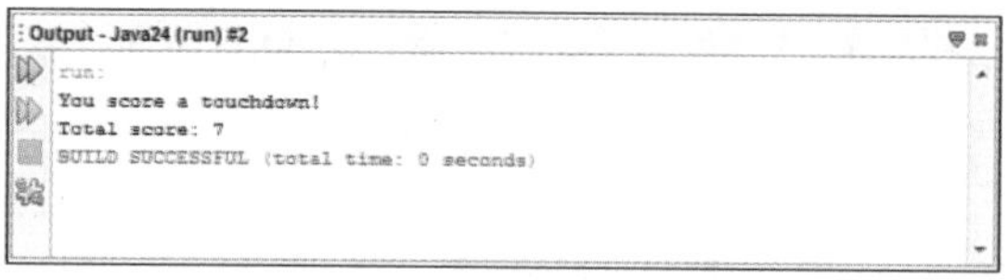

FIGURE 7.1
The output of the Game program.

You can use block statements in `if` statements to make the computer do more than one thing if a condition is true. The following is an example of an `if` statement that includes a block statement:

```
int playerScore = 12000;
int playerLives = 3;
int difficultyLevel = 10;

if (playerScore > 9999) {
    playerLives++;
    System.out.println("Extra life!");
    difficultyLevel = difficultyLevel + 5;
}
```

The brackets are used to group all statements that are part of the if statement. If the variable playerScore is greater than 9,999, three things happen:

▶ The value of the playerLives variable increases by one (because the increment operator ++ is used).

▶ The text "Extra life!" is displayed.

▶ The value of the difficultyLevel variable is increased by 5.

If the variable playerScore is not greater than 9,999, nothing happens. All three statements inside the if statement block are ignored.

if-else **Statements**

There are times when you want to do something if a condition is true and something else if the condition is false. You can do this by using the else statement in addition to the if statement, as in the following example:

```java
int answer = 17;
int correctAnswer = 13;

if (answer == correctAnswer) {
    score += 10;
    System.out.println("That's right. You get 10 points");
} else {
    score -= 5;
    System.out.println("Sorry, that's wrong. You lose 5 points");
}
```

for two items, first is "if", second is "else"

The else statement does not have a condition listed alongside it, unlike the if statement. The else statement is matched with the if statement that immediately precedes it. You also can use else to chain several if statements together, as in the following example:

```java
if (grade == 'A') {
    System.out.println("You got an A. Great job!");
} else if (grade == 'B') {
    System.out.println("You got a B. Good work!");
} else if (grade == 'C') {
    System.out.println("You got a C. What went wrong?");
} else {
    System.out.println("You got an F. You'll do well in Congress!");
}
```

for more than two items, first is "if", last is "else", everything in between is "else if"

By putting together several different if and else statements in this way, you can handle a variety of conditions. The preceding example sends a specific message to A students, B students, C students, and future legislators.

switch **Statements**

The if and else statements are good for situations with two possible conditions, but there are times when you have more than two conditions.

With the preceding grade example, you saw that if and else statements can be chained to handle several different conditions.

Another way to do this is with the switch statement, which can test for a variety of different conditions and respond accordingly. In the following code, the grading example has been rewritten with a switch statement:

```
switch (grade) {
    case 'A':
        System.out.println("You got an A. Great, job!");
        break;   — needed between each case
    case 'B':
        System.out.println("You got a B. Good work!");
        break;
    case 'C':
        System.out.println("You got a C. What went wrong?");
        break;
    default:
        System.out.println("You got an F. You'll do well in Congress!");
}   what happens if none of the cases match
```

(handwritten margin notes: goes through what variable you want to test; If variable equals case, the information is outputted)

The first line of the switch statement specifies the variable that is tested—in this example, grade. Then, the switch statement uses the { and } brackets to form a block statement.

Each case statement checks the test variable in the switch statement against a specific value. The value used in a case statement can be a character, an integer, or a string. In the preceding example, there are case statements for the characters A, B, and C. Each has one or two statements that follow it. When one of these case statements matches the variable in switch, the computer handles the statements after the case statement until it encounters a break statement.

For example, if the grade variable has the value of B, the text "You got a B. Good work!" is displayed. The next statement is break, so nothing else in the switch statement is executed. The break statement tells the computer to break out of the switch statement.

The default statement is used as a catch-all if none of the preceding case statements is true. In this example, it occurs if the grade variable does not equal A, B, or C. You do not have to use a default statement with every switch block statement you use in your programs. If it is omitted, nothing happens if none of the case statements has the correct value.

Java 7 adds support for using strings as the test variable in a switch-case statement. The Commodity class in Listing 7.2 uses this statement to either buy or sell an unspecified commodity. The commodity costs $20 when purchased and earns $15 when sold.

A switch-case statement tests the value of a string named command, running one block if it equals "BUY" and another if it equals "SELL".

LISTING 7.2   The Commodity Program

```
 1: public class Commodity {
 2:     public static void main(String[] arguments) {
 3:         String command = "BUY";
 4:         int balance = 550;
 5:         int quantity = 42;
 6:
 7:         switch (command) {
 8:             case "BUY":
 9:                 quantity += 5;
10:                 balance -= 20;
11:                 break;
12:             case "SELL":
13:                 quantity -= 5;
14:                 balance += 15;
15:         }
16:         System.out.println("Balance: " + balance + "\n"
17:             + "Quantity: " + quantity);
18:     }
19: }
```

This application sets the command string to "BUY" in line 3. When the switch is tested, the case block in lines 9–11 is run. The quantity of the commodity increases by 5 and the balance is lowered by $20.

You might encounter an error when writing this program that prevents it from being compiled and run. NetBeans might not be configured to employ features of the language introduced in Java 7. If you use a string in a switch statement, you might see a red alert icon to the left of the source code editor pane on line 7. The error message could be "strings in switch are not supported," which indicates that some configuration is needed.

Java 7 features are enabled on a project-by-project basis in NetBeans. Follow these steps to do this:

1. In the Projects pane, right-click the Java24 item (or whatever you named your project) and click Properties from the pop-up menu. The Project Properties dialog opens.

2. In the Categories pane, click Sources if it is not already selected. The dialog displays source code properties (see Figure 7.2).

3. In the Source/Binary Format drop-down, choose JDK 7 and click OK.

FIGURE 7.2
Setting up the NetBeans editor to support Java 7.

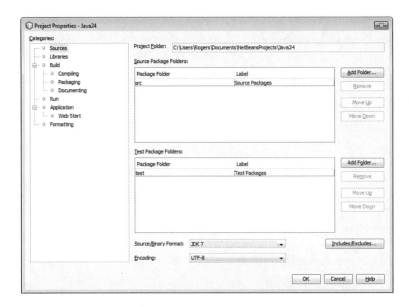

This sets up the source code editor for all programs in the project to work with Java 7.

When the Commodity program is run, it produces the following output:

```
Balance: 530
Quantity: 47
```

The Conditional Operator

The most complicated conditional statement in Java is the ternary operator ?.

You can use the ternary operator when you want to assign a value or display a value based on a condition. For example, consider a video game that sets the numberOfEnemies variable based on whether the skillLevel variable is greater than 5. One way you can do this is an if-else statement:

```
if (skillLevel > 5) {
    numberOfEnemies = 10;
```

```
} else {
    numberOfEnemies = 5;
}
```

A shorter way to do this is to use the ternary operator. A ternary expression has five parts:

▶ The condition to test, surrounded by parentheses, as in (`skillLevel > 5`)

▶ A question mark (?)

▶ The value to use if the condition is true

▶ A colon (:)

▶ The value to use if the condition is false

To use the ternary operator to set `numberOfEnemies` based on `skillLevel`, you could use the following statement:

```
int numberOfEnemies = (skillLevel > 5) ? 10 : 5;
```

← *says if skillLevel is greater than 5, number of enemies equals 10, but if not, 5, good for comparison of two items*

You also can use the ternary operator to determine what information to display. Consider the example of a program that displays the text "Mr." or "Ms." depending on the value of the `gender` variable. Here's a statement that accomplishes this:

```
System.out.print( (gender.equals("male")) ? "Mr." : "Ms." );
```

The ternary operator can be useful, but it's also the hardest conditional in Java to understand. As you learn Java, you don't encounter any situations where the ternary operator must be used instead of `if-else` statements.

Watching the Clock

The next project gives you another look at each of the conditional tests you can use in your programs. For this project, you use Java's built-in time-keeping feature, which keeps track of the current date and time, and present this information in sentence form.

Run NetBeans (or another program to create Java programs) and give a new class the name `Clock`. This program is long, but most of it consists of long conditional statements. Type the full text of Listing 7.3 into the source code editor, and save the file.

importants everything except utility package *(handwritten)*

LISTING 7.3   The Clock Program

```
 1: import java.util.*;
 2:
 3: class Clock {
 4:     public static void main(String[] arguments) {
 5:         // get current time and date
 6:         Calendar now = Calendar.getInstance();
 7:         int hour = now.get(Calendar.HOUR_OF_DAY);
 8:         int minute = now.get(Calendar.MINUTE);
 9:         int month = now.get(Calendar.MONTH) + 1;
10:         int day = now.get(Calendar.DAY_OF_MONTH);
11:         int year = now.get(Calendar.YEAR);
12:
13:         // display greeting
14:         if (hour < 12) {
15:             System.out.println("Good morning.\n");
16:         } else if (hour < 17) {
17:             System.out.println("Good afternoon.\n");
18:         } else {
19:             System.out.println("Good evening.\n");
20:         }
21:
22:         // begin time message by showing the minutes
23:         System.out.print("It's");
24:         if (minute != 0) {
25:             System.out.print(" " + minute + " ");
26:             System.out.print( (minute != 1) ? "minutes" :
27:                 "minute");
28:             System.out.print(" past");
29:         }
30:
31:         // display the hour
32:         System.out.print(" ");
33:         System.out.print( (hour > 12) ? (hour - 12) : hour );
34:         System.out.print(" o'clock on ");
35:
36:         // display the name of the month
37:         switch (month) {
38:             case 1:
39:                 System.out.print("January");
40:                 break;
41:             case 2:
42:                 System.out.print("February");
43:                 break;
44:             case 3:
45:                 System.out.print("March");
46:                 break;
47:             case 4:
48:                 System.out.print("April");
49:                 break;
50:             case 5:
51:                 System.out.print("May");
```

(handwritten annotation lines 7–11: self explanatory)

LISTING 7.3   Continued

```
52:               break;
53:           case 6:
54:               System.out.print("June");
55:               break;
56:           case 7:
57:               System.out.print("July");
58:               break;
59:           case 8:
60:               System.out.print("August");
61:               break;
62:           case 9:
63:               System.out.print("September");
64:               break;
65:           case 10:
66:               System.out.print("October");
67:               break;
68:           case 11:
69:               System.out.print("November");
70:               break;
71:           case 12:
72:               System.out.print("December");
73:       }
74:
75:       // display the date and year
76:       System.out.println(" " + day + ", " + year + ".");
77:   }
78: }
```

After the program compiles correctly, look it over to get a good idea about how the conditional tests are being used.

With the exception of Line 1 and Lines 6–11, the Clock program contains material that has been covered up to this point. After a series of variables are set up to hold the current date and time, a series of if or switch conditionals are used to determine what information should be displayed.

This program contains several uses of System.out.println() and System.out.print() to display strings.

Lines 6–11 refer to a Calendar variable called now. The Calendar variable type is capitalized because Calendar is an object.

You learn how to create and work with objects during Hour 10, "Creating Your First Object." For this hour, focus on what's taking place in those lines rather than how it's happening.

The `Clock` program is made up of the following sections:

- ▶ Line 1 enables your program to use a class that is needed to track the current date and time: `java.util.Calendar`.

- ▶ Lines 3–4 begin the `Clock` program and its `main()` statement block.

- ▶ Line 6 creates a `Calendar` object called `now` that contains the current date and time of your system. The `now` object changes each time you run this program. (Unless the physical laws of the universe are altered and time stands still).

- ▶ Lines 7–11 create variables to hold the `hour`, `minute`, `month`, `day`, and `year`. The values for these variables are pulled from the `Calendar` object, which is the storehouse for all this information.

- ▶ Lines 14–20 display one of three possible greetings: "Good morning.", "Good afternoon.", or "Good evening." The greeting to display is selected based on the value of the `hour` variable.

- ▶ Lines 23–29 display the current minute along with some accompanying text. First, the text "It's" is displayed in Line 23. If the value of `minute` is equal to 0, Lines 25–28 are ignored because of the `if` statement in Line 24. This statement is necessary because it would not make sense for the program to tell someone that it's 0 minutes past an hour. Line 25 displays the current value of the `minute` variable. A ternary operator is used in Lines 26–27 to display either the text "minutes" or "minute," depending on whether `minute` is equal to 1. Finally, in Line 28 the text `past` is displayed.

- ▶ Lines 32–34 display the current hour by using another ternary operator. This ternary conditional statement in Line 33 causes the hour to be displayed differently if it is larger than 12, which prevents the computer from stating times like "15 o'clock."

- ▶ Lines 37–73, almost half of the program, are a long `switch` statement that displays a different name of the month based on the integer value stored in the `month` variable.

- ▶ Line 76 finishes off the display by showing the current date and the year.

- ▶ Lines 77–78 close out the `main()` statement block and then the entire `Clock` program.

When you run this program, the output should display a sentence based on the current date and time. The output of the application is shown in the Output pane in Figure 7.3.

FIGURE 7.3
The output of the Clock program.

Run the program several times to see how it keeps up with the clock.

Summary

Now that you can use conditional statements, the overall intelligence of your Java programs has improved greatly. Your programs can evaluate information and use it to react differently in different situations, even if information changes as the program is running. They can decide between two or more alternatives based on specific conditions.

Programming a computer forces you to break a task down into a logical set of steps to undertake and decisions that must be made. Using the if statement and other conditionals in programming also promotes a type of logical thinking that can reap benefits in other aspects of your life:

▶ "*If* he is elected president in November, I will seek a Cabinet position, *else* I will move to Canada."

▶ "*If* my blind date is attractive, I'll pay for dinner at an expensive restaurant, *else* we will go to Pizza Hut."

▶ "*If* I violate my probation, the only team that will draft me is the Philadelphia Eagles."

Q&A

Q. The `if` statement seems like the one that's most useful. Is it possible to use only `if` statements in programs and never use the others?

A. It's possible to do without `else` or `switch`, and many programmers never use the ternary operator `?`. However, `else` and `switch` often are beneficial to use in your programs because they make the programs easier to understand. A set of `if` statements chained together can become unwieldy.

Q. In the `Clock` program, why is 1 added to `Calendar.MONTH` to get the current month value?

A. This is necessary because of a quirk in the way that the Calendar class represents months. Instead of numbering them from 1 to 12 as you might expect, Calendar numbers months beginning with 0 in January and ending with 11 in December. Adding 1 causes months to be represented numerically in a more understandable manner.

Q. During this hour, opening and closing brackets { and } are not used with an `if` statement if it is used in conjunction with only one statement. Isn't it mandatory to use brackets?

A. No. Brackets can be used as part of any `if` statement to surround the part of the program that's dependent on the conditional test. Using brackets is a good practice to get into because it prevents a common error that might take place when you revise the program. If you add a second statement after an `if` conditional and don't add brackets, unexpected errors occur when the program is run.

Q. Does `break` have to be used in each section of statements that follow a `case`?

A. You don't have to use `break`. If you do not use it at the end of a group of statements, all the remaining statements inside the switch block statement are handled, regardless of the case value they are being tested with. However, in most cases you're likely to want a `break` statement at the end of each group.

Q. Why did the Thompson Twins get that name when they were a trio, they were not related, and none of them was named Thompson?

A. Band members Tom Bailey, Alannah Currie, and Joe Leeway called themselves the Thompson Twins in honor of Thomson and Thompson, a pair of bumbling detectives featured in the Belgian comic books *The Adventures of Tintin*.

The bowler-wearing detectives were physically indistinguishable except for a minor difference in the shape of their mustaches. Despite being terrible at their jobs, they were inexplicably assigned to important and sensitive missions. They often pursued Tintin for crimes that he did not commit.

As their names would indicate, the detectives were not related either.

Workshop

The following questions see what condition you're in after studying conditional statements in Java.

Quiz

1. Conditional tests result in either a `true` or `false` value. Which variable type does this remind you of?

    A. None. Stop pestering me with all these questions.

    B. The `long` variable type.

    C. The `boolean` type.

2. Which statement is used as a catch-all category in a `switch` block statement?

    A. `default`

    B. `otherwise`

    C. `onTheOtherHand`

3. What's a conditional?

    A. The thing that repairs messy split ends and tangles after you shampoo.

    B. Something in a program that tests whether a condition is true or false.

    C. The place where you confess your sins to a religious authority figure.

Answers

1. **C.** The `boolean` variable type only can equal `true` or `false`, making it similar to conditional tests. If you answered A., I'm sorry, but there's only 17 hours left and we've got a lot left to cover. Java doesn't teach itself.

2. **A.** `default` statements are handled if none of the other `case` statements matches the `switch` variable.

3. **B.** The other answers describe conditioner and a confessional.

Activities

To improve your conditioning in terms of Java conditionals, review the topics of this hour with the following activities:

▶ Add `//` in front of a `break` statement on one of the lines in the `Clock` program to make it a comment, and then compile it and see what happens when you run it. Try it again with a few more `break` statements removed.

▶ Create a short program that stores a value of your choosing from 1 to 100 in an integer variable called `grade`. Use this `grade` variable with a conditional statement to display a different message for all A, B, C, D, and F students. Try it first with an `if` statement, and then try it with a `switch` statement.

To see Java programs that implement these activities, visit the book's website at www.java24hours.com.

Repeating an Action with Loops

One of the more annoying punishments for schoolchildren is to make them write something over and over again on a chalkboard. On *The Simpsons*, in one of his frequent trips to the board, Bart Simpson had to write, "The art teacher is fat, not pregnant," dozens of times. This punishment might work on children, but a computer can repeat a task with ease.

Computer programs are ideally suited to do the same thing over and over because of loops. A *loop* is a statement or block that is repeated in a program. Some loops run a fixed number of times. Others run indefinitely.

There are three loop statements in Java: `for`, `do`, and `while`. Each can work like the others, but it's beneficial to learn how all three operate. You often can simplify a loop section of a program by choosing the right statement.

for **Loops**

In your programming, you find many circumstances in which a loop is useful. You can use them to keep doing something several times, such as an antivirus program that opens each new email received to look for viruses. You also can use loops to cause the computer to do nothing for a brief period, such as an animated clock that displays the current time once per minute.

A loop statement causes a computer program to return to the same place more than once, like a stunt plane completing an acrobatic loop.

Java's most complex loop statement is `for`. A `for` loop repeats a section of a program a fixed number of times. The following is an example:

WHAT YOU'LL LEARN IN THIS HOUR:

- ▶ Using the `for` loop
- ▶ Using the `while` loop
- ▶ Using the `do-while` loop
- ▶ Exiting a loop prematurely
- ▶ Naming a loop

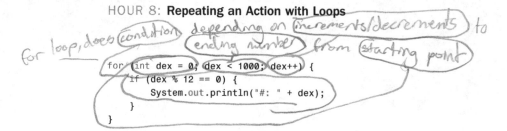

```
for (int dex = 0; dex < 1000; dex++) {
    if (dex % 12 == 0) {
        System.out.println("#: " + dex);
    }
}
```

This loop displays every number from 0 to 999 evenly divisible by 12.

Every for loop has a variable that determines when the loop should begin and end. This variable is called the counter (or index). The counter in the preceding loop is the variable dex.

The example illustrates the three parts of a for statement:

▶ The initialization section: In the first part, the dex variable is given an initial value of 0.

▶ The conditional section: In the second part, there is a conditional test like one you might use in an if statement: dex < 1000.

▶ The change section: The third part is a statement that changes the value of the dex variable, in this example by using the increment operator.

In the initialization section, you set up the counter variable. You can create the variable in the for statement, as the preceding example does with the integer variable dex. You also can create the variable elsewhere in the program. In either case, you should give the variable a starting value in this section of the for statement. The variable has this value when the loop starts.

The conditional section contains a test that must remain true for the loop to continue looping. When the test is false, the loop ends. In this example, the loop ends when the dex variable is equal to or greater than 1,000.

The last section of the for statement contains a statement that changes the value of the counter variable. This statement is handled each time the loop goes around. The counter variable has to change in some way or the loop never ends. In the example, dex is incremented by one in the change section. If dex was not changed, it would stay at its original value of 0 and the conditional dex < 1000 always would be true.

The for statement's block is executed during each trip through the loop.

The preceding example had the following statements in the block:

```
if (dex % 12 == 0) {
    System.out.println("#: " + dex);
}
```

These statements are executed 1,000 times. The loop starts by setting the dex variable equal to 0. It then adds 1 to dex during each pass through the loop and stops looping when dex is no longer less than 1,000.

As you have seen with if statements, a for loop does not require brackets if it contains only a single statement. This is shown in the following example:

```
for (int p = 0; p < 500; p++)
    System.out.println("I will not sell miracle cures");
```

This loop displays the text "I will not sell miracle cures" 500 times. Although brackets are not required around a single statement inside a loop, you can use them to make the block easier to spot.

The first program you create during this hour displays the first 200 multiples of 9: 9×1, 9×2, 9×3, and so on, up to 9×200. In NetBeans, create a new empty Java file named Nines and enter the text in Listing 8.1. When you save the file, it is stored as Nines.java.

LISTING 8.1   The Full Text of Nines.java

```
1: class Nines {
2:     public static void main(String[] arguments) {
3:         for (int dex = 1; dex <= 200; dex++) {
4:             int multiple = 9 * dex;
5:             System.out.print(multiple + " ");
6:         }
7:     }
8: }
```

The Nines program contains a for statement in Line 3. This statement has three parts:

▶ Initialization: int dex = 1, which creates an integer variable called dex and gives it an initial value of 1.

▶ Conditional: dex <= 200, which must be true during each trip through the loop. When it is not true, the loop ends.

▶ Change: dex++, which increments the dex variable by one during each trip through the loop.

Run the program by choosing Run, Run File in NetBeans. The program produces the following output:

NOTE

An unusual term you might hear in connection with loops is *iteration*. An iteration is a single trip through a loop. The counter variable that is used to control the loop is called an *iterator*.

Output ▼

```
9 18 27 36 45 54 63 72 81 90 99 108 117 126 135 144 153 162 171
180 189 198 207 216 225 234 243 252 261 270 279 288 297 306 315
324 333 342 351 360 369 378 387 396 405 414 423 432 441 450 459
468 477 486 495 504 513 522 531 540 549 558 567 576 585 594 603
612 621 630 639 648 657 666 675 684 693 702 711 720 729 738 747
756 765 774 783 792 801 810 819 828 837 846 855 864 873 882 891
900 909 918 927 936 945 954 963 972 981 990 999 1008 1017 1026
1035 1044 1053 1062 1071 1080 1089 1098 1107 1116 1125 1134 1143
1152 1161 1170 1179 1188 1197 1206 1215 1224 1233 1242 1251 1260
1269 1278 1287 1296 1305 1314 1323 1332 1341 1350 1359 1368 1377
1386 1395 1404 1413 1422 1431 1440 1449 1458 1467 1476 1485 1494
1503 1512 1521 1530 1539 1548 1557 1566 1575 1584 1593 1602 1611
1620 1629 1638 1647 1656 1665 1674 1683 1692 1701 1710 1719 1728
1737 1746 1755 1764 1773 1782 1791 1800
```

The output window in NetBeans does not wrap text, so all the numbers appear on a single line. To make the text wrap, right-click the output pane and choose Wrap text from the pop-up menu.

while **Loops**

The while loop does not have as many different sections as a for loop. The only thing it needs is a conditional test, which accompanies the while statement. The following is an example of a while loop:

```
while (gameLives > 0) {
    // the statements inside the loop go here
}
```

This loop continues repeating until the gameLives variable is no longer greater than 0.

The while statement tests the condition at the beginning of the loop before any statements in the loop have been handled. If the tested condition is false when a program reaches the while statement for the first time, the statements inside the loop are ignored.

If the while condition is true, the loop goes around once and tests the while condition again. If the tested condition never changes inside the loop, the loop keeps looping indefinitely.

The following statements cause a while loop to display the same line of text several times:

```
int limit = 5;
int count = 1;
while (count < limit) {
    System.out.println("Pork is not a verb");
    count++;
}
```

A while loop uses one or more variables set up before the loop statement. In this example, two integer variables are created: limit, which has a value of 5, and count, which has a value of 1.

The while loop displays the text "Pork is not a verb" four times. If you gave the count variable an initial value of 6 instead of 1, the text never would be displayed.

do-while **Loops**

The do-while loop is similar to the while loop, but the conditional test goes in a different place. The following is an example of a do-while loop:

```
do {
    // the statements inside the loop go here
} while (gameLives > 0);
```

do-while loop, same as while loop except it does the stuff inside then the condition.

Like the while loop, this loop continues looping until the gameLives variable is no longer greater than 0. The do-while loop is different because the conditional test is conducted after the statements inside the loop, instead of before them.

When the do loop is reached for the first time as a program runs, the statements between the do and while are handled automatically, and then the while condition is tested to determine whether the loop should be repeated. If the while condition is true, the loop goes around one more time. If the condition is false, the loop ends. Something must happen inside the do and while statements that changes the condition tested with while, or the loop continued indefinitely. The statements inside a do-while loop always are handled at least once.

The following statements cause a do-while loop to display the same line of text several times:

```
int limit = 5;
int count = 1;
do {
    System.out.println("I will not Xerox my butt");
    count++;
} while (count < limit);
```

Like a while loop, a do-while loop uses one or more variables that are set up before the loop statement.

The loop displays the text "I will not Xerox my butt" four times. If you gave the count variable an initial value of 6 instead of 1, the text would be displayed once, even though count is never less than limit.

In a do-while loop, the statements inside the loop are executed at least once even if the loop condition is false the first time around.

Exiting a Loop

The normal way to exit a loop is for the tested condition to become false. This is true of all three types of loops in Java. There might be times when you want a loop to end immediately, even if the condition being tested is still true. You can accomplish this with a break statement, as shown in the following code:

```
int index = 0;
while (index <= 1000) {
    index = index + 5;
    if (index == 400) {
        break;
    }
}
```

exits loop

A break statement ends the loop that contains the statement.

In this example, the while loop loops until the index variable is greater than 1,000. However, a special case causes the loop to end earlier than that: If index equals 400, the break statement is executed, ending the loop immediately.

Another special-circumstance statement you can use inside a loop is continue. The continue statement causes the loop to exit its current trip through the loop and start over at the first statement of the loop. Consider the following loop:

```
int index = 0;
while (index <= 1000) {
    index = index + 5;
    if (index == 400)
        continue;
    System.out.println("The index is " + index);
}
```

allows you to go back to beginning of loop!

In this loop, the statements are handled normally unless the value of index equals 400. In that case, the continue statement causes the loop to go back to the while statement instead of proceeding normally to the System.out.println() statement. Because of the continue statement, the loop never displays the following text:

```
The index is 400
```

You can use the break and continue statements with all three kinds of loops.

The break statement makes it possible to create a loop in your program that's designed to run forever, as in this example:

```
while (true) {
    if (quitKeyPressed == true) {
        break;
    }
}
```

Naming a Loop

Like other statements in Java programs, you can place loops inside each other. The following shows a for loop inside a while loop:

```
int points = 0;
int target = 100;
while (target <= 100) {
    for (int i = 0; i < target; i++) {
        if (points > 50)
            break;
        points = points + i;
    }
}
```

In this example, the break statement causes the for loop to end if the points variable is greater than 50. However, the while loop never ends because target is never greater than 100.

In some cases, you might want to break out of both loops. To make this possible, you have to give the outer loop—in this example, the while statement—a name. To name a loop, put the name on the line before the beginning of the loop and follow it with a colon (:).

When the loop has a name, use the name after the break or continue statement to indicate the loop to which the break or continue statement applies. The following example repeats the previous one with the exception of one thing: If the points variable is greater than 50, both loops end.

```
int points = 0;
int target = 100;
targetLoop:
While (target <= 100) {
    for (int i = 0; i < target; i++) {
        if (points > 50)
            break targetLoop;
        points = points + i;
    }
}
```

(handwritten: naming loop; has to be before)

(handwritten: indication for breakage)

When a loop's name is used in a `break` or `continue` statement, the name does not include a colon.

Complex `for` Loops

A `for` loop can be more complex, including more than one variable in its initialization, conditional, and change sections. Each section of a `for` loop is set off from the other sections with a semicolon (`;`). A `for` loop can have more than one variable set up during the initialization section and more than one statement in the change section, as in the following code:

```
int i, j;
for (i = 0, j = 0; i * j < 1000; i++, j += 2) {
    System.out.println(i + " * " + j + " = " + (i * j));
}
```

In each section of the `for` loop, commas are used to separate the variables as in `i = 0, j = 0`. The example loop displays a list of equations where the i and j variables are multiplied together. The i variable increases by one, and the j variable increases by two during each trip through the loop. When i multiplied by j is equal or greater than 1,000, the loop ends.

Sections of a `for` loop also can be empty. An example of this is when a loop's counter variable already has been created with an initial value in another part of the program, as in the following:

```
for ( ; displayCount < endValue; displayCount++) {
    // loop statements would be here
}
```

(handwritten: don't rely on it)

(handwritten: can be initialized before)

Testing Your Computer Speed

This hour's workshop is a Java program that performs a *benchmark*, a test that measures how fast computer hardware or software is operating. The

Benchmark program uses a loop statement to repeatedly perform the following mathematical expression:

```
double x = Math.sqrt(index);
```

This statement calls the `Math.sqrt()` method to find the square root of a number. You learn how methods work during Hour 11, "Describing What Your Object Is Like."

The benchmark you're creating sees how many times a Java program can calculate a square root in one minute.

Use NetBeans to create a new empty Java file called Benchmark. Enter the text of Listing 8.2 and save the program when you're done.

LISTING 8.2   The Full Source Code of Benchmark.java

```
 1: class Benchmark {
 2:     public static void main(String[] arguments) {
 3:         long startTime = System.currentTimeMillis();    get milliseconds
 4:         long endTime = startTime + 60000;
 5:         long index = 0;
 6:         while (true) {
 7:             double x = Math.sqrt(index);
 8:             long now = System.currentTimeMillis();
 9:             if (now > endTime) {
10:                 break;
11:             }
12:             index++;
13:         }
14:         System.out.println(index + " loops in one minute.");
15:     }
16: }
```

The following things take place in the program:

▶ Lines 1–2: The Benchmark class is declared and the main() block of the program begins.

▶ Line 3: The startTime variable is created with the current time in milliseconds as its value, measured by calling the currentTimeMillis() method of Java's System class.

▶ Line 4: The endTime variable is created with a value 60,000 higher than startTime. Because one minute equals 60,000 milliseconds, this sets the variable one minute past startTime.

▶ Line 5: A long named index is set up with an initial value of 0.

▶ Line 6: The `while` statement begins a loop using `true` as the conditional, which causes the loop to continue forever (in other words, until something else stops it).

▶ Line 7: The square root of `index` is calculated and stored in the `x` variable.

▶ Line 8: Using `currentTimeMillis()`, the now variable is created with the current time.

▶ Lines 9–11: If `now` is greater than `endTime`, this signifies that the loop has been running for one minute and `break` ends the `while` loop. Otherwise, it keeps looping.

▶ Line 12: The `index` variable is incremented by 1 with each trip through the loop.

▶ Lines 14: Outside the loop, the program displays the number of times it performed the square root calculation.

The output of the application is shown in the Output pane in Figure 8.1.

FIGURE 8.1
The output of the `Benchmark` program.

The `Benchmark` program is an excellent way to see whether your computer is faster than mine. During the testing of this program, my computer performed around 4.5 billion calculations. If your computer has better results, don't just send me your condolences. Buy more of my books so I can upgrade.

Summary

Loops are a fundamental part of most programming languages. Animation created by displaying several graphics in sequence is one of many tasks you could not accomplish in Java or any other programming language without loops.

Every one of Bart Simpson's chalkboard punishments has been documented on the Web. Visit www.snpp.com/guides/chalkboard.openings.html to see the list along with a Java program that runs on the page drawing Bart's sayings on a green chalkboard.

Q&A

Q. The term *initialization* has been used in several places. What does it mean?

A. It means to give something an initial value and set it up. When you create a variable and assign a starting value to it, you are initializing the variable.

Q. If a loop never ends, how does the program stop running?

A. Usually in a program where a loop does not end, something else in the program is set up to stop execution in some way. For example, a loop in a game program could continue indefinitely while the player still has lives left.

One bug that crops up often as you work on programs is an *infinite loop*, a loop that never stops because of a programming mistake. If one of the Java programs you run becomes stuck in an infinite loop, press the red alert icon to the left of the Output pane.

Q. How can I buy stock in the Green Bay Packers?

A. Unless the publicly owned NFL team decides to hold another stock sale, the only way to become a stockholder is to inherit shares in a will.

The Packers have sold stock in 1923, 1935, 1950, and 1997. Approximately 112,000 people own 4.7 million shares in the team, despite the fact that they have very limited rights associated with the stock.

Holders don't earn a dividend and can't profit from their shares. They only can sell them back to the team and lose money in the deal. No individual can own more than 200,000 shares.

They do receive exclusive team merchandise offers and can attend an annual meeting to elect the seven-member board that manages the team.

In the 1923 stock sale that formed the franchise, 1,000 fans bought shares for $5 each. The 1997 sale raised $24 million for the Lambeau Field renovation.

More information on the stock can be found on the Web at www.packers.com/community/shareholders.html.

Workshop

The following questions test your knowledge of loops. In the spirit of the subject matter, repeat each of these until you get them right.

Quiz

1. What must be used to separate each section of a `for` statement?

    A. Commas

    B. Semicolons

    C. Off-duty police officers

2. Which statement causes a program to go back to the statement that began a loop and then keep going from there?

    A. `continue`

    B. `next`

    C. `skip`

3. Which loop statement in Java always runs at least once?

    A. `for`

    B. `while`

    C. `do-while`

Answers

1. B. Commas are used to separate things within a section, but semicolons separate sections.

2. A. The `break` statement ends a loop entirely, and `continue` skips to the next go-round of the loop.

3. C. The `do-while` conditional isn't evaluated until after the first pass through the loop.

Activities

If your head isn't going in circles from all this looping, review the topics of this hour with the following activities:

▶ Modify the `Benchmark` program to test the execution of simple mathematical calculation such as multiplication or division.

▶ Write a short program using loops that finds the first 400 numbers that are multiples of 13.

To see Java programs that implement these activities, visit the book's website at www.java24hours.com.

HOUR 9
Storing Information with Arrays

No one benefited more from the development of the computer than Santa Claus. For centuries, humankind has put an immense burden on him to gather and process information. Old St. Nick has to keep track of the following things:

- Naughty children

- Nice children

- Gift requests

- Homes with impassable chimneys

- Women who want more from Santa than Mrs. Claus is willing to let him give

- Countries that shoot unidentified aircraft first and ask questions later

Computers were a great boon to the North Pole. They are ideal for the storage, categorization, and study of information.

The most basic way that information is stored in a computer program is by putting it into a variable. The list of naughty children is an example of a collection of similar information. To keep track of a list of this kind, you can use arrays.

Arrays are groups of related variables that share the same type. Any type of information that can be stored as a variable can become the items stored in an array. Arrays can be used to keep track of more sophisticated types of information than a single variable, but they are almost as easy to create and manipulate as variables.

WHAT YOU'LL LEARN IN THIS HOUR:

- Creating an array
- Setting the size of an array
- Giving a value to an array element
- Changing the information in an array
- Making multidimensional arrays
- Sorting an array

NOTE

Java is flexible about where the square brackets are placed when an array is being created. You can put them after the variable name instead of the variable type, as in the following:

```
String niceChild[];
```

To make arrays easier for humans to spot in your programs, you should stick to one style rather than switching back and forth. Examples in this book always place the brackets after the variable or class type.

Creating Arrays

Arrays are variables grouped together under a common name. The term array should be familiar to you—think of a salesperson showing off her array of products or a game show with a dazzling array of prizes. Like variables, arrays are created by stating the type of variable being organized into the array and the name of the array. A pair of square brackets ([ ]) follow the type to distinguish arrays from variables.

You can create arrays for any type of information that can be stored as a variable. For example, the following statement creates an array of string variables:

```
String[] naughtyChild;
```

Here are two more examples:

```
int[] reindeerWeight;
boolean[] hostileAirTravelNations;
```

The previous examples create arrays, but they do not store any values in them. To do this, you can use the new keyword along with the variable type or store values in the array within { and } marks. When using new, you must specify how many different items are stored in the array. Each item in an array is called an *element*. The following statement creates an array and sets aside space for the values that it holds:

```
int[] elfSeniority = new int[250];
```

This example creates an array of integers called elfSeniority. The array has 250 elements that can store the months that each of Santa's elves has been employed at the Pole. If Santa runs a union shop, this information is extremely important to track.

When you create an array with the new statement, you must specify the number of elements. Each element of the array is given an initial value that depends on the type of the array. All numeric arrays have the initial value 0, char arrays equal '\0', and boolean arrays have the value false. A String array and all other objects are created with the initial value of null.

For arrays that are not extremely large, you can set up their initial values at the same time that you create them. The following example creates an array of strings and gives them initial values:

```
String[] reindeerNames = { "Dasher", "Dancer", "Prancer", "Vixen",
    "Comet", "Cupid", "Donder", "Blitzen" };
```

The information that should be stored in elements of the array is placed between { and } brackets with commas separating each element. The number of elements in the array is set to the number of elements in the comma-separated list. Each element of the array must be of the same type. The preceding example uses a string to hold each of the reindeer names.

After the array is created, you cannot make room for more elements. Even if you recall the most famous reindeer of all, you couldn't add "Rudolph" as the ninth element of the reindeerNames array. The Java compiler won't let poor Rudolph join in any reindeerNames.

Using Arrays

You use arrays in a program as you would any variable, except for the element number between the square brackets next to the array's name. You can use an array element anywhere a variable could be used. The following statements all use arrays that have already been defined in this hour's examples:

```
elfSeniority[193] += 1;
niceChild[9428] = "Eli";
if (hostileAirTravelNations[currentNation] == true) {
    sendGiftByMail();
}
```

The first element of an array is numbered 0 instead of 1. This means that the highest number is one less than you might expect. Consider the following statement:

```
String[] topGifts = new String[10];
```

This statement creates an array of string variables numbered from 0 to 9. If you referred to topGifts[10] somewhere else in the program, you would get an error message referring to an ArrayIndexOutOfBoundsException.

Exceptions are another word for errors in Java programs. This exception is an "array index out of bounds" error, which means that a program tried to use an array element that doesn't exist within its defined boundaries. You learn more about exceptions during Hour 18, "Handling Errors in a Program."

If you want to check the upper limit of an array so you can avoid going beyond that limit, a variable called length is associated with each array that is created. The length variable is an integer that contains the number of elements an array holds. The following example creates an array and then reports its length:

```
String[] reindeerNames = { "Dasher", "Dancer", "Prancer", "Vixen",
    "Comet", "Cupid", "Donder", "Blitzen", "Rudolph" };
System.out.println("There are " + reindeerNames.length + " reindeer.");
```

gives integer value of array

In this example, the value of `reindeerNames.length` is 9, which means that the highest element number you can specify is 8.

You can work with text in Java as a string or an array of characters. When you're working with strings, one useful technique is to put each character in a string into its own element of a character array. To do this, call the string's `toCharArray()` method, which produces a `char` array with the same number of elements as the length of the string.

This hour's first project uses both of the techniques introduced in this section. The `SpaceRemover` program displays a string with all space characters replaced with periods (.).

To get started, open the Java24 project in NetBeans, choose File, New File and create a new Empty Java File called `SpaceRemover`. Enter Listing 9.1 in the source editor and save it when you're done.

LISTING 9.1   The Full Text of `SpaceRemover.java`

holds characters for loop

```
 1: class SpaceRemover {
 2:     public static void main(String[] args) {
 3:         String mostFamous = "Rudolph the Red-Nosed Reindeer";
 4:         char[] mfl = mostFamous.toCharArray();      turns string
 5:         for (int dex = 0; dex < mfl.length; dex++) {
 6:             char current = mfl[dex];                array into character array
 7:             if (current != ' ') {
 8:                 System.out.print(current);
 9:             } else {
10:                 System.out.print('.');
11:             }
12:         }
13:         System.out.println();
14:     }
15: }
```

Run the program with the command Run, Run File to see the output shown in Figure 9.1.

The `SpaceRemover` application stores the text "Rudolph the Red-Nosed Reindeer" in two places—a string called `mostFamous` and a `char` array called `mfl`. The array is created in Line 4 by calling the `toCharArray()` method of `mostFamous`, which fills an array with one element for each character in the text. The character "R" goes into element 0, "u" into element 1, and so on, up to "r" in element 29.

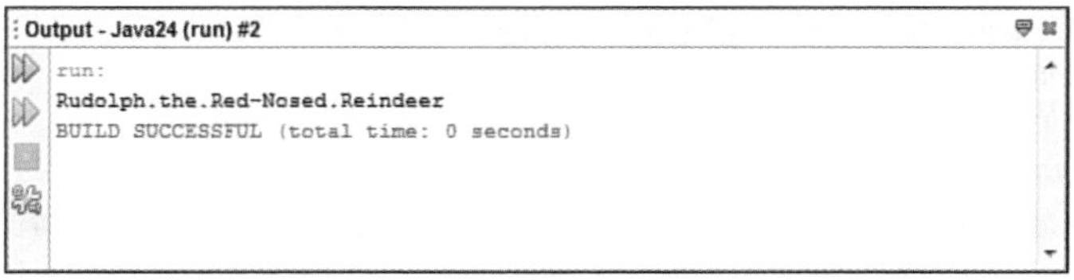

```
Output - Java24 (run) #2
 run:
 Rudolph.the.Red-Nosed.Reindeer
 BUILD SUCCESSFUL (total time: 0 seconds)
```

FIGURE 9.1
The output of the SpaceRemover
program.

The for loop in Lines 5–12 looks at each character in the mfl array. If the character is not a space, it is displayed. If it is a space, a . character is displayed instead.

Multidimensional Arrays

The arrays thus far in the hour all have one dimension, so you can retrieve an element using a single number. Some types of information require more dimensions to store adequately as arrays, such as points in an (x,y) coordinate system. One dimension of the array could store the x coordinate, and the other dimension could store the y coordinate.

To create an array that has two dimensions, you must use an additional set of square brackets when creating and using the array, as in these statements:

```
boolean[][] selectedPoint = new boolean[50][50];
selectedPoint[4][13] = true;
selectedPoint[7][6] = true;
selectedPoint[11][22] = true;
```

[handwritten annotations: Creates multidimensional boolean array; set amount for multidimensional array; sets it to true]

This example creates an array of Boolean values called selectedPoint. The array has 50 elements in its first dimension and 50 elements in its second dimension, so 2,500 individual array elements can hold values (50 multiplied by 50). When the array is created, each element is given the default value of false. Three elements are given the value true: a point at the (x,y) position of 4,13, one at 7,6, and one at 11,22.

Arrays can have as many dimensions as you need, but keep in mind that they take up a lot of memory if they're extremely large. Creating the 50 by 50 selectedPoint array was equivalent to creating 2,500 individual variables.

Sorting an Array

When you have grouped a bunch of similar items together into an array, one thing you can do is rearrange items. The following statements swap the values of two elements in an integer array called numbers:

```
int temp = numbers[5];
numbers[5] = numbers[6];
numbers[6] = temp;
```

These statements result in numbers[5] and numbers[6] trading values with each other. The integer variable called temp is used as a temporary storage place for one of the values being swapped. Sorting is the process of arranging a list of related items into a set order, such as when a list of numbers is sorted from lowest to highest.

Santa Claus could use sorting to arrange the order of gift recipients by last name with Willie Aames and Hank Aaron raking in their Yuletide plunder much earlier than alphabetical unfortunates Dweezil Zappa and Jim Zorn.

Sorting an array is easy in Java because the Arrays class does all of the work. Arrays, which is part of the java.util group of classes, can rearrange arrays of all variable types.

To use the Arrays class in a program, use the following steps:

1. Use the import java.util.* statement to make all the java.util classes available in the program.

2. Create the array.

3. Use the sort() method of the Arrays class to rearrange an array.

An array of variables that is sorted by the Arrays class are rearranged into ascending numerical order. Characters and strings are arranged in alphabetical order.

To see this in action, create a new Empty Java File named Name and enter the text of Listing 9.2, a short program that sorts names, in the source editor.

LISTING 9.2   The Full Source Code of Name.java

```
 1: import java.util.*;
 2:
 3: class Name {
 4:     public static void main(String[] args) {
 5:         String names[] = { "Lauren", "Audrina", "Heidi", "Whitney",
 6:             "Stephanie", "Spencer", "Lisa", "Brody", "Frankie",
 7:             "Holly", "Jordan", "Brian", "Jason" };
 8:         System.out.println("The original order:");
 9:         for (int i = 0; i < names.length; i++) {
10:             System.out.print(i + ": " + names[i] + " ");
11:         }
12:         Arrays.sort(names);
13:         System.out.println("\nThe new order:");
```

Sorts array in alphabetical order

LISTING 9.2   Continued

```
14:          for (int i = 0; i < names.length; i++) {
15:              System.out.print(i + ": " + names[i] + " ");
16:          }
17:          System.out.println();
18:      }
19: }
```

[handwritten annotation: allow you to all the individual indexes.]

When you run this Java program, it displays a list of 13 names in their original order, sorts the names, and then redisplays the list. Here's the output:

Output ▼

```
The original order:
0: Lauren 1: Audrina 2: Heidi 3: Whitney 4: Stephanie 5: Spencer
6: Lisa 7: Brody 8: Frankie 9: Holly 10: Jordan 11: Brian
12: Jason
The new order:
0: Audrina 1: Brian 2: Brody 3: Frankie 4: Heidi 5: Holly
6: Jason 7: Jordan 8: Lauren 9: Lisa 10: Spencer 11: Stephanie 12:
Whitney
```

When you're working with strings and the basic types of variables such as integers and floating-point numbers, you only can sort them by ascending order using the Arrays class. You can write code to do your own sorts by hand if you desire a different arrangement of elements during a sort, or you want better efficiency than the Arrays class provides.

Counting Characters in Strings

The letters that appear most often in English are E, R, S, T, L, N, C, D, M, and O, in that order. This is a fact worth knowing if you ever find yourself on the syndicated game show *Wheel of Fortune*.

The next program you create this hour counts letter frequency in as many different phrases and expressions as you care to type. An array is used to count the number of times that each letter appears. When you're done, the program presents the number of times each letter appeared in the phrases.

Create a new Empty Java File in NetBeans called Wheel.java, fill it with the contents of Listing 9.3 and save the file when you're finished. Feel free to add additional phrases between Lines 17 and 18, formatting them exactly like Line 17.

NOTE

If you're unfamiliar with the show, *Wheel of Fortune* is a game in which three contestants guess the letters of a phrase, name, or quote. If they get a letter right and it's a consonant, they win the amount of money spun on a big wheel. To re-create the experience, play hangman with your friends in front of a studio audience, hand out random amounts of money when someone guesses a letter correctly, and give the winner a new Amana stove.

LISTING 9.3   The Full Source Code of `Wheel.java`

```
 1: class Wheel {
 2:     public static void main(String[] args) {
 3:         String phrase[] = {
 4:             "A STITCH IN TIME SAVES NINE",
 5:             "DON'T EAT YELLOW SNOW",
 6:             "JUST DO IT",
 7:             "EVERY GOOD BOY DOES FINE",
 8:             "I WANT MY MTV",
 9:             "I LIKE IKE",
10:             "PLAY IT AGAIN, SAM",
11:             "FROSTY THE SNOWMAN",
12:             "ONE MORE FOR THE ROAD",
13:             "HOME FIELD ADVANTAGE",
14:             "VALENTINE'S DAY MASSACRE",
15:             "GROVER CLEVELAND OHIO",
16:             "SPAGHETTI WESTERN",
17:             "AQUA TEEN HUNGER FORCE",
18:             "IT'S A WONDERFUL LIFE"
19:         };
20:         int[] letterCount = new int[26];
21:         for (int count = 0; count < phrase.length; count++) {
22:             String current = phrase[count];
23:             char[] letters = current.toCharArray();
24:             for (int count2 = 0; count2 < letters.length; count2++) {
25:                 char lett = letters[count2];
26:                 if ( (lett >= 'A') & (lett <= 'Z') ) {
27:                     letterCount[lett - 'A']++;
28:                 }
29:             }
30:         }
31:         for (char count = 'A'; count <= 'Z'; count++) {
32:             System.out.print(count + ": " +
33:                 letterCount[count - 'A'] +
34:                 " ");
35:         }
36:         System.out.println();
37:     }
38: }
```

If you run the program without adding your own phrases, the output should resemble Listing 9.4.

LISTING 9.4   Output of the `Wheel` Program

```
A: 22 B: 1 C: 4 D: 10 E: 33 F: 7 G: 6 H: 7 I: 18
J: 1 K: 2 L: 10 M: 8 N: 19 O: 20 P: 2 Q: 1 R: 12
S: 15 T: 20 U: 4 V: 7 W: 6 X: 0 Y: 7 Z: 0
```

The following things are taking place in the Wheel program:

- Lines 3–19: Phrases are stored in a string array called phrase.

- Line 20: An integer array called letterCount is created with 26 elements. This array is used to store the number of times each letter appears. The order of the elements is from A to Z. letterCount[0] stores the count for letter A, letterCount[1] stores the count for B, and so on, up to letterCount[25] for Z.

- Line 21: A for loop cycles through the phrases stored in the phrase array. The phrase.length variable is used to end the loop after the last phrase is reached.

- Line 22: A string variable named current is set with the value of the current element of the phrase array.

- Line 23: A character array is created and stores all the characters in the current phrase.

- Line 24: A for loop cycles through the letters of the current phrase. The letters.length variable is used to end the loop after the last letter is reached.

- Line 25: A character variable called lett is created with the value of the current letter. In addition to their text value, characters have a numeric value. Because elements of an array are numbered, the numeric value of each character is used to determine its element number.

- Lines 26–28: An if statement weeds out all characters that are not part of the alphabet, such as punctuation and spaces. An element of the letterCount array is increased by 1 depending on the numeric value of the current character, which is stored in lett. The numeric values of the alphabet range from 65 for 'A' to 90 for 'Z'. Because the letterCount array begins at 0 and ends at 25, 'A' (65) is subtracted from lett to determine which array element to increase.

- Line 31: A for loop cycles through the alphabet from 'A' to 'Z'.

- Lines 32–34: The current letter is displayed followed by a semicolon and the number of times the letter appeared in the phrases stored in the phrase array.

This project shows how two nested for loops can be used to cycle through a group of phrases one letter at a time. Java attaches a numeric value to each character; this value is easier to use than the character inside arrays.

explains how to count array while in their own way (handwritten margin note)

NOTE

The numeric values associated with each of the characters from A to Z are those used by the ASCII character set. The ASCII character set is part of Unicode, the full character set supported by the Java language. Unicode includes support for more than 60,000 different characters used in the world's written languages. ASCII is limited to just 256.

Summary

Arrays make it possible to store complicated types of information in a program and manipulate that information. They're ideal for anything that can be arranged in a list and can be accessed easily using the loop statements that you learned about during Hour 8, "Repeating an Action with Loops."

To be honest, the information processing needs of Santa Claus probably have outgrown arrays. More children are manufactured each year, and the gifts they want are increasing in complexity and expense.

Your programs are likely to use arrays to store information that is unwieldy to work with using variables, even if you're not making any lists or checking them twice.

Q&A

Q. Is the numeric range of the alphabet, from 65 for A to 90 for Z, part of the basic Java language? If so, what are 1 through 64 reserved for?

A. The numbers 1 through 64 include numerals, punctuation marks, and some unprintable characters, such as linefeed, newline, and backspace. A number is associated with each printable character that can be used in a Java program, as well as some unprintable ones. Java uses the Unicode numbering system. The first 127 characters are from the ASCII character set, which you might have used in another programming language.

Q. Why are some errors called exceptions?

A. The significance of the term is that a program normally runs without any problems, and the exception signals an exceptional circumstance that must be dealt with. Exceptions are warning messages that are sent from within a Java program. In the Java language, the term *error* is sometimes confined to describe error conditions that take place within the interpreter running a program. You learn more about both subjects during Hour 18.

Q. In a multidimensional array, is it possible to use the `length` variable to measure different dimensions other than the first?

A. You can test any dimension of the array. For the first dimension, use `length` with the name of the array, as in `x.length`. Subsequent dimensions can be measured by using `length` with the `[0]` element of that dimension. Consider an array called `data` that was created with the following statement:

```
int[][][] data = new int[12][13][14];
```

The dimensions of this array can be measured by using the `data.length` variable for the first dimension, `data[0].length` for the second, and `data[0][0].length` for the third.

Q. Why does New England Patriots head coach Bill Belichick always wear that ridiculous hoodie on the sidelines?

A. Sportswriters believe that Belichick began wearing the attire in response to an NFL deal with Reebok that required all coaches to wear licensed team apparel.

"He decided that if they were going to make him wear team apparel then he'd sift through the options and put on the absolute ugliest thing he could find," Dan Wetzel of Yahoo! Sports explained in 2007. "He chose a grey sweatshirt, often with a hood."

Belichick's passive-aggressive fashion statement has turned the hoodie into one of the team's best-selling items.

Workshop

If the brain were an array, you could test its `length` by answering each of the following questions about arrays.

Quiz

1. What types of information are arrays best suited for?

   A. Lists

   B. Pairs of related information

   C. Trivia

2. What variable can you use to check the upper boundary of an array?

   A. top

   B. length

   C. limit

3. How many reindeer does Santa have, including Rudolph?

   A. 8

   B. 9

   C. 10

Answers

1. **A.** Lists that contain nothing but the same type of information—strings, numbers, and so on—are well-suited for storage in arrays.

2. **B.** The `length` variable contains a count of the number of elements in an array.

3. **B.** Santa had "eight tiny reindeer," according to Clement Clarke Moore's "A Visit from St. Nicholas," so Rudolph makes nine.

Activities

To give yourself an array of experiences to draw from later, you can expand your knowledge of this hour's topics with the following activities:

- ▶ Create a program that uses a multidimensional array to store student grades. The first dimension should be a number for each student, and the second dimension should be for each student's grades. Display the average of all the grades earned by each student and an overall average for every student.

- ▶ Write a program that stores the first 400 numbers that are multiples of 13 in an array.

To see Java programs that implement these activities, visit the book's website at www.java24hours.com.

HOUR 10
Creating Your First Object

One of the more fearsome examples of jargon that you encounter during these 24 hours is *object-oriented programming* (OOP). This complicated term describes, in an elegant way, what a computer program is and how it works.

Before OOP, a computer program was usually described under the simplest definition you've learned in this book: a set of instructions listed in a file and handled in some kind of reliable order.

By thinking of a program as a collection of objects, you can figure out the tasks a program must accomplish and assign the tasks to the objects where they best belong.

How Object-Oriented Programming Works

You can think of the Java programs you create as objects, just like physical objects that exist in the real world. Objects exist independently of other objects, interact in specific ways, and can be combined with other objects to form something bigger. If you think of a computer program as a group of objects that interact with each other, you can design a program that's more reliable, easier to understand, and reusable in other projects.

In Hour 23, "Creating Java2D Graphics," you create a Java program that displays pie graphs—circles with different-colored pie slices to represent data (see Figure 10.1). A *pie chart* is an object that is made up of smaller objects—individual slices of different colors, a legend identifying what each slice represents, and a title.

FIGURE 10.1
A Java program that displays a pie
chart.

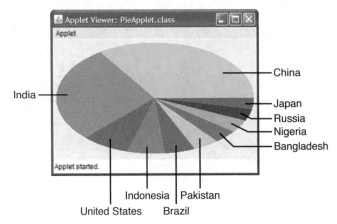

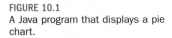

Each object has things that make it different than other objects. Pie charts are circular, whereas bar graphs represent data as a series of rectangles. If you break down computer programs in the same way a pie chart is broken down, you're engaging in OOP. In OOP, an object contains two things: attributes and behavior. *Attributes* are things that describe the object and show how it is different than other objects. *Behavior* is what an object does.

You create objects in Java by using a class as a template. A *class* is a master copy of the object that determines the attributes and behavior an object should have. The term *class* should be familiar to you because Java programs are called classes. Every program you create with Java is a class that you can use as a template for the creation of new objects. As an example, any Java program that uses strings is using objects created from the String class. This class contains attributes that determine what a String object is and behavior that controls what String objects can do.

With OOP, a computer program is a group of objects that work together to get something done. Some simple programs might seem as though they consist of only one object: the class file. However, even those programs are using other objects to get work done.

Objects in Action

Consider the case of the program that displays a pie chart. A PieChart object could consist of the following:

▸ Behavior to calculate the size of each pie slice

▸ Behavior to draw the chart

▸ An attribute to store the title of the chart

It might seem odd to ask the `PieChart` object to draw itself because graphs don't draw themselves in the real world. Objects in OOP work for themselves whenever possible. This quality makes it easier to incorporate them in other programs. If a `PieChart` object did not know how to draw itself, for instance, every time you used that `PieChart` object in another program, you would have to create behavior to draw it.

For another example of OOP, consider the autodialer program that Matthew Broderick's character used in the movie *WarGames* to find computers he could break into.

Using an autodialer today would attract the attention of your local phone company or law enforcement. Back in the '80s, it was a good way to be rebellious without leaving the house. David Lightman (the character portrayed by Broderick) used his autodialer to look for a video game company's private computer system—he wanted to play the company's new game before it was released. Instead, Lightman found a secret government computer that could play everything from chess to Global Thermonuclear War.

An autodialer, like any computer program, can be thought of as a group of objects that work together. It could be broken down into the following:

> ▶ A `Modem` object, which knows its attributes such as speed, and has behavior—for example, it can make the modem dial a number and detect that another computer system has answered a call

> ▶ A `Monitor` object, which keeps track of what numbers are called and which ones are successful

Each object exists independently of the other.

One advantage of designing a completely independent `Modem` object is that it could be used in other programs that need modem functionality.

Another reason to use self-contained objects is that they are easier to debug. Computer programs quickly become unwieldy in size. If you're debugging something like a `Modem` object and you know it's not dependent on anything else, you can focus on making sure the `Modem` object does the job it's supposed to do and holds the information that it needs to do its job.

Learning an object-oriented language such as Java as your first programming language can be advantageous because you're not unlearning the habits of other styles of programming.

NOTE

An *autodialer* is software that uses a modem to dial a series of phone numbers in sequence. The purpose of such a program is to find other computers that answer the phone, so you can call them later to see what they are.

What Objects Are

Objects are created by using a class of objects as a template. The following statements create a class:

```
public class Modem {
}
```

An object created from this class can't do anything because it doesn't have any attributes or behavior. You need to add those to make the class useful, as in the following statements:

```
public class Modem {
    int speed;

    public void displaySpeed() {
        System.out.println("Speed: " + speed);
    }
}
```

creates method (handwritten annotation)

The Modem class now should be starting to look like programs you've written during Hours 1 through 9. The Modem class begins with a class statement, except that it has public in it. This means that the class is available for use by the public—in other words, by any program that wants to use Modem objects.

The first part of the Modem class creates an integer variable called speed. This variable is an attribute of the object.

The second part of the Modem class is a method called displaySpeed(). This method is part of the object's behavior. It contains one statement, System.out.println(), which reveals the modem's speed value.

An object's variables often are called instance variables or member variables.

If you want to use a Modem object in a program, you create the object with the following statement:

```
Modem device = new Modem();
```

creates object. objects are used to pull variables and methods from other classes (handwritten annotation)

This statement creates a Modem object called device. After you have created an object, you can set its variables and call its methods. Here's how to set the value of the speed variable of the device object:

```
device.speed = 28800;
```

sets the speed variable universal to 28800 (handwritten annotation)

To make this modem display its speed by calling the `displaySpeed()` method, you call the method:

```
device.displaySpeed();
```
~displays method in other program class.

The `Modem` object named `device` would respond to this statement by displaying the text "Speed: 28800."

Understanding Inheritance

A big advantage to OOP is *inheritance*, which enables one object to inherit behavior and attributes from another object.

When you start creating objects, you sometimes find that a new object you want is a lot like an object you already have.

What if David Lightman wanted an object that could handle error correction and other advanced modem features that weren't around in 1983 when *WarGames* was released? Lightman could create a new `ErrorCorrectionModem` object by copying the statements of the `Modem` object and revising them. However, if most of the behavior and attributes of `ErrorCorrectionModem` are the same as those of `Modem`, this is a lot of unnecessary work. It also means that Lightman would have two separate programs to update if something needed to be changed later.

Through inheritance, a programmer can create a new class of objects by defining how they are different than an existing class. Lightman could make `ErrorCorrectionModem` inherit from `Modem`, and all he would need to write are things that make error-correction modems different than modems.

A class of objects inherits from another class by using the `extends` statement. The following is a skeleton of an `ErrorCorrectionModem` class that inherits from the `Modem` class:

```
public class ErrorCorrectionModem extends Modem {
    // program goes here
}
```
`allows inheritance, inheritance allows you to create similar programs.`

Building an Inheritance Hierarchy

Inheritance, which enables a variety of related classes to be developed without redundant work, makes it possible for code to be passed down from one class to another class to another class. This grouping of classes is called a *class hierarchy*, and all the standard classes you can use in your Java programs are part of a hierarchy.

Understanding a hierarchy is easier if you understand subclasses and superclasses. A class that inherits from another class is called a *subclass*. The class that is inherited from is called a *superclass*.

In the preceding *WarGames* example, the Modem class is the superclass of the ErrorCorrectionModem class. ErrorCorrectionModem is the subclass of Modem.

A class can have more than one class that inherits from it in the hierarchy—another subclass of Modem could be ISDNModem because ISDN modems have behavior and attributes that make them different from error-correcting modems. If there was a subclass of ErrorCorrectionModem such as InternalErrorCorrectionModem, it would inherit from all classes above it in the hierarchy—both ErrorCorrectionModem and Modem. These inheritance relationships are shown in Figure 10.2.

FIGURE 10.2
An example of a class hierarchy.

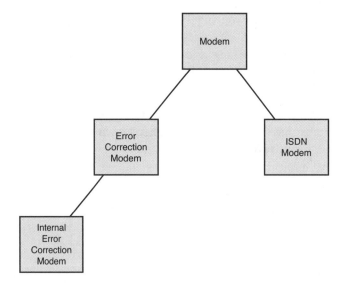

The classes that make up the standard Java language make full use of inheritance, so understanding it is essential. You learn more about inheritance during Hour 12, "Making the Most of Existing Objects."

Converting Objects and Simple Variables

One of the most common tasks you need to accomplish in Java is to convert information from one form into another. Several types of conversions you can do include

▶ Converting an object into another object

▶ Converting a simple variable into another type of variable

▶ Using an object to create a simple variable

▶ Using a simple variable to create an object

Simple variables are the basic data types you learned about during Hour 5, "Storing and Changing Information in a Program." These types include int, float, char, long, and double.

When using a method or an expression in a program, you must use the right type of information that's expected by these methods and expressions. A method that expects a Calendar object must receive a Calendar object, for instance. If you used a method that takes a single integer argument and you sent it a floating-point number instead, an error would occur when you attempted to compile the program.

Converting information to a new form is called *casting*. Casting produces a new value that is a different type of variable or object than its source. You don't actually change the value when casting. Instead, a new variable or object is created in the format you need.

The terms *source* and *destination* are useful when discussing the concept of casting. The source is some kind of information in its original form—whether it's a variable or an object. The destination is the converted version of the source in a new form.

Casting Simple Variables

With simple variables, casting occurs most commonly between numeric variables such as integers and floating-point numbers. One type of variable that cannot be used in any casting is Boolean values.

NOTE

When a method such as System.out.println() requires a string argument, you can use the + operator to combine several different types of information in that argument. As long as one of the things being combined is a string, the combined argument is converted into a string.

To cast information into a new format, you precede it with the new format surrounded by parentheses marks. For example, if you want to cast something into a long variable, you precede it with (long). The following statements cast a float value into an int:

```
float source = 7.06F;
int destination = (int) source;
```

casting converts number after into num inside.

In variable casting where the destination holds larger values than the source, the value is converted easily, such as when a byte is cast into an int. A byte holds values from –128 to 127, whereas an int holds values from –2.1 billion to 2.1 billion. No matter what value the byte variable holds, the new int variable has plenty of room for it.

You sometimes can use a variable in a different format without casting it at all. For example, you can use char variables as if they were int variables. Also, you can use int variables as if they were long variables, and anything can be used as a double.

In most cases, because the destination provides more room than the source, the information is converted without changing its value. The main exceptions occur when an int or long variable is cast to a float, or a long is cast into a double.

When you are converting information from a larger variable type into a smaller type, you must explicitly cast it, as in the following statements:

```
int xNum = 103;
byte val = (byte) xNum;
```

Here, casting converts an integer value called xNum into a byte variable called val. This is an example where the destination variable holds a smaller range of values than the source variable. A byte holds integer values ranging from –128 to 127, and an int holds a much larger range of integer values.

When the source variable in a casting operation has a value that isn't enabled in the destination variable, Java changes the value to make the cast fit successfully. This can produce unexpected results if you're not expecting the change.

Casting Objects

You can cast objects into other objects when the source and destination are related by inheritance. One class must be a subclass of the other.

Some objects do not require casting at all. You can use an object where any of its superclasses are expected. All objects in Java are subclasses of the `Object` class, so you can use any object as an argument when an `Object` is expected.

You also can use an object where one of its subclasses is expected. However, because subclasses usually contain more information than their superclasses, you might lose some of this information. If the object doesn't have a method that the subclass would contain, an error results if that missing method is used in the program.

To use an object in place of one of its subclasses, you must cast it explicitly with statements such as the following:

```
Graphics comp = new Graphics();
Graphics2D comp2D = (Graphics2D) comp;
```

This casts a `Graphics` object called `comp` into a `Graphics2D` object. You don't lose any information in the cast, but you gain all the methods and variables the subclass defines.

Converting Simple Variables to Objects and Back

One thing you can't do is cast an object to a simple variable or a simple variable to an object. There are classes in Java for each of the simple variable types include `Boolean`, `Byte`, `Character`, `Double`, `Float`, `Integer`, `Long`, and `Short`. All these classes are capitalized because they are objects, not simple variable types.

Using methods defined in each of these classes, you can create an object using a variable's value as an argument. The following statement creates an Integer object with the value 5309: *creates object of variable*

```
Integer suffix = new Integer(5309);
```

After you have created an object like this, you can use it like any other object. When you want to use that value again as a simple variable, the class has methods to perform that conversion. To get an `int` value from the preceding `suffix` object, the following statement could be used: *converts object back to simple variable*

```
int newSuffix = suffix.intValue();
```

This statement causes the `newSuffix` variable to have the value 5309, expressed as an `int` value. One common casting from an object to a variable is to use a string in a numeric expression. When the string's value could become an integer, this can be done using the parseInt() method of the Integer class, as in this example:

```
String count = "25";
int myCount = Integer.parseInt(count); — converts
                                          string to
                                          integer specifically
```

This converts a string with the text "25" into an integer with the value 25. If the string value was not a valid integer, the conversion would not work.

The next project you create is an application that converts a string value in a command-line argument to a numeric value, a common technique when you're taking input from a user at the command line.

Return to your Java24 project in NetBeans, choose File, New File, and then create a new Empty Java File named NewRoot. Enter Listing 10.1 in the source editor and remember to save the file.

LISTING 10.1   The Full Text of NewRoot.java

```
 1: class NewRoot {
 2:     public static void main(String[] args) {
 3:         int number = 100;
 4:         if (args.length > 0) {
 5:             number = Integer.parseInt(args[0]);
 6:         }
 7:         System.out.println("The square root of "
 8:             + number
 9:             + " is "
10:             + Math.sqrt(number) );
11:     }
12: }
```

Before you run the program, you must configure NetBeans to run it with a command-line argument. Choose the menu command Run, Set Project Configuration, Customize. The Project Properties window opens. Enter NewRoot as the Main Class and 169 in the Arguments field. Click OK to close the dialog.

To run the program, choose Run, Run Main Project (instead of Run, Run File). The program displays the number and its square root, as shown in Figure 10.3.

The NewRoot application is an expansion of an earlier tutorial from Hour 4, "Understanding How Java Programs Work," that displayed the square root of the integer 225.

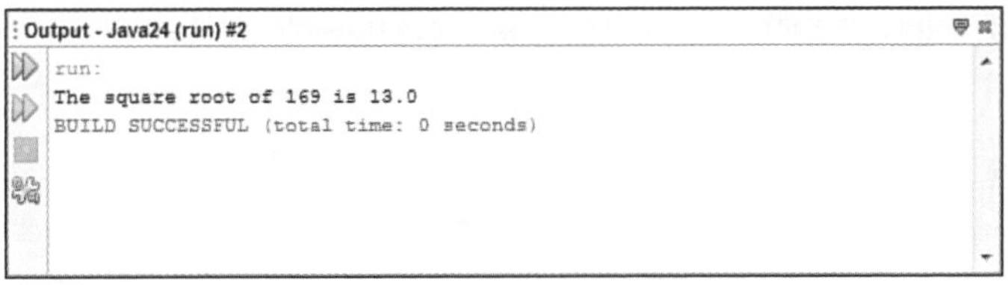

Output - Java24 (run) #2

run:
The square root of 169 is 13.0
BUILD SUCCESSFUL (total time: 0 seconds)

FIGURE 10.3
The output of the NewRoot
program.

That program would have been more useful if it took a number submitted by a user and displayed its square root. This requires conversion from a string to an integer. All command-line arguments are stored as elements of a String array, so you must cast them to numbers before using them in mathematical expressions.

To create an integer value based on the contents of a string, the Integer.parseInt() method is called with the string as the only argument, as in Line 5:

```
number = Integer.parseInt(args[0]);
```

The args[0] array element holds the first command-line argument submitted when the application is run. When the program was run with "169" as an argument, the string "169" was cast to the int 169.

Autoboxing and Unboxing

Every one of the basic data types in Java has a corresponding object class: boolean (Boolean class), byte (Byte), char (Character), double (Double), float (Float), int (Integer), long (Long), and short (Short).

For each of these pairs, the information has identical value. The only difference between them is the format the value takes. An integer value such as 413 could be represented by either an int or the Integer class.

Java's autoboxing and unboxing capabilities make it possible to use the basic data type and object forms of a value interchangeably.

Autoboxing casts a simple variable value to the corresponding class.

Unboxing casts an object to the corresponding simple value.

These features work behind the scenes, assuring that when you are expecting a simple data type like float, an object is converted to the matching data type with the same value. When you're expecting an object like Float, a data type is converted to an object as necessary.

because they are
are object variable
parts) java
automatically
converts them together
when used

The following statements show where autoboxing and unboxing come in handy:

```
Float total = new Float(1.3F);
float sum = total / 5;
```

In early versions of Java (before Java 1.5), this would be an error—the use of a `Float` object in the second statement is not possible. Java now unboxes `total` to make the statement work, resulting in `sum` being equal to 0.26.

Creating an Object

To see a working example of classes and inheritance, in the next project you create classes that represent two types of objects: cable modems, which are implemented as the `CableModem` class, and DSL modems, which are implemented as the `DslModem` class. The workshop focuses on simple attributes and behavior for these objects:

▶ Each object should have a speed that it can display.

▶ Each object should be able to connect to the Internet.

One thing that cable modems and DSL modems have in common is that they both have a speed. Because this is something they share, it can be put into a class that is the superclass of both the `CableModem` and `DslModem` classes. Call this class `Modem`. In NetBeans, create a new empty Java class called `Modem`. Enter Listing 10.2 in the source editor and save the file.

LISTING 10.2   The Full Text of `Modem.java`

```
1: public class Modem {
2:     int speed;
3:
4:     public void displaySpeed() {
5:         System.out.println("Speed: " + speed);
6:     }
7: }
```

This file is compiled automatically as `Modem.class`. You cannot run this program directly, but you can use it in other classes. The `Modem` class can handle one of the things that the `CableModem` and `DslModem` classes have in common. By using the `extends` statement when you are creating the `CableModem` and `DslModem` classes, you can make each of them a subclass of `Modem`.

Start a new empty Java file in NetBeans with the class name `CableModem`. Enter Listing 10.3 and save the file.

LISTING 10.3   The Full Text of `CableModem.java`

```
1: public class CableModem extends Modem {
2:     String method = "cable connection";
3:
4:     public void connect() {
5:         System.out.println("Connecting to the Internet ...");
6:         System.out.println("Using a " + method);
7:     }
8: }
```

Create a third file in NetBeans named `DslModem`. Enter Listing 10.4 and save the file.

LISTING 10.4   The Full Text of `DslModem.java`

```
1: public class DslModem extends Modem {
2:     String method = "DSL phone connection";
3:
4:     public void connect() {
5:         System.out.println("Connecting to the Internet ...");
6:         System.out.println("Using a " + method);
7:     }
8: }
```

If there were no errors, you now have three class files: `Modem.class`, `CableModem.class`, and `DslModem.class`. However, you cannot run any of these class files because they do not have `main()` blocks like the ones in other programs you've created. You need to create a short application to test out the class hierarchy you have just built.

Return to your NetBeans and create a new empty Java file with the class name `ModemTester`. Enter Listing 10.5 in the source editor and save the file.

LISTING 10.5   The Full Text of `ModemTester.java`

```
 1: public class ModemTester {
 2:     public static void main(String[] args) {
 3:         CableModem surfBoard = new CableModem();
 4:         DslModem gateway = new DslModem();
 5:         surfBoard.speed = 500000;
 6:         gateway.speed = 400000;
 7:         System.out.println("Trying the cable modem:");
 8:         surfBoard.displaySpeed();
 9:         surfBoard.connect();
10:         System.out.println("Trying the DSL modem:");
11:         gateway.displaySpeed();
12:         gateway.connect();
13:     }
14: }
```

because they are inherited, the variables don't have to repeat themselves and can use the method. [handwritten annotation]

When you run the program, you should see output matching Figure 10.4.

FIGURE 10.4
The output of the ModemTester program.

The following things are taking place in Listing 10.5:

► Lines 3–4: Two new objects are created—a CableModem object called surfBoard and a DslModem object called gateway.

► Line 5: The speed variable of the CableModem object named surfBoard is set to 500000.

► Line 6: The speed variable of the DslModem object named gateway is set to 400000.

► Line 8: The displaySpeed() method of the surfBoard object is called. This method is inherited from Modem—even though it isn't present in the CableModem class, you can call it.

► Line 9: The connect() method of the surfBoard object is called.

► Line 11: The displaySpeed() method of the gateway object is called.

► Line 12: The connect() method of the gateway object is called.

Summary

After creating your first class of objects and arranging several classes into a hierarchy, you ought to be more comfortable with the term *object-oriented programming* (OOP). You learn more about object behavior and attributes in the next two hours as you start creating more sophisticated objects.

Terms such as program, class, and object make more sense as you become more experienced with this style of development. OOP is a concept that takes some time to get used to. When you have mastered it, you find that it's an effective way to design, develop, and debug computer programs.

Q&A

Q. Can classes inherit from more than one class?

A. It's possible with some programming languages (such as C++), but not Java. Multiple inheritance is a powerful feature, but it also makes OOP a bit harder to learn and use. Java's developers decided to limit inheritance to one superclass for any class, although a class can have numerous subclasses. One way to compensate for this limitation is to inherit methods from a special type of class called an interface. You learn more about interfaces during Hour 19, "Creating a Threaded Program."

Q. When would you want to create a method that isn't `public`?

A. The main time you would not want to make a method available to other programs is when the method is strictly for the use of one program you're writing. If you're creating a game program and your `shootRayGun()` method is highly specific to the game you're writing, it could be a private method. To keep a method from being `public`, leave off the `public` statement in front of the method's name.

Q. Why is it possible to use `char` values as if they were `int` values?

A. A character can be used as an `int` variable because each character has a corresponding numeric code that represents its position in the character set. If you have a variable named k with the value 67, the cast `(char) k` produces the character value `'C'` because the numeric code associated with a capital C is 67, according to the ASCII character set. The ASCII character set is part of the Unicode character standard adopted by the Java language.

Q. Does Tabasco hot sauce spoil?

A. No it doesn't, though if you keep an opened bottle around for several years it will change color. The ingredients of vinegar, red pepper, and salt are an extremely inhospitable environment for bacterial growth.

McIlhenny Company, the makers of Tabasco, say the original brand has a shelf life of five years. Other versions have a shelf life from 18 months to three years.

As a huge fan of the product, I find it hard to believe anyone is keeping a bottle of Tabasco around long enough to ask this question.

Workshop

The following questions test your knowledge of objects and the programs that use them.

Quiz

1. What statement is used to enable one class to inherit from another class?

    A. `inherits`

    B. `extends`

    C. `handItOverAndNobodyGetsHurt`

2. Why are compiled Java programs saved with the `.class` file extension?

    A. Java's developers think it's a classy language.

    B. It's a subtle tribute to the world's teachers.

    C. Every Java program is a class.

3. What are the two things that make up an object?

    A. Attributes and behavior

    B. Commands and data files

    C. Spit and vinegar

Answers

1. B. The `extends` statement is used because the subclass is an extension of the attributes and behavior of the superclass and of any superclasses above that in the class hierarchy.

2. C. Your programs are always made up of at least one main class and any other classes that are needed.

3. A. In a way, B also is true because commands are comparable to behavior, and data files are analogous to attributes.

Activities

If you don't object, you can `extends` your knowledge of this hour's topics with the following activities:

▶ Create an `AcousticModem` class with a speed of 300 and its own connect() method.

▶ Add a `disconnect()` method to one of the classes in the `Modem` project, deciding where it should go to support modem disconnection in cable, DSL, and acoustic modems.

To see Java programs that implement these activities, visit the book's website at www.java24hours.com.

Describing What Your Object Is Like

As you learned during last hour's introduction to object-oriented programming (OOP), an object is a way of organizing a program so that it has everything it needs to accomplish a task. Objects consist of attributes and behavior.

Attributes are the information stored within an object. They can be variables such as integers, characters, and Boolean values, or objects such as String and Calendar objects. *Behavior* is the groups of statements used to handle specific jobs within the object. Each of these groups is called a *method*.

Up to this point, you have been working with methods and variables of objects without knowing it. Any time your statement had a period in it that wasn't a decimal point or part of a string, an object was involved.

Creating Variables

In this hour, you are looking at a class of objects called Virus whose sole purpose in life is to reproduce in as many places as possible—much like some people I knew in college. A Virus has several different things it needs to do its work, and these are implemented as the behavior of the class. The information that's needed for the methods are stored as attributes.

The attributes of an object represent variables needed for the object to function. These variables could be simple data types such as integers, characters, and floating-point numbers, or they could be arrays or objects of classes such as String or Calendar. You can use an object's variables throughout its class, in any of the methods the object contains. By convention, you create variables immediately after the class statement that creates the class and before any methods.

WHAT YOU'LL LEARN IN THIS HOUR:

- ▶ Creating variables for an object or class
- ▶ Using methods with objects and classes
- ▶ Calling a method and returning a value
- ▶ Creating constructors
- ▶ Sending arguments to a method
- ▶ Using this to refer to an object
- ▶ Creating new objects

One of the things that a Virus object needs is a way to indicate that a file already has been infected. Some computer viruses change the field that stores the time a file was last modified; for example, a virus might move the time from 13:41:20 to 13:41:61. Because no normal file would be saved on the 61st second of a minute, the time signifies that the file was infected. The Virus object uses the impossible seconds value 86 in an integer variable called newSeconds.

The following statements begin a class called Virus with an attribute called newSeconds and two other attributes:

```
public class Virus {
    public int newSeconds = 86;
    public String author = "Sam Snett";
    int maxFileSize = 30000;
}
```

All three variables are attributes for the class: newSeconds, maxFileSize, and author.

Putting a statement such as public in a variable declaration statement is called *access control* because it determines how other objects made from other classes can use that variable—or if they can use it at all.

Making a variable public makes it possible to modify the variable from another program that is using the Virus object.

If the other program attaches special significance to the number 92, for instance, it can change newSeconds to that value. The following statements create a Virus object called influenza and set its newSeconds variable:

```
Virus influenza = new Virus();
influenza.newSeconds = 92;
```

In the Virus class, the author variable also is public, so it can be changed freely from other programs. The other variable, maxFileSize, can be used only within the class itself.

When you make a variable in a class public, the class loses control over how that variable is used by other programs. In many cases, this might not be a problem. For example, the author variable can be changed to any name or pseudonym that identifies the author of the virus. The name might eventually be used on court documents if the author is prosecuted, so you don't want to pick a dumb one. *The State of Ohio v. LoveHandles* doesn't have the same ring to it as *Ohio v. MafiaBoy*.

Restricting access to a variable keeps errors from occurring if the variable is set incorrectly by another program. With the Virus class, if newSeconds is set to a value of 60 or less, it isn't reliable as a way to tell that a file is infected. Some files might be saved with that number of seconds regardless of the virus. If the Virus class of objects needs to guard against this problem, you need to do these two things:

▶ Switch the variable from public to protected or private, two other statements that provide more restrictive access.

▶ Add behavior to change the value of the variable and report the value of the variable to other programs.

You can use a protected variable only in the same class as the variable, any subclasses of that class, or classes in the same package. A *package* is a group of related classes that serve a common purpose. An example is the java.util package, which contains classes that offer useful utilities such as date and time programming and file archiving. When you use the import statement in a Java program with an asterisk, as in import java.util.*, you are making it easier to refer to the classes of that package in a program.

A private variable is restricted even further than a protected variable—you can use it only in the same class. Unless you know that a variable can be changed to anything without affecting how its class functions, you should make the variable private or protected.

The following statement makes newSeconds a private variable:

```
private int newSeconds = 86;
```

If you want other programs to use the newSeconds variable in some way, you have to create behavior that makes it possible. This task is covered later in the hour.

There also is another type of access control: the lack of any public, private, or protected statement when the variable is created.

In most of the programs you have created prior to this hour, you didn't specify any access control. When no access control is set, the variable is available only to classes in the same package. This is called default or package access.

Creating Class Variables

When you create an object, it has its own version of all variables that are part of the object's class. Each object created from the Virus class of objects has its own version of the `newSeconds`, `maxFileSize`, and `author` variables. If you modified one of these variables in an object, it would not affect the same variable in another `Virus` object.

There are times when an attribute should describe an entire class of objects instead of a specific object itself. These are called *class variables*. If you want to keep track of how many `Virus` objects are being used in a program, you could use a class variable to store this information. Only one copy of the variable exists for the whole class. The variables you have been creating for objects thus far can be called *object variables* because they are associated with a specific object.

Both types of variables are created and used in the same way, but `static` is part of the statement that creates class variables. The following statement creates a class variable for the `Virus` example:

```
static int virusCount = 0;
```
~~creates class variable~~

Changing the value of a class variable is no different than changing an object's variables. If you have a `Virus` object called `tuberculosis`, you could change the class variable `virusCount` with the following statement:

```
tuberculosis.virusCount++;
```

Because class variables apply to an entire class, you also can use the name of the class instead:

```
Virus.virusCount++;
```

Both statements accomplish the same thing, but an advantage to using the name of the class when working with class variables is that it shows immediately that `virusCount` is a class variable instead of an object variable. If you always use object names when working with class variables, you aren't able to tell whether they are class or object variables without looking carefully at the source code.

Class variables also are called *static* variables.

Creating Behavior with Methods

Attributes are the way to keep track of information about a class of objects, but for a class to do the things it was created to do, you must create behavior. Behavior describes the parts of a class that accomplish specific tasks. Each of these sections is called a *method*.

You have been using methods throughout your programs up to this point without knowing it, including one in particular: println(). This method displays text onscreen. Like variables, methods are used in connection with an object or a class. The name of the object or class is followed by a period and the name of the method, as in screen2D.drawString() or Integer.parseInt().

Declaring a Method

You create methods with a statement that looks similar to the statement that begins a class. Both can take arguments between parentheses after their names, and both use { and } marks at the beginning and end. The difference is that methods can send back a value after they are handled. The value can be one of the simple types such as integers or Boolean values, or it can be a class of objects.

The following is an example of a method the Virus class can use to infect files:

```
public boolean infectFile(String filename) {
    boolean success = false;
    // file-infecting statements go here
    return success;
}
```

[handwritten: creates boolean method with string argument]

This method takes a single argument: a string variable called filename, which is a variable that represents the file that should be attacked. If the infection is a success, the success variable is set to true.

In the statement that begins the method, boolean precedes the name of the method, infectFile. This statement signifies that a boolean value is sent back after the method is handled. The return statement is what actually sends a value back. In this method, the value of success is returned.

If a method should not return a value, use the keyword void.

When a method returns a value, you can use the method as part of an expression. For example, if you created a Virus object called malaria, you could use statements such as these:

[handwritten: if it returns true]

```
if (malaria.infectFile(currentFile)) {
    System.out.println(currentFile + " has been infected!");
} else {
    System.out.println("Curses! Foiled again!");
}
```

NOTE

The System.out.println() method might seem confusing because it has two periods instead of one. This is because two classes are involved in the statement—the System class and the PrintStream class. The System class has a variable called out that is a PrintStream object. println() is a method of the PrintStream class. The System.out.println() statement means, in effect, "Use the println() method of the out variable of the System class." You can chain together references in this way.

You can use any method that returns a value at any place in the program where you could use a variable.

Earlier in the hour, you switched the newSeconds variable to private to prevent it from being read or modified by other programs. There's still a way to make it possible for newSeconds to be used elsewhere: Create public methods in the Virus class that get the value of newSeconds and set newSeconds to a new value. These new methods should be public, unlike the newSeconds variable itself, so they can be called in other programs.

Consider the following two methods:

```
public int getSeconds() {
    return newSeconds;
}

public void setSeconds(int newValue) {
    if (newValue > 60) {
        newSeconds = newValue;
    }
}
```

These methods are called *accessor* methods because they enable the newSeconds variable to be accessed from other objects.

The getSeconds() method is used to retrieve the current value of newSeconds. The getSeconds() method does not have any arguments, but it still must have parentheses after the method name. The setSeconds() method takes one argument, an integer called newValue. This argument is the new value of newSeconds. If newValue is greater than 60, the change will be made.

In this example, the Virus class controls how the newSeconds variable can be used by other classes. This process is called *encapsulation*, and it's a fundamental concept of OOP. The better your objects are able to protect themselves against misuse, the more useful they are when you use them in other programs.

Though newSeconds is private, the new methods getSeconds() and setSeconds() are able to work with newSeconds because they are in the same class.

Similar Methods with Different Arguments

As you have seen with the setSeconds() method, you can send arguments to a method to affect what it does. Different methods in a class can have different names, but methods also can have the same name if they have different arguments.

Two methods can have the same name if they have a different number of arguments or the arguments are of different variable types. For example, it might be useful for the Virus class of objects to have two tauntUser() methods. One could have no arguments and would deliver a generic taunt. The other could specify the taunt as a string argument. The following statements implement these methods:

```
void tauntUser() {
    System.out.println("That has gotta hurt!");
}

void tauntUser(String taunt) {
    System.out.println(taunt);
}
```

The methods have the same name, but the arguments differ—one has no argument, the other has a single String argument. The arguments to a method are called the method's *signature*. A class can have different methods with the same name as long as each method has a different signature.

Constructor Methods

When you want to create an object in a program, the new statement is used, as in the following example:

```
Virus typhoid = new Virus();
```

This statement creates a new Virus object called typhoid. When you use the new statement, a special method of that object's class is called. This method is called a *constructor* because it handles the work required to create the object. The purpose of a constructor is to set up any variables and call the methods that must take place for the object to function properly.

Constructors are defined like other methods, except they cannot return a value. The following are two constructors for the Virus class of objects:

```
public Virus() {
    String author = "Ignoto";
    int maxFileSize = 30000;
}

public Virus(String name, int size) {
    author = name;
    maxFileSize = size;
}
```

Like other methods, constructors can use the arguments they are sent as a way to define more than one constructor in a class. In this example, the first constructor would be called when a new statement such as the following is used:

```
Virus mumps = new Virus();
```

The other constructor could be called only if a string and an integer are sent as arguments with the new statement, as in this example:

```
Virus rubella = new Virus("April Mayhem", 60000);
```

If you don't include any constructor methods in a class, it inherits a single constructor method with no arguments from its superclass. There also might be other constructor methods that it inherits, depending on the superclass used.

In any class, there must be a constructor method that has the same number and type of arguments as the new statement that's used to create objects of that class. In the example of the Virus class, which has Virus() and Virus(String name, int size) constructors, you only could create Virus objects with two different types of new statements: one without arguments and one with a string and an integer as the only two arguments.

Class Methods

Like class variables, class methods are a way to provide functionality associated with an entire class instead of a specific object. Use a class method when the method does nothing that affects an individual object of the class. In the previous hour, "Creating Your First Object," you used the parseInt() method of the Integer class to convert a string to a variable of the type int:

```
int fontSize = Integer.parseInt(fontText);
```

creates class method

This is a class method. To make a method into a class method, use static in front of the method name, as in the following code:

```
static void showVirusCount() {
    System.out.println("There are " + virusCount + " viruses");
}
```

The virusCount class variable was used earlier to keep track of how many Virus objects have been created by a program. The showVirusCount() method is a class method that displays this total, and you can call it with a statement such as the following:

```
Virus.showVirusCount();
```

calls method

Variable Scope Within Methods

When you create a variable or an object inside a method in one of your classes, it is usable only inside that method. The reason for this is the concept of *variable scope*. Scope is the block in which a variable exists in a program. If you go outside of the part of the program defined by the scope, you can no longer use the variable.

The { and } statements in a program define the boundaries for a variable's scope. Any variable created within these marks cannot be used outside of them. For example, consider the following statements:

```
if (numFiles < 1) {
    String warning = "No files remaining.";
}
System.out.println(warning);
```

This code does not work—and does not compile in NetBeans—because the warning variable was created inside the brackets of the if block. Those brackets define the scope of the variable. The warning variable does not exist outside of the brackets, so the System.out.println() method cannot use it as an argument.

When you use a set of brackets inside another set of brackets, you need to pay attention to the scope of the enclosed variables. Take a look at the following example:

```
if (infectedFiles < 5) {
    int status = 1;
    if (infectedFiles < 1) {
        boolean firstVirus = true;
        status = 0;
    } else {
        firstVirus = false;
    }
}
```

See any problems? In this example the status variable can be used anywhere, but the statement that assigns a value to the firstVirus variable causes a compiler error. Because firstVirus is created within the scope of the if (infectedFiles < 1) statement, it doesn't exist inside the scope of the else statement that follows.

To fix the problem, firstVirus must be created outside both of these blocks so that its scope includes both of them. One solution is to create firstVirus one line after status is created.

Rules that enforce scope make programs easier to debug because scope limits the area in which you can use a variable. This reduces one of the most common errors that can crop up in programming—using the same variable two different ways in different parts of a program.

The concept of scope also applies to methods because they are defined by an opening bracket and closing bracket. A variable created inside a method cannot be used in other methods. You only can use a variable in more than one method if it was created as an object variable or class variable.

Putting One Class Inside Another

Although a Java program is called a class, there are many occasions when a program requires more than one class to get its work done. These programs consist of a main class and any helper classes that are needed.

When you divide a program into multiple classes, there are two ways to define the helper classes. One way is to define each class separately, as in the following example:

```
public class Wrecker {
    String author = "Ignoto";

    public void infectFile() {
        VirusCode vic = new VirusCode(1024);
    }
}

class VirusCode {
    int vSize;

    VirusCode(int size) {
        vSize = size;
    }
}
```

In this example, the `VirusCode` class is a helper class for the `Wrecker` class. Helper classes often are defined in the same source code file as the class they're assisting. When the source file is compiled, multiple class files are produced. The preceding example produces the files `Wrecker.class` and `VirusCode.class` when compiled.

When creating a main class and a helper class, you also can put the helper inside the main class. When this is done, the helper class is called an *inner class*.

You place an inner class within the opening bracket and closing bracket of another class.

```
public class Wrecker {
    String author = "Ignoto";

    public void infectFile() {
        VirusCode vic = new VirusCode(1024);
    }

    class VirusCode {
        int vSize;

        VirusCode(int size) {
            vSize = size;
        }
    }
}
```

You can use an inner class in the same manner as any other kind of helper class. The main difference—other than its location—is what happens after the compiler gets through with these classes. Inner classes do not get the name indicated by their class statement. Instead, the compiler gives them a name that includes the name of the main class.

In the preceding example, the compiler produces Wrecker.class and Wrecker$VirusCode.class.

Using the this Keyword

Because you can refer to variables and methods in other classes along with variables and methods in your own classes, the variable you're referring to can become confusing in some circumstances. One way to make things more clear is with the this statement—a way to refer within a program to the program's own object.

When you are using an object's methods or variables, you put the name of the object in front of the method or variable name, separated by a period. Consider these examples:

```
Virus chickenpox = new Virus();
chickenpox.name = "LoveHandles";
chickenpox.setSeconds(75);
```

These statements create a new Virus object called chickenpox, set the name variable of chickenpox, and then call the setSeconds() method of chickenpox.

There are times in a program when you need to refer to the current object—in other words, the object represented by the program itself. For example, inside the Virus class, you might have a method that has its own variable called author:

```
public void checkAuthor() {
    String author = null;
}
```

A variable called author exists within the scope of the checkAuthor() method, but it isn't the same variable as an object variable called author. If you want to refer to the current object's author variable, you have to use the this statement, as in the following:

```
System.out.println(this.author);
```

By using this, you make it clear to which variable or method you are referring. You can use this anywhere in a class that you would refer to an object by name. If you want to send the current object as an argument in a method, for example, you could use a statement such as the following:

```
verifyData(this);
```

In many cases, the this statement is not needed to make it clear that you're referring to an object's variables and methods. However, there's no detriment to using this any time you want to be sure you're referring to the right thing.

The this keyword comes in handy in a constructor when setting the value of an object's instance variables. Consider a Virus object that has author and maxFileSize variables. This constructor sets them:

```
public Virus(String author, int maxFileSize) {
    this.author = author;
    this.maxFileSize = maxFileSize;
}
```

Using Class Methods and Variables

At the insistence of our attorney, the next project is not the creation of a working virus. Instead, you create a simple Virus object that can count the number of Virus objects that a program has created and report the total.

Choose File, New File in NetBeans and create a new Empty Java File called Virus. Enter Listing 11.1 in the source editor.

Listing 11.1   The Full Text of `Virus.java`

```
 1: public class Virus {
 2:     static int virusCount = 0;
 3:
 4:     public Virus() {
 5:         virusCount++;
 6:     }
 7:
 8:     static int getVirusCount() {
 9:         return virusCount;
10:     }
11: }
```

Save the file, which NetBeans compiles automatically. This class lacks a `main()` method and thus cannot be run directly. To test out this new `Virus` class, you need to create a second class that can create `Virus` objects.

The `VirusLab` class is a simple application that creates `Virus` objects and then counts the number of objects that have been created with the `getVirusCount()` class method of the `Virus` class.

Open a new file with your word processor and enter Listing 11.2. Save the file as `VirusLab.java` when you're done.

Listing 11.2   The Full Text of `VirusLab.java`

```
 1: public class VirusLab {
 2:     public static void main(String[] args) {
 3:         int numViruses = Integer.parseInt(args[0]);
 4:         if (numViruses > 0) {
 5:             Virus[] virii = new Virus[numViruses];
 6:             for (int i = 0; i < numViruses; i++) {
 7:                 virii[i] = new Virus();
 8:             }
 9:             System.out.println("There are " + Virus.getVirusCount()
10:                 + " viruses.");
11:         }
12:     }
13: }
```

The `VirusLab` class is an application that takes one argument when you run it at the command line: the number of `Virus` objects to create. To specify the command-line argument in NetBeans, do the following:

1. Choose Run, Set Project Configuration, Customize. The Project Properties dialog opens.

2. Enter VirusLab in the Main Class field, and enter the number of Virus objects you'd like the program to create in the Arguments field.

3. Click OK to close the dialog.

To run a program you've configured in this manner, choose Run, Run Main Project in NetBeans.

Arguments are read into an application using a string array that's sent to the main() method. In the VirusLab class, this occurs in Line 2.

To work with an argument as an integer, it must be converted from a String object to an integer. This requires the use of the parseInt() class method of the Integer class. In Line 3, an int variable named numViruses is created from the first argument sent to the program on the command line.

If the numViruses variable is greater than 0, the following things take place in the VirusLab application:

▶ Line 5: An array of Virus objects is created with the numViruses variable determining the number of objects in the array.

▶ Lines 6–8: A for loop is used to call the constructor method for each Virus object in the array.

▶ Lines 9–10: After all the Virus objects have been constructed, the getVirusCount() class method of the Virus class is used to count the number of its objects that have been created. This should match the argument that was set when you ran the VirusLab application.

If the numViruses variable is not greater than 0, nothing happens in the VirusLab application.

After the VirusLab.java file has been compiled, test it with any command-line argument you'd like to try. The number of Virus objects that can be created depends on the memory that's available on your system when you run the VirusLab application. On the author's system, anything greater than 5.5 million viruses causes the program to crash after displaying an OutOfMemoryError message.

If you don't specify more Virus objects than your system can handle, the output should be something like Figure 11.1.

FIGURE 11.1
The output of the VirusLab
program.

Summary

You now have completed two of the three hours devoted to object-oriented concepts in this book. You've learned how to create an object, give behavior and attributes to the object and its class of objects, and convert objects and variables into other forms by using casting.

Thinking in terms of objects is one of the tougher challenges of the Java programming language. When you start to understand it, however, you realize that the entire language makes use of objects and classes.

During the next hour, you learn how to give your objects parents and children.

Q&A

Q. Do you have to create an object to use class variables or methods?

A. Because class variables and methods aren't associated with a specific object, you don't need to create an object solely for the purpose of using them. The use of the `Integer.parseInt()` method is an example of this because you don't have to create a new `Integer` object just to convert a string to an `int` value.

Q. Is there a list of all the built-in methods that Java supports?

A. Oracle offers full documentation for all classes in the Java language, including all public methods you can use, on the Web at http://download.oracle.com/javase/7/docs/api.

Q. What do I have to do to be ranked in men's tennis?

A. There are currently 1,847 male tennis players ranked in the ATP World Tour tennis rankings. If your goal is to do at least as well as the lowest ranked player, you must reach the round of 16 in an ITF Futures tournament.

At the time of this writing, Tilen Zitnik is ranked in 1,847th place among men's singles players. Zitnik achieved this distinction by earning only one point in the 15 tournaments he's entered the past 52 weeks. Several hundred other players also have earned one point, but they did it in fewer tournaments.

Zitnik, a 19-year-old from Slovenia, played the Ukraine F3 futures tournament in March 2011. There was a 48-player qualifier and a 32-player field. Zitnik beat Matteo Marfa of Italy in three sets. He had the misfortune of drawing No. 1 seed Artem Smirnov of the Ukraine in the second round and lost in two sets. His year-to-date prize winnings are $1,260.

There's probably a Futures tournament near you. More than 500 take place around the world each year. Visit www.itftennis.com for the calendar and entry information.

Good luck! If you make it, I want a share of your earnings.

Workshop

The following questions see if you have the attributes and behavior to understand OOP techniques.

Quiz

1. In a Java class, a method is an example of what?

    A. Attributes

    B. Statements

    C. Behavior

2. If you want to make a variable a class variable, what statement must you use when it is created?

    A. `new`

    B. `public`

    C. `static`

3. What is the name for the part of a program in which a variable lives?

    A. Its nest

    B. The scope

    C. Variable valley

Answers

1. **C.** A method is made up of statements, but it's an example of behavior.

2. **C.** If the `static` statement is left off, the variable is an object variable instead of a class variable.

3. **B.** The compiler fails with an error when a variable is used outside of its scope.

Activities

If all this talk of viruses didn't make you sick, you can increase your knowledge of this hour's topics with the following activity:

▶ Add a `private` variable to the `Virus` class that stores an integer called `newSeconds`. Create methods to return the value of `newSeconds` and change the value of `newSeconds` only if the new value is between 60 and 100.

▶ Write a Java application that takes an argument as a string, converts it to a float variable, converts that to a `Float` object, and finally turns that into an `int` variable. Run it a few times with different arguments to see how the results change.

To see Java programs that implement these activities, visit the book's website at www.java24hours.com.

Making the Most of Existing Objects

Java objects are ideally suited for childbearing. When you create an object—a set of attributes and behavior—you have designed something that's ready to pass these qualities on to offspring. These child objects take on a lot of the same attributes and behavior of the parent. They also can do some things differently than the parent.

This system is called *inheritance*, and it's something every superclass (parent) gives to its subclasses (children). Inheritance is one of the most useful aspects of object-oriented programming (OOP), and you learn about it during this hour.

Another useful aspect of OOP is the capability to create an object that you can use with different programs. Reusability makes it easier to develop error-free, reliable programs.

The Power of Inheritance

You have used inheritance every time you worked with one of the standard Java classes such as String or Integer. Java classes are organized into a pyramid-shaped hierarchy of classes in which all classes descend from the Object class.

A class of objects inherits from all superclasses that are above it. To get a working idea of how this operates, consider the JApplet class. This class is a superclass of all applets, browser-based Java programs that use a graphical user interface framework called Swing. The JApplet class is a subclass of Applet.

A partial family tree of JApplet is shown in Figure 12.1. Each of the boxes is a class, and the lines connect a superclass to any subclasses below it.

WHAT YOU'LL LEARN IN THIS HOUR:

▶ Designing superclasses and subclasses

▶ Forming an inheritance hierarchy

▶ Overriding methods

FIGURE 12.1
The family tree of the JApplet
class.

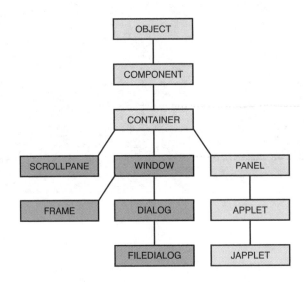

At the top is the Object class. JApplet has five superclasses above it in the hierarchy: Applet, Panel, Container, Component, and Object.

The JApplet class inherits attributes and behavior from each of these classes because each is directly above it in the hierarchy of superclasses. JApplet does not inherit anything from the five green classes in Figure 12.1, which include Dialog and Frame, because they are not above it in the hierarchy.

If this seems confusing, think of the hierarchy as a family tree. JApplet inherits from its parent, the parent's parent, and on upward. It even might inherit some things from its great-great-great-grandparent, Object. The JApplet class doesn't inherit from its siblings or its cousins, however.

Creating a new class boils down to the following task: You only have to define the ways in which it is different from an existing class. The rest of the work is done for you.

Inheriting Behavior and Attributes

The behavior and attributes of a class are a combination of two things: its own behavior and attributes and all the behavior and attributes it inherits from its superclasses.

The following are some of the behavior and attributes of JApplet:

> ▶ The equals() method determines whether a JApplet object has the same value as another object.

- The setBackground() method sets the background color of the applet window.

- The add() method adds user interface components such as buttons and text fields to the applet.

- The setLayout() method defines how the applet's graphical user interface is organized.

applet necesoties

The JApplet class can use all these methods, even though setLayout() is the only one it didn't inherit from another class. The equals() method is defined in Object, setBackground() comes from Component, and add() comes from Container.

Overriding Methods

Some methods defined in the JApplet class of objects also are defined in one of its superclasses. As an example, the update() method is part of both the JApplet class and the Component class. When a method is defined in a subclass and its superclass, the subclass method is used. This enables a subclass to change, replace, or completely wipe out some of the behavior or attributes of its superclasses. In the case of update(), the purpose is to wipe out some behavior present in a superclass.

— this is in inheritance

Creating a new method in a subclass to change behavior inherited from a superclass is called *overriding* the method. You need to override a method any time the inherited behavior produces an undesired result.

Establishing Inheritance

A class is defined as the subclass of another class using the extends statement, as in the following:

```
class AnimatedLogo extends JApplet {
    // behavior and attributes go here
}
```

The extends statement establishes the AnimatedLogo class of objects as a subclass of JApplet. As you see during Hour 17, "Creating Interactive Web Programs," all Swing applets must be subclasses of JApplet. They need the functionality this class provides to run when presented on a web page.

One method that AnimatedLogo must override is the paint() method, which is used to draw everything within the program's window. The paint() method, implemented by the Component class, is passed all the way down to AnimatedLogo. However, the paint() method does not do anything. It exists so that subclasses of Component have a method they can use when something must be displayed.

To override a method, you must declare the method in the same way it was declared in the superclass from which it was inherited. A public method must remain public, the value sent back by the method must be the same, and the number and type of arguments to the method must not change.

The paint() method of the Component class begins as follows:

```
public void paint(Graphics g) {
```

When AnimatedLogo overrides this method, it must begin with a statement like this:

```
public void paint(Graphics screen) {
```

The only difference lies in the name of the Graphics object, which does not matter when determining if the methods are created in the same way. These two statements match because the following things match:

- ▶ Both paint() methods are public.

- ▶ Both methods return no value, as declared by the use of the void statement.

- ▶ Both have a Graphics object as their only argument.

Using this **and** super **in a Subclass**

Two keywords that are extremely useful in a subclass are this and super.

As you learned during the previous hour, the this keyword is used to refer to the current object. When you're creating a class and you need to refer to the specific object created from that class, you can use this, as in the following statement:

```
this.title = "Cagney";
```

This statement sets the object's title variable to the text "Cagney."

The super keyword serves a similar purpose: It refers to the immediate superclass of the object. You can use super in several different ways:

- ▶ To refer to a constructor method of the superclass, as in
  super("Adam", 12);

▶ To refer to a variable of the superclass, as in `super.hawaii = 50`

▶ To refer to a method of the superclass, as in `super.dragnet()`

One way you use the `super` keyword is in the constructor method of a subclass. Because a subclass inherits the behavior and attributes of its superclass, you have to associate each constructor method of that subclass with a constructor method of its superclass. Otherwise, some of the behavior and attributes might not be set up correctly, and the subclass isn't able to function properly.

To associate the constructors, the first statement of a subclass constructor method must be a call to a constructor method of the superclass. This requires the `super` keyword, as in the following statements:

```
public readFiles(String name, int length) {
    super(name, length);
}
```

This example is the constructor method of a subclass, which is using `super(name, length)` to call a comparable constructor in its superclass. *calls constructor of superclass*

If you don't use `super` to call a constructor method in the superclass, Java automatically calls `super()` with no arguments when the subclass constructor begins. If this superclass constructor doesn't exist or provides unexpected behavior, errors result, so it's better to call a superclass constructor yourself.

Working with Existing Objects

OOP encourages reuse. If you develop an object for use with one Java programming project, it should be possible to incorporate that object into another project without modification.

If a Java class is well designed, it's possible to make that class available for use in other programs. The more objects available for use in your programs, the less work you have to do when creating your own software. If there's an excellent spell-checking object that suits your needs, you can use it instead of writing your own. Ideally, you can even give your boss a false impression about how long it took to add spell-checking functionality to your project, and use this extra time to make personal long-distance calls from the office.

NOTE

The author of this book, like many in his profession, is self-employed and works out of his home. Please keep this in mind when evaluating his advice on how to conduct yourself in the workplace.

When Java was first introduced, the system of sharing objects was largely an informal one. Programmers developed their objects to be as independent as possible and protected them against misuse through the use of private variables and public methods to read and write those variables.

Sharing objects becomes more powerful when there's a standard approach to developing reusable objects.

The benefits of a standard include the following:

▶ There's less need to document how an object works because anyone who knows the standard already knows a lot about how it functions.

▶ You can design development tools that follow the standard, making it possible to work more easily with these objects.

▶ Two objects that follow the standard are able to interact with each other without special programming to make them compatible.

Storing Objects of the Same Class in Vectors

An important decision to make when writing a computer program is where to store data. In the first half of this book, you've found three useful places to keep information: basic data types such as int and char, arrays, and String objects.

Any Java class can hold data. One of the most useful is Vector, a data structure that holds objects of the same class.

Vectors are like arrays, which also hold elements of related data, but they can grow or shrink in size at any time.

The Vector class belongs to the java.util package of classes, one of the most useful in the Java class library. An import statement makes it available in your program:

```
import java.util.Vector;
```

A vector holds objects that either belong to the same class or share the same superclass. They are created by referencing two classes—the Vector class and the class the vector holds.

The name of the class held by the vector is placed within < and > characters, as in this statement:

```
Vector<String> victor = new Vector<String>();
```
[handwritten: sets a vector that holds string, can switch string into other data types and objects.]

The preceding statement creates a vector that holds strings. Identifying a
vector's class in this manner utilizes generics, a way to indicate the kind of
objects a data structure like vector holds. If you are using vectors with an
older version of Java, you'd write a constructor like this:

```
Vector victor = new Vector();
```

Although you can still do this, generics make your code more reliable
because they give the compiler a way to prevent you from misusing a vector. If you attempt to put an `Integer` object in a vector that's supposed to
hold `String` objects, the compiler fails with an error.

Unlike arrays, vectors aren't created with a fixed number of elements they
hold. The vector is created with 10 elements. If you know you're storing a
lot more objects than that, you can specify a size as an argument to the
constructor. Here's a statement that creates a 300-element vector:

```
Vector<String> victoria = new Vector<String>(300);
```
[handwritten: specifies amount of elements/objects]

You can add an object to a vector by calling its `add()` method, using the
object as the only argument:

```
victoria.add("Vance");
victoria.add("Vernon");
victoria.add("Velma");
```
[handwritten: add method]

You add objects in order, so if these are the first three objects added to
`victoria`, element 0 is "Vance", element 1 is "Vernon", and element 2 is
"Velma".

You retrieve elements from vectors by calling their `get()` method with the
element's index number as the argument:

```
String name = victoria.get(1);
```
[handwritten: vectors go from 0 and up so this is 2nd num. Also this calls that number]

This statement stores "Vernon" in the name string.

To see if a vector contains an object in one of its elements, call its
`contains()` method with that object as an argument:

```
if (victoria.contains("Velma")) {
    System.out.println("Velma found");
}
```
[handwritten: returns true if object is in vector, false if not]

You can remove an object from a vector using itself or an index number:

```
victoria.remove(0);
victoria.remove("Vernon");
```

These two statements leave "Velma" as the only string in the vector.

Looping Through a Vector

Java includes a special `for` loop that makes it easy to load a vector and examine each of its elements in turn.

This loop has two parts, one less than the `for` loops you learned about in Hour 8, "Repeating an Action with Loops."

The first part is the initialization section: the class and name of a variable that holds each object retrieved from the vector. This object should belong to the same class that holds the vector.

The second part identifies the vector.

Here's code that loops through the `victoria` vector, displaying each name to the screen:

```
for (String name : victoria) {
    System.out.println(name);
}
```

The hour's first project takes vectors and the special `for` loop for a spin, presenting a list of strings in alphabetical order. The list comes from an array and command-line arguments.

With your Java24 project open within NetBeans, choose File, New File, and then create a new Empty Java File named `StringLister`. Enter Listing 12.1 in the source editor and save the file.

LISTING 12.1   The Full Text of `StringLister.java`

```
 1: import java.util.*;
 2:
 3: public class StringLister {
 4:     String[] names = { "Spanky", "Alfalfa", "Buckwheat", "Daria",
 5:         "Stymie", "Marianne", "Scotty", "Tommy", "Chubby" };
 6:
 7:     public StringLister(String[] moreNames) {
 8:         Vector<String> list = new Vector<String>();
 9:         for (int i = 0; i < names.length; i++) {
10:             list.add(names[i]);
11:         }
12:         for (int i = 0; i < moreNames.length; i++) {
```

```
13:                    list.add(moreNames[i]);
14:            }
15:            Collections.sort(list);
16:            for (String name : list) {
17:                System.out.println(name);
18:            }
19:        }
20:
21:        public static void main(String[] args) {
22:            StringLister lister = new StringLister(args);
23:        }
24: }
```

[handwritten margin notes]: takes all items in vector and substitutes with wrable until vector has no more. Then it wes into to everything in parameter

Before you run the application (choose Run, Run File), you should use the Run, Set Project Configuration, Customize command to set the main class to StringLister and the argument to one or more names separated by spaces, such as Jackie Mickey Farina Woim.

The names specified at the command line are added to the names stored in an array in Lines 4–5. Because the total number of names is not known until the program runs, a vector serves as a better storage place for these strings than an array.

The vector's strings are sorted in alphabetical order using a method of the Collections class:

```
Collections.sort(list);
```
[handwritten margin note]: — sorts vectors

This class, like Vector, belongs to the java.util package. Vectors and other useful data structures are called collections in Java.

When you run the program, the output should be a list of names in alphabetical order (see Figure 12.2). The flexible size of vectors enables your additional names to be added to the data structure and sorted along with the others.

```
Output - Java24 (run) #2
 Alfalfa
 Buckwheat
 Chubby
 Daria
 Marianne
 Scotty
 Spanky
 Stymie
 Tommy
 BUILD SUCCESSFUL (total time: 0 seconds)
```

FIGURE 12.2
The output of the StringLister program.

Creating a Subclass

To see an example of inheritance at work, in the next project you create a class called `Point3D` that represents a point in three-dimensional space. You can express a two-dimensional point with an (x,y) coordinate. Applets use an (x,y) coordinate system to determine where text and graphics should be displayed. Three-dimensional space adds a third coordinate, which can be called z.

The `Point3D` class of objects should do three things:

▶ Keep track of an object's (x,y,z) coordinate

▶ Move an object to a new (x,y,z) coordinate when needed

▶ Move an object by a certain amount of x, y, and z values as needed

Java already has a standard class that represents two-dimensional points; it's called `Point`.

It has two integer variables called x and y that store a `Point` object's (x,y) location. It also has a `move()` method to place a point at the specified location, and a `translate()` method to move an object by an amount of x and y values.

In the Java24 projects in NetBeans, create a new empty file called `Point3D` and enter the text of Listing 12.2 into the file. Save it when you're done.

LISTING 12.2   The Full Text of `Point3D.java`

```
 1: import java.awt.*;
 2:
 3: public class Point3D extends Point {
 4:     public int z;
 5:
 6:     public Point3D(int x, int y, int z) {
 7:         super(x,y);
 8:         this.z = z;
 9:     }
10:
11:     public void move(int x, int y, int z) {
12:         this.z = z;
13:         super.move(x, y);
14:     }
15:
16:     public void translate(int x, int y, int z) {
17:         this.z += z;
18:         super.translate(x, y);
19:     }
20: }
```

The `Point3D` class does not have a `main()` block statement, so you cannot run it with a Java interpreter, but you can use it in Java programs anywhere a three-dimensional point is needed.

The `Point3D` class only has to do work that isn't being done by its superclass, `Point`. This primarily involves keeping track of the integer variable `z` and receiving it as an argument to the `move()` method, `translate()` method, and `Point3D()` constructor method.

All the methods use the keywords `super` and `this`. The `this` statement is used to refer to the current `Point3D` object, so `this.z = z;` in Line 8 sets the object variable `z` equal to the `z` value that is sent as an argument to the method in Line 6.

The `super` statement refers to the current object's superclass, `Point`. It is used to set variables and call methods that are inherited by `Point3D`. The statement `super(x,y)` in Line 7 calls the `Point(x,y)` constructor in the superclass, which then sets the (x,y) coordinates of the `Point3D` object. Because `Point` already is equipped to handle the x and y axes, it would be redundant for the `Point3D` class of objects to do the same thing.

To test out the `Point3D` class you have compiled, create a program that uses `Point` and `Point3D` objects and moves them around. Create a new file in NetBeans called `PointTester` and enter Listing 12.3 into it. The file compiles automatically when it is saved.

LISTING 12.3   The Full Text of `PointTester.java`

```
 1: import java.awt.*;
 2:
 3: class PointTester {
 4:     public static void main(String[] args) {
 5:         Point object1 = new Point(11,22);
 6:         Point3D object2 = new Point3D(7,6,64);
 7:
 8:         System.out.println("The 2D point is located at (" + object1.x
 9:             + ", " + object1.y + ")");
10:         System.out.println("\tIt's being moved to (4, 13)");
11:         object1.move(4,13);
12:         System.out.println("The 2D point is now at (" + object1.x
13:             + ", " + object1.y + ")");
14:         System.out.println("\tIt's being moved -10 units on both the x "
15:             + "and y axes");
16:         object1.translate(-10,-10);
17:         System.out.println("The 2D point ends up at (" + object1.x
18:             + ", " + object1.y + ")\n");
19:
```

LISTING 12.3   Continued

```
20:         System.out.println("The 3D point is located at (" + object2.x
21:             + ", " + object2.y + ", " + object2.z + ")");
22:         System.out.println("\tIt's being moved to (10, 22, 71)");
23:         object2.move(10,22,71);
24:         System.out.println("The 3D point is now at (" + object2.x
25:             + ", " + object2.y + ", " + object2.z + ")");
26:         System.out.println("\tIt's being moved -20 units on the x, y "
27:             + "and z axes");
28:         object2.translate(-20,-20,-20);
29:         System.out.println("The 3D point ends up at (" + object2.x
30:             + ", " + object2.y + ", " + object2.z + ")");
31:     }
32: }
```

When you run the file by choosing Run, Run File, you see the output shown in Figure 12.3 if the program compiled properly. If not, look for the red icon alongside the source editor that indicates the line that triggered an error.

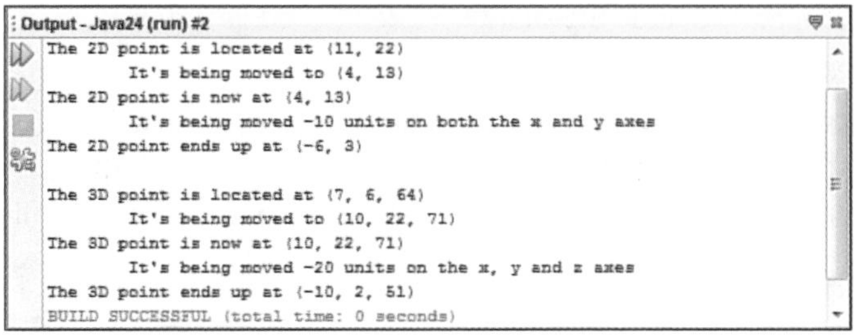

FIGURE 12.3
The output of the PointTester program.

```
Output - Java24 (run) #2
The 2D point is located at (11, 22)
        It's being moved to (4, 13)
The 2D point is now at (4, 13)
        It's being moved -10 units on both the x and y axes
The 2D point ends up at (-6, 3)

The 3D point is located at (7, 6, 64)
        It's being moved to (10, 22, 71)
The 3D point is now at (10, 22, 71)
        It's being moved -20 units on the x, y and z axes
The 3D point ends up at (-10, 2, 51)
BUILD SUCCESSFUL (total time: 0 seconds)
```

Summary

When people talk about the miracle of birth, they're probably not speaking of the way a superclass in Java can give birth to subclasses or the way behavior and attributes are inherited in a hierarchy of classes.

If the real world worked the same way that OOP does, every descendant of Mozart could choose to be a brilliant composer. All descendants of Mark Twain could be poetic about Mississippi riverboat life. Every skill your ancestors worked to achieve would be handed to you without an ounce of toil.

On the scale of miracles, inheritance isn't quite up to par with continuing the existence of a species or throwing consecutive no-hitters. However, it's an effective way to design software with a minimum of redundant work.

Q&A

Q. Most Java programs we've created up to this point have not used `extends` to inherit from a superclass. Does this mean they exist outside of the class hierarchy?

A. All classes you create in Java are part of the hierarchy because the default superclass for the programs you write is `Object` when you aren't using the `extends` keyword. The `equals()` and `toString()` methods of all classes are part of the behavior that automatically is inherited from `Object`.

Q. Why do people yell "eureka!" when they've discovered something?

A. Eureka is borrowed from ancient Greek, where it meant "I have found it!" The phrase was supposedly exclaimed by the Greek scholar Archimedes when he stepped into a bath.

What did the Greek discover in the bath? The rising water level, which led him to understand that the volume of displaced water must equal the volume of his body parts.

The story about Archimedes was spread two centuries later by Vitruvius in his multivolume *De Architectura*, a book about architecture.

"Eureka" has been in the California state seal since 1849, referring to the discovery of gold near Sutter's Mill a year earlier.

Workshop

To determine what kind of knowledge you inherited from the past hour's work, answer the following questions.

Quiz

1. If a superclass handles a method in a way you don't want to use in the subclass, what can you do?

    A. Delete the method in the superclass.

    B. Override the method in the subclass.

    C. Write a nasty letter to the editor of the *San Jose Mercury News* hoping that Java's developers read it.

2. What methods can you use to retrieve an element stored in a vector?

   A. get()

   B. read()

   C. elementAt()

3. What statement can you use to refer to the methods and variables of the current object?

   A. this

   B. that

   C. theOther

Answers

1. B. Because you can override the method, you don't have to change any aspect of the superclass or the way it works.

2. A. The get() method has one argument—the index number of the element.

3. A. The this keyword refers to the object in which it appears.

Activities

If a fertile imagination has birthed in you a desire to learn more, you can spawn more knowledge of inheritance with the following activities:

▶ Create a Point4D class that adds a t coordinate to the (x,y,z) coordinate system created by the Point3D class. The t coordinate stands for time, so you need to ensure that it is never set to a negative value.

▶ Take the members of a football team's offense: lineman, wide receiver, tight end, running back, and quarterback. Design a hierarchy of classes that represent the skills of these players, putting common skills higher up in the hierarchy. For example, blocking is behavior that probably should be inherited by the linemen and tight end classes, and speed is something that should be inherited by wide receivers and running backs.

To see Java programs that implement these activities, visit the book's website at www.java24hours.com.

Building a Simple User Interface

Things are going to get pretty gooey during this hour. You will make an enormous mess creating your first graphical user interface (GUI) with Java.

Computer users have come to expect their software to feature a GUI, take user input from a mouse, and work like other programs. Although some users still work in command-line environments such as MS-DOS or a Linux shell, most would be confused by software that does not offer a point-and-click, drag-and-drop graphical interface like in Microsoft Windows or MacOS.

Java supports this kind of software with Swing, a collection of Java classes that represent all the different buttons, text fields, sliders, and other components that can be part of a GUI, as well as the classes needed to take user input from those components.

During this hour and the next, you create and organize GUIs in Java. Afterward in Hour 15, "Responding to User Input," you enable those interfaces to receive mouse clicks and other user input.

Swing and the Abstract Windowing Toolkit

Because Java is a cross-platform language that enables you to write programs for many different operating systems, its graphical user software must be flexible. Instead of catering only to the Windows style or the Mac version, it must handle both along with other platforms.

With Java, the development of a program's user interface is based on Swing and an earlier set of classes called the Abstract Windowing Toolkit. These classes enable you to create a GUI and receive input from the user.

WHAT YOU'LL LEARN IN THIS HOUR:

▶ Creating user interface components such as buttons

▶ Creating labels, text fields, and other components

▶ Grouping components together

▶ Putting components inside other components

▶ Opening and closing windows

Swing includes everything you need to write programs that use a GUI. With Java's user interface classes, you can create a GUI that includes all the following and more:

- ▶ Buttons, check boxes, labels, and other simple components
- ▶ Text fields, sliders, and other more complex components
- ▶ Pull-down menus and pop-up menus
- ▶ Windows, frames, dialog boxes, panels, and applet windows

Using Components

In Java, every part of a GUI is represented by a class in the Swing package. There is a JButton class for buttons, a JWindow class for windows, a JTextField class for text fields, and so on.

To create and display an interface, you create objects, set their variables, and call their methods. The techniques are the same as those you used during the previous three hours as you were introduced to object-oriented programming (OOP).

When you are putting a GUI together, you work with two kinds of objects: components and containers. A *component* is an individual element in a user interface, such as a button or slider. A *container* is a component that you can use to hold other components.

The first step in creating an interface is to create a container that can hold components. In an application, this container is often a window or a frame.

Windows and Frames

Windows and frames are containers that can be displayed in a user interface and hold other components. *Windows* are simple containers that do not have a title bar or any of the other buttons normally along the top edge of a GUI. *Frames* are windows that include all the common windowing features users expect to find when they run software—such as buttons to close, expand, and shrink the window.

You create these containers using Swing's JWindow and JFrame classes. To make the Swing package of classes available in a Java program, use the following statement:

```
import javax.swing.*;
```

One way to make use of a frame in a Java application is to make the application a subclass of JFrame. Your program inherits the behavior it needs to function as a frame. The following statements create a subclass of JFrame:

```java
import javax.swing.*;

public class MainFrame extends JFrame {
    public MainFrame() {
        // set up the frame
    }
}
```

makes class a subclass of JFrame and allows it to access JFrame resources.

This class creates a frame but doesn't set it up completely. In the frame's constructor, you must do several things when creating a frame:

▶ Call a constructor of the superclass, JFrame.

▶ Set up the title of the frame.

▶ Set up the size of the frame.

▶ Set the frame's look and feel.

▶ Define what happens when the frame is closed by a user.

how to create interfaces

You also must make the frame visible, unless for some reason it should not be displayed when the application begins running.

Most of these things can be handled in the frame's constructor. The first thing the method must contain is a call to one of the constructors of JFrame, using the super statement. Here's an example:

```java
super();
```
— calls JFrame constructor

needed to start creating things in JFrame

The preceding statement calls the JFrame constructor with no arguments. You also can call it with the title of your frame as an argument:

```java
super("Main Frame");
```
this one adds title

This sets the title of the frame, which appears in the title bar along the top edge, to the specified string. In this example, the text greeting "Main Frame" appears.

If you don't set up a title in this way, you can call the frame's setTitle() method with a string as an argument:

```java
setTitle("Main Frame");
```
sets title if not with constructor

The size of the frame can be established by calling its setSize() method with two arguments: the width and height. The following statement sets up a frame that is 350 pixels wide and 125 pixels tall:

sets dimensions of window

```
setSize(350, 125);
        width  height
```

Another way to set the size of a frame is to fill it with components, and then call the frame's pack() method with no arguments:

```
pack();
```

The pack() method sets the frame big enough to hold the preferred size of each component inside the frame (but no bigger). Every interface component has a preferred size, though this is sometimes disregarded, depending on how components have been arranged within an interface. You don't need to explicitly set the size of a frame before calling pack()—the method sets it to an adequate size before the frame is displayed.

Every frame is displayed with a button along the title bar that can be used to close the frame. On a Windows system, this button appears as an X in the upper-right corner of the frame. To define what happens when this button is clicked, call the frame's setDefaultCloseOperation() method with one of four JFrame class variables as an argument:

Events that happen due to x button in top right

▸ setDefaultCloseOperation(JFrame.EXIT_ON_CLOSE)—Exit the program when the button is clicked.

▸ setDefaultCloseOperation(JFrame.DISPOSE_ON_CLOSE)—Close the frame and keep running the application.

▸ setDefaultCloseOperation(JFrame.DO_NOTHING_ON_CLOSE)—Keep the frame open and continue running.

▸ setDefaultCloseOperation(JFrame.HIDE_ON_CLOSE)—Close the frame and continue running.

A graphical user interface created with Swing can customize its appearance with a look and feel, a visual theme that controls how buttons and other components appear and how they behave.

Java 7 introduces an enhanced look and feel called Nimbus, but it must be turned on to be used in a class. You set a look and feel by calling the setLookAndFeel() method of the UIManager class in the main Swing package. The method takes one argument: the full name of the look and feel's class.

The following statement sets Nimbus as the look and feel:

```
UIManager.setLookAndFeel(
    "com.sun.java.swing.plaf.nimbus.NimbusLookAndFeel"
);
```

One last thing is required to make the frame visible: Call its `setVisible()` method with `true` as an argument:

```
setVisible(true);
```

This opens the frame at the defined width and height. You also can call it with `false` to stop displaying a frame.

Listing 13.1 contains the source code described in this section. In an empty Java file named `SalutonFrame`, enter these statements.

LISTING 13.1 The Full Text of `SalutonFrame.java`

```
 1: import javax.swing.*;
 2:
 3: public class SalutonFrame extends JFrame {
 4:     public SalutonFrame() {
 5:         super("Saluton mondo!");
 6:         setLookAndFeel();
 7:         setSize(350, 100);
 8:         setDefaultCloseOperation(JFrame.EXIT_ON_CLOSE);
 9:         setVisible(true);
10:     }
11:
12:     private void setLookAndFeel() {
13:         try {
14:             UIManager.setLookAndFeel(
15:                 "com.sun.java.swing.plaf.nimbus.NimbusLookAndFeel"
16:             );
17:         } catch (Exception exc) {
18:             // ignore error
19:         }
20:     }
21:
22:     public static void main(String[] arguments) {
23:         SalutonFrame sal = new SalutonFrame();
24:     }
25: }
```

code for interface on next page.

Lines 22–24 of Listing 13.1 contain a `main()` method, which turns this frame class into an application. When you run the class, you see the frame shown in Figure 13.1.

FIGURE 13.1
Displaying a frame in an
application.

The only thing that SalutonFrame displays is a title—the Esperanto greeting "Saluton mondo!" The frame is an empty window because it doesn't contain any other components yet.

To add components to a frame, you must create the component and add it to the container. Each container has an add() method that takes one argument: the component to display.

The SalutonFrame class includes a setLookAndFeel() method that designates Nimbus as the frame's look and feel. The setLookAndFeel() method of the UIManager class is called in lines 14–16 to accomplish this.

The call to this method is placed inside a try-catch block, which enables errors that might occur to be handled. The try and catch statements are new because they haven't been introduced yet. Dealing with errors using these statements is covered in Hour 18, "Handling Errors in a Program."

At this point, all you need to know is that calling UIManager.setLookAndFeel() sets a GUI's look and feel. Any error that might occur as a result will just cause a program to keep the default look and feel instead of Nimbus.

Buttons

One simple component you can add to a container is a JButton object. JButton, like the other components you are working with during this hour, is part of the java.awt.swing package. A JButton object is a clickable button with a label that describes what clicking the button does. This label can be text, graphics, or both. The following statement creates a JButton called okButton and gives it the text label OK:

```
JButton okButton = new JButton("OK");
```

After a component such as JButton is created, it should be added to a container by calling its add() method:

```
add(okButton);
```

When you add components to a container, you do not specify the place in the container where the component should be displayed. The arrangement of components is decided by an object called a layout manager. The simplest of these managers is the FlowLayout class, which is part of the java.awt package.

To make a container use a specific layout manager, you must first create an object of that layout manager's class. You create a FlowLayout object with a statement, such as the following: — creates layout manager

```
FlowLayout flo = new FlowLayout();
```

After you create a layout manager, you call the container's setLayout() method to associate the manager with the container. The only argument to this method should be the layout manager object, as in the following example:

```
pane.setLayout(flo);
```
sets layout object to have the pane style

This statement designates the flo object as the layout manager for the pane container.

The next application you create, a class called Playback, is a Java application that displays a frame with three buttons. Enter the text from Listing 13.2 into a new empty Java file and save the file.

LISTING 13.2   The Full Text of Playback.java

```
 1: import javax.swing.*;
 2: import java.awt.*;
 3:
 4: public class Playback extends JFrame {
 5:     public Playback() {
 6:         super("Playback");
 7:         setLookAndFeel();
 8:         setSize(225, 80);
 9:         setDefaultCloseOperation(JFrame.EXIT_ON_CLOSE);
10:         FlowLayout flo = new FlowLayout();
11:         setLayout(flo);
12:         JButton play = new JButton("Play");
13:         JButton stop = new JButton("Stop");
14:         JButton pause = new JButton("Pause");
15:         add(play);
16:         add(stop);
17:         add(pause);
18:         setVisible(true);   — needed for all windows
19:     }
20:
21:     private void setLookAndFeel() {
22:         try {
23:             UIManager.setLookAndFeel(
```

LISTING 13.2   Continued

```
24:                    "com.sun.java.swing.plaf.nimbus.NimbusLookAndFeel"
25:              );
26:          } catch (Exception exc) {
27:              // ignore error
28:          }
29:      }
30:
31:      public static void main(String[] arguments) {
32:          Playback pb = new Playback();
33:      }
34: }
```

The Playback program creates a FlowLayout layout manager in line 10 and sets the frame to employ it in line 11. When three buttons are added to the frame in lines 15–17, they're arranged by this manager.

When you run the application, your output should resemble Figure 13.2. You can click each of the buttons, but nothing happens in response because your program does not contain any methods to receive user input—that's covered during Hour 15.

You can add many Swing user components to a container in this manner.

FIGURE 13.2
Displaying buttons on a GUI.

NOTE

Because so many different user interface components must be introduced during this hour, the full source code used to create each figure is not listed here. You can find full versions of each program on the book's website at www.java24hours. com on the Hour 13 page.

Labels and Text Fields

A JLabel component displays information that the user cannot modify. This information can be text, a graphic, or both. These components are often used to label other components in an interface, hence the name. They often identify text fields.

A JTextField component is an area where a user can enter a single line of text. You can set up the width of the box when you create the text field.

The following statements create a JLabel component and JTextField object and add them to a container:

```
JLabel pageLabel = new JLabel("Web page address: ", JLabel.RIGHT);
JTextField pageAddress = new JTextField(20);
FlowLayout flo = new FlowLayout();
setLayout(flo);
add(pageLabel);
add(pageAddress);
```

Figure 13.3 shows this label and text field side-by-side. Both of the statements in this example use an argument to configure how the component should look.

FIGURE 13.3
Displaying labels and text fields.

The pageLabel label is set up with the text "Web page address:" and a JLabel.RIGHT argument. This last value indicates that the label should appear flush right. JLabel.LEFT aligns the label text flush left, and JLabel. CENTER centers it. The argument used with JTextField indicates the text field should be approximately 20 characters wide. You also can specify default text that appears in the text field with a statement such as the following:

```
JTextField country = new JTextField("US", 29);
```
default text that appears automatically"

This statement would create a JTextField object that is 20 characters wide and has the text US in the field.

You can retrieve the text contained within the object with the getText() method, which returns a string:

```
String countryChoice = country.getText();
```
retrieve text that is in it currently (this includes what's entered on default)

As you might have guessed, you also can set the text with a corresponding method:

```
country.setText("Separate Customs Territory of Taiwan, Penghu, Kinmen,
and Matsu");
```
sets default text

This sets the text to the official name of Chinese Taipei, which is the longest country name in the world.

Check Boxes

A JCheckBox component is a box next to a line of text that can be checked or unchecked by the user. The following statements create a JCheckBox object and add it to a container:

```
JCheckBox jumboSize = new JCheckBox("Jumbo Size");
FlowLayout flo = new FlowLayout();
setLayout(flo);
add(jumboSize);
```
name label

The argument to the JCheckBox() constructor indicates the text to be displayed alongside the box. If you want the box to be checked, you use the following statement instead:

```
JCheckBox jumboSize = new JCheckBox("Jumbo Size", true);
```

You can present a JCheckBox singly or as part of a group. In a group of check boxes, only one can be checked at a time. To make a JCheckBox object part of a group, you have to create a ButtonGroup object. Consider the following:

```
JCheckBox frogLegs = new JCheckBox("Frog Leg Grande", true);
JCheckBox fishTacos = new JCheckBox("Fish Taco Platter", false);
JCheckBox emuNuggets = new JCheckBox("Emu Nuggets", false);
FlowLayout flo = new FlowLayout();
ButtonGroup meals = new ButtonGroup();
meals.add(frogLegs);
meals.add(fishTacos);
meals.add(emuNuggets);
setLayout(flo);
add(jumboSize);
add(frogLegs);
add(fishTacos);
add(emuNuggets);
```

This creates three check boxes that are all grouped under the ButtonGroup object called meals. The Frog Leg Grande box is checked initially, but if the user checked one of the other meal boxes, the check next to Frog Leg Grande would disappear automatically. Figure 13.4 shows the different check boxes from this section.

FIGURE 13.4
Displaying check box components.

Combo Boxes

A JComboBox component is a pop-up list of choices that also can be set up to receive text input. When both options are enabled, you can select an item with your mouse or use the keyboard to enter text instead. The combo box serves a similar purpose to a group of check boxes, except that only one of the choices is visible unless the pop-up list is being displayed.

To create a JComboBox object, you have to add each of the choices after creating the object, as in the following example:

```
JComboBox profession = new JComboBox();
FlowLayout flo = new FlowLayout();
profession.addItem("Butcher");
profession.addItem("Baker");
profession.addItem("Candlestick maker");
profession.addItem("Fletcher");
profession.addItem("Fighter");
profession.addItem("Technical writer");
setLayout(flo);
add(profession);
```

This example creates a single JComboBox component that provides six choices from which the user can select. When one is selected, it appears in the display of the component. Figure 13.5 shows this example while the pop-up list of choices is being displayed.

FIGURE 13.5
Displaying combo box components.

To enable a JComboBox component to receive text input, you must call its setEditable() method with an argument of true:

```
profession.setEditable(true);
```
— so people can edit text

You must call this method before the component is added to a container.

Text Areas

A JTextArea component is a text field that enables the user to enter more than one line of text. You can specify the width and height of the component. The following statements create and add a JTextArea component with a width of 40 characters and a height of 8 lines and to a container:

```
JTextArea comments = new JTextArea(8, 40);
FlowLayout flo = new FlowLayout();
setLayout(flo);
add(comments);
```
40 = character width

Figure 13.6 shows this example in a frame.

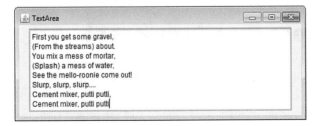

FIGURE 13.6
Displaying text area components.

Text area components behave in ways you might not expect—they expand in size when the user reaches the bottom of the area, and do not include scroll-bars along the right edge or bottom edge. To implement the kind of text areas you see in other GUI software, you must place the area inside a container called a scroll pane, as you see in Hour 16, "Building a Complex User Interface."

You can specify a string in the JTextArea() constructor to be displayed in the text area, using the newline character (\n) to send text to the next line, as in the following:

```
JTextArea comments = new JTextArea("I should have been a pair\n"
    + "of ragged claws.", 10, 25);
```

Panels

The last components you learn to create during this hour are panels, which are created in Swing using the JPanel class. JPanel objects are the simplest kind of container you can use in a Swing interface. The purpose of JPanel objects is to subdivide a display area into different groups of components. When the display is divided into sections, you can use different rules for how each section is organized.

You can create a JPanel object and add it to a container with the following statements:

```
JPanel topRow = new JPanel();
FlowLayout flo = new FlowLayout();
setLayout(flo);
add(topRow);
```

Panels are often used when arranging the components in an interface, as you see in Hour 14, "Laying Out a User Interface."

You add components to a panel by calling its add() method. You can assign a layout manager directly to the panel by calling its setLayout() method.

You can also use panels when you need an area in an interface to draw something, such as an image from a graphics file.

Another convenient use of JPanel is to create your own components that can be added to other classes. This is demonstrated in this hour's workshop.

Creating Your Own Component

An advantage of OOP is the capability to reuse classes in different projects. For the next project, you create a special panel component that you can reuse in other Java programs. The component, ClockPanel, displays the current date and time in a manner similar to the ClockTalk project from Hour 7, "Using Conditional Tests to Make Decisions."

The first step in creating your own user interface component is to decide the existing component from which to inherit. The ClockPanel component is a subclass of JPanel.

The ClockPanel class is defined in Listing 13.3. This class represents panel components that include a label displaying the current date and time. Enter the text from Listing 13.3 into a new empty Java file and save the file.

LISTING 13.3   The Full Text of ClockPanel.java

```java
 1: import javax.swing.*;
 2: import java.awt.*;
 3: import java.util.*;
 4:
 5: public class ClockPanel extends JPanel {
 6:     public ClockPanel() {
 7:         super();
 8:         String currentTime = getTime();
 9:         JLabel time = new JLabel("Time: ");
10:         JLabel current = new JLabel(currentTime);
11:         add(time);
12:         add(current);
13:     }
14:
15:     final String getTime() {
16:         String time;
17:         // get current time and date
18:         Calendar now = Calendar.getInstance();
19:         int hour = now.get(Calendar.HOUR_OF_DAY);
20:         int minute = now.get(Calendar.MINUTE);
21:         int month = now.get(Calendar.MONTH) + 1;
22:         int day = now.get(Calendar.DAY_OF_MONTH);
23:         int year = now.get(Calendar.YEAR);
24:
25:         String monthName = "";
26:         switch (month) {
27:             case (1):
28:                 monthName = "January";
29:                 break;
30:             case (2):
31:                 monthName = "February";
32:                 break;
33:             case (3):
34:                 monthName = "March";
35:                 break;
36:             case (4):
37:                 monthName = "April";
38:                 break;
39:             case (5):
40:                 monthName = "May";
41:                 break;
42:             case (6):
```

LISTING 13.3   Continued

```
43:                    monthName = "June";
44:                    break;
45:                case (7):
46:                    monthName = "July";
47:                    break;
48:                case (8):
49:                    monthName = "August";
50:                    break;
51:                case (9):
52:                    monthName = "September";
53:                    break;
54:                case (10):
55:                    monthName = "October";
56:                    break;
57:                case (11):
58:                    monthName = "November";
59:                    break;
60:                case (12):
61:                    monthName = "December";
62:            }
63:        time = monthName + " " + day + ", " + year + " "
64:            + hour + ":" + minute;
65:        return time;
66:    }
67: }
```

The getTime() method in ClockPanel contains the same technique for retrieving the current date and time as the ClockTalk application from Hour 7. This method has the keyword final when it is declared in line 15:

```
final String getTime() {
    // ...
}
```

Using final prevents the method from being overridden in a subclass. This is required for ClockPanel to be a GUI component.

The panel is created in the constructor in Lines 6–13. The following things are taking place:

- ► Line 8—The date and time are retrieved by calling getTime() and storing the string it returns in the currentTime variable.

- ► Line 9—A new label named time is created with the text "Time: ".

- ► Line 10—currentTime is used as the text of new label component called current.

▶ Line 11—The `time` label is added to the clock panel by calling the panel's `add()` method with the label as an argument.

▶ Line 12—The `current` label is added to the panel in the same manner.

To try out this panel, create the `ClockFrame` application, which is defined in Listing 13.4.

LISTING 13.4   The Full Text of `ClockFrame.java`

```
 1: import java.awt.*;
 2: import javax.swing.*;
 3:
 4: public class ClockFrame extends JFrame {
 5:     public ClockFrame() {
 6:         super("Clock");
 7:         setLookAndFeel();
 8:         setSize(225, 125);
 9:         setDefaultCloseOperation(JFrame.EXIT_ON_CLOSE);
10:         FlowLayout flo = new FlowLayout();
11:         setLayout(flo);
12:         ClockPanel time = new ClockPanel();
13:         add(time);
14:         setVisible(true);
15:     }
16:
17:     private void setLookAndFeel() {
18:         try {
19:             UIManager.setLookAndFeel(
20:                 "com.sun.java.swing.plaf.nimbus.NimbusLookAndFeel"
21:             );
22:         } catch (Exception exc) {
23:             // ignore error
24:         }
25:     }
26:
27:     public static void main(String[] arguments) {
28:         ClockFrame clock = new ClockFrame();
29:     }
30: }
```

When you run the application, it should resemble Figure 13.7.

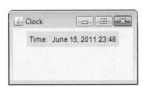

FIGURE 13.7
Displaying a clock panel component.

Summary

Users have come to expect a point-and-click, visual environment for the programs they run. This expectation makes creating software more of a challenge, but Java puts these capabilities into your hands with Swing, which provides all the classes you need to provide a working, useful GUI—regardless of what kind of setup you're using to run Java programs.

During the next hour, you learn more about the design of a GUI as you work with layout managers, classes that are used to specify how components are arranged within a container.

Q&A

Q. How are components arranged if I don't assign a layout manager to a container?

A. In a simple container such as a panel, components are arranged using `FlowLayout` by default. Each component is added in the same manner that words are displayed on a page in English, from left to right, then down to the next line when there's no more room. Frames, windows, and applets use the `GridLayout` default layout style you learn about during the next hour.

Q. Why do so many of the graphical user interface classes have names preceded by a J, such as `JFrame` and `JLabel`?

A. These classes are a part of the Swing framework, which was the second attempt at graphical user interface classes in the Java class library. The Abstract Windowing Toolkit (AWT) was first, and it had simpler class names like `Frame` and `Label`.

The AWT classes belong to the `java.awt` package and related packages, while Swing belong to `javax.swing` and the like, so they could have the same class names. The use of the J names keeps the classes from being mistaken for each other.

Swing classes also are called Java Foundation Classes (JFC).

Q. Where can I buy an uncut sheet of $1 bills?

A. The U.S. Bureau of Engraving and Printing sells sheets of real $1, $10, $20 and $50 bills at the website www.moneyfactorystore.gov.

A sheet of 32 $1 bills sells for $55, 16 $10 bills for $269, 16 $20 bills for $409, and 16 $50 bills for $900.

The bureau also sells a five-pound bag containing $10,000 of shredded bills for $45.

Workshop

If your brain hasn't been turned into a GUI mush with this hour's toil, test your skills by answering the following questions.

Quiz

1. Which user component is used as a container to hold other components?

    A. TupperWare

    B. JPanel

    C. Choice

2. Which of the following must be done first within a container?

    A. Establish a layout manager.

    B. Add components.

    C. Doesn't matter.

3. What method determines how components are arranged within a container?

    A. setLayout()

    B. setLayoutManager()

    C. setVisible()

Answers

1. B. JPanel. You can add components to the panel and then add the panel to another container such as a frame.

2. A. You must specify the layout manager before the components so you can add them in the correct way.

3. A. The setLayout() method takes one argument: the layout manager object that has the job of deciding where components should be displayed.

Activities

To interface further with the subject of GUI design, undertake the following activities:

▶ Modify the SalutonFrame application so that it displays "Saluton Mondo!" in the frame's main area instead of the title bar.

▶ Create a frame that contains another frame and make both of them visible at the same time.

To see Java programs that implement these activities, visit the book's website at www.java24hours.com.

HOUR 14
Laying Out a User Interface

When you begin designing graphical user interfaces (GUI) for your Java programs, one obstacle you face is that your components can move around. Whenever a container changes size—such as when a user resizes a frame—the components it holds may rearrange themselves to fit its new dimensions.

This fluidity works in your favor because it takes into account the differences in how interface components are displayed on different operating systems. A clickable button might look different in Windows than it does in Linux or Mac OS.

Components are organized in an interface by using a set of classes called *layout managers*. These classes define how components are displayed within a container. Each container in an interface can have its own layout manager.

WHAT YOU'LL LEARN IN THIS HOUR:

▶ Creating a layout manager
▶ Assigning a layout manager to a container
▶ Using panels to organize components in an interface
▶ Working with unusual layouts
▶ Creating a prototype for a Java application

Using Layout Managers

In Java, the placement of components within a container depends on the size of other components and the height and width of the container. The layout of buttons, text fields, and other components can be affected by the following things:

▶ The size of the container

▶ The size of other components and containers

▶ The layout manager that is being used

There are several layout managers you can use to affect how components are shown. The default manager for panels is the FlowLayout class in the java.awt package, which was used during the previous hour.

Under `FlowLayout`, components are dropped onto an area in the same way words are organized on a page in English—from left to right, and then down to the next line when there's no more space.

The following example could be used in a frame so that it employs flow layout when components are added:

```
FlowLayout topLayout = new FlowLayout();
setLayout(topLayout);
```

You also can set up a layout manager to work within a specific container, such as a `JPanel` object. You can do this by using the `setLayout()` method of that container object.

The `Crisis` application has a GUI with five buttons. Create a new empty Java file for a class named `Crisis`. Enter text from Listing 14.1 into the file and save the file.

LISTING 14.1   The Full Text of `Crisis.java`

```
 1: import java.awt.*;
 2: import javax.swing.*;
 3:
 4: public class Crisis extends JFrame {
 5:     JButton panicButton;
 6:     JButton dontPanicButton;
 7:     JButton blameButton;
 8:     JButton mediaButton;
 9:     JButton saveButton;
10:
11:     public Crisis() {
12:         super("Crisis");
13:         setLookAndFeel();
14:         setSize(348, 128);
15:         setDefaultCloseOperation(JFrame.EXIT_ON_CLOSE);
16:         FlowLayout flo = new FlowLayout();
17:         setLayout(flo);
18:         panicButton = new JButton("Panic");
19:         dontPanicButton = new JButton("Don't Panic");
20:         blameButton = new JButton("Blame Others");
21:         mediaButton = new JButton("Notify the Media");
22:         saveButton = new JButton("Save Yourself");
23:         add(panicButton);
24:         add(dontPanicButton);
25:         add(blameButton);
26:         add(mediaButton);
27:         add(saveButton);
28:         setVisible(true);
29:     }
30:
```

LISTING 14.1   Continued

```
31:     private void setLookAndFeel() {
32:         try {
33:             UIManager.setLookAndFeel(
34:                 "com.sun.java.swing.plaf.nimbus.NimbusLookAndFeel"
35:             );
36:         } catch (Exception exc) {
37:             // ignore error
38:         }
39:     }
40:
41:     public static void main(String[] arguments) {
42:         Crisis cr = new Crisis();
43:     }
44: }
```

Figure 14.1 shows the application running.

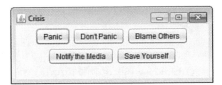

FIGURE 14.1
Arranging components using flow layout.

The FlowLayout class uses the dimensions of its container as the only guideline for how to lay out components. Resize the window of the application to see how components are instantly rearranged. Make the window twice as wide, and you see all of the JButton components are now shown on the same line.

The GridLayout **Manager**

The GridLayout class in the java.awt package organizes all components in a container into a specific number of rows and columns. All components are allocated the same amount of size in the display area, so if you specify a grid that is three columns wide and three rows tall, the container is divided into nine areas of equal size.

GridLayout places all components as they are added into a place on a grid. Components are added from left to right until a row is full, and then the leftmost column of the next grid is filled.

The following statements create a container and set it to use a grid layout that is two rows wide and three columns tall:

(handwritten: sets layout to grid style)

```
GridLayout grid = new GridLayout(2, 3);
setLayout(grid);
```

(handwritten: height width)

Figure 14.2 shows what the Crisis application would look like if it used grid layout.

Some labels in Figure 14.2 display text that has been shortened. If the text is wider than the area available in the component, the label is shortened using ellipses (…).

The BorderLayout **Manager**

The BorderLayout class, also in java.awt, arranges components at specific positions within the container that are identified by one of five directions: north, south, east, west, or center.

The BorderLayout manager arranges components into five areas: four denoted by compass directions and one for the center area. When you add a component under this layout, the add() method includes a second argument to specify where the component should be placed. This argument should be one of five class variables of the BorderLayout class: NORTH, SOUTH, EAST, WEST, and CENTER are used for this argument.

Like the GridLayout class, BorderLayout devotes all available space to the components. The component placed in the center is given all the space that isn't needed for the four border components, so it's usually the largest.

The following statements create a container that uses border layout:

```
BorderLayout crisisLayout = new BorderLayout();
setLayout(crisisLayout);
add(panicButton, BorderLayout.NORTH);
add(dontPanicButton, BorderLayout.SOUTH);
add(blameButton, BorderLayout.EAST);
add(mediaButton, BorderLayout.WEST);
add(saveButton, BorderLayout.CENTER);
```

(handwritten: sets positions based on directions)

Figure 14.3 shows how this looks in the Crisis application.

FIGURE 14.3
Arranging components using
border layout.

The BoxLayout Manager

Another handy layout manager, BoxLayout in the javax.swing package,
makes it possible to stack components in a single row horizontally or
vertically.

To employ this layout, create a panel to hold components, and then create
a layout manager with two arguments:

▶ The component to organize in box layout

▶ The value BoxLayout.Y_AXIS for vertical alignment and
BoxLayout.X_AXIS for horizontal alignment

Here's code to stack the Crisis components:

```
JPanel pane = new JPanel();
BoxLayout box = new BoxLayout(pane, BoxLayout.Y_AXIS);
pane.setLayout(box);
pane.add(panicButton);
pane.add(dontPanicButton);
pane.add(blameButton);
pane.add(mediaButton);
pane.add(saveButton);
add(pane);
```

(handwritten annotations: "— determines vertical or horizontal positioning)", "component")

FIGURE 14.4
Stacking components using box
layout.

Figure 14.4 shows how this turns out.

Separating Components with Insets

As you are arranging components within a container, you can move components away from the edges of the container using Insets, an object that
represents the border area of a container.

The Insets class, which is part of the java.awt package, has a constructor
that takes four arguments: the space to leave at the top, left, bottom, and
right of the container. Each argument is specified using pixels, the same
unit of measure employed when defining the size of a frame.

The following statement creates an `Insets` object:

```
Insets around = new Insets(10, 6, 10, 3);
```

top, bottom, left, right (handwritten annotations)

The `around` object represents a container border that is 10 pixels inside the top edge, 6 pixels inside the left, 10 pixels inside the bottom, and 3 pixels inside the right.

To make use of an `Insets` object in a container, you must override the container's `getInsets()` method. This method has no arguments and returns an `Insets` object, as in the following example:

how to override it (handwritten annotation)

```
public Insets getInsets() {
    Insets squeeze = new Insets(50, 15, 10, 15);
    return squeeze;
}
```

Figure 14.5 shows how this would change the `FlowLayout`-managed interface shown in Figure 14.1.

FIGURE 14.5
Using insets to add space around components.

The container shown in Figure 14.5 has an empty border that's 15 pixels from the left edge, 10 pixels from the bottom edge, 15 pixels from the right edge, and 50 pixels from the top edge.

Laying Out an Application

The layout managers you have seen thus far were applied to an entire frame; the `setLayout()` method of the frame was used, and all components followed the same rules. This setup can be suitable for some programs, but as you try to develop a GUI with Swing, you often find that none of the layout managers fit.

One way around this problem is to use a group of `JPanel` objects as containers to hold different parts of a GUI. You can set up different layout rules for each of these parts by using the `setLayout()` methods of each `JPanel`. After these panels contain all the components they need to contain, you can add the panels directly to the frame.

The next project develops a full interface for the program you write during the next hour. The program is a Lotto number cruncher that assesses a user's chance of winning one of the multimillion dollar Lotto contests in the span of a lifetime. This chance is determined by running random six-number Lotto drawings again and again until the user's numbers turn up as the big winner. Figure 14.6 shows the GUI you are developing for the application.

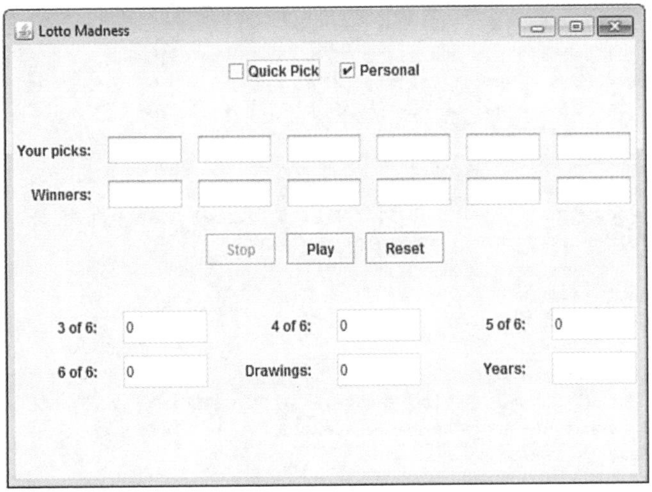

FIGURE 14.6
Displaying the GUI of the LottoMadness application.

Create a new empty Java file called LottoMadness, enter text from Listing 14.2 into the source editor, and save the file.

LISTING 14.2   The Full Text of LottoMadness.java

```
 1: import java.awt.*;
 2: import javax.swing.*;
 3:
 4: public class LottoMadness extends JFrame {
 5:
 6:     // set up row 1
 7:     JPanel row1 = new JPanel();
 8:     ButtonGroup option = new ButtonGroup();
 9:     JCheckBox quickpick = new JCheckBox("Quick Pick", false);
10:     JCheckBox personal = new JCheckBox("Personal", true);
11:     // set up row 2
12:     JPanel row2 = new JPanel();
13:     JLabel numbersLabel = new JLabel("Your picks: ", JLabel.RIGHT);
14:     JTextField[] numbers = new JTextField[6];
15:     JLabel winnersLabel = new JLabel("Winners: ", JLabel.RIGHT);
16:     JTextField[] winners = new JTextField[6];
```

LISTING 14.2   Continued

```
17:     // set up row 3
18:     JPanel row3 = new JPanel();
19:     JButton stop = new JButton("Stop");
20:     JButton play = new JButton("Play");
21:     JButton reset = new JButton("Reset");
22:     // set up row 4
23:     JPanel row4 = new JPanel();
24:     JLabel got3Label = new JLabel("3 of 6: ", JLabel.RIGHT);
25:     JTextField got3 = new JTextField("0");
26:     JLabel got4Label = new JLabel("4 of 6: ", JLabel.RIGHT);
27:     JTextField got4 = new JTextField("0");
28:     JLabel got5Label = new JLabel("5 of 6: ", JLabel.RIGHT);
29:     JTextField got5 = new JTextField("0");
30:     JLabel got6Label = new JLabel("6 of 6: ", JLabel.RIGHT);
31:     JTextField got6 = new JTextField("0", 10);
32:     JLabel drawingsLabel = new JLabel("Drawings: ", JLabel.RIGHT);
33:     JTextField drawings = new JTextField("0");
34:     JLabel yearsLabel = new JLabel("Years: ", JLabel.RIGHT);
35:     JTextField years = new JTextField();
36:
37:     public LottoMadness() {
38:         super("Lotto Madness");
39:         setLookAndFeel();
40:         setSize(550, 400);
41:         setDefaultCloseOperation(JFrame.EXIT_ON_CLOSE);
42:         GridLayout layout = new GridLayout(5, 1, 10, 10);
43:         setLayout(layout);
44:
45:         FlowLayout layout1 = new FlowLayout(FlowLayout.CENTER,
46:             10, 10);
47:         option.add(quickpick);
48:         option.add(personal);
49:         row1.setLayout(layout1);
50:         row1.add(quickpick);
51:         row1.add(personal);
52:         add(row1);
53:
54:         GridLayout layout2 = new GridLayout(2, 7, 10, 10);
55:         row2.setLayout(layout2);
56:         row2.add(numbersLabel);
57:         for (int i = 0; i < 6; i++) {
58:             numbers[i] = new JTextField();
59:             row2.add(numbers[i]);
60:         }
61:         row2.add(winnersLabel);
62:         for (int i = 0; i < 6; i++) {
63:             winners[i] = new JTextField();
64:             winners[i].setEditable(false);
65:             row2.add(winners[i]);
66:         }
67:         add(row2);
```

LISTING 14.2   Continued

```
 68:
 69:          FlowLayout layout3 = new FlowLayout(FlowLayout.CENTER,
 70:              10, 10);
 71:          row3.setLayout(layout3);
 72:          stop.setEnabled(false);
 73:          row3.add(stop);
 74:          row3.add(play);
 75:          row3.add(reset);
 76:          add(row3);
 77:
 78:          GridLayout layout4 = new GridLayout(2, 3, 20, 10);
 79:          row4.setLayout(layout4);
 80:          row4.add(got3Label);
 81:          got3.setEditable(false);
 82:          row4.add(got3);
 83:          row4.add(got4Label);
 84:          got4.setEditable(false);
 85:          row4.add(got4);
 86:          row4.add(got5Label);
 87:          got5.setEditable(false);
 88:          row4.add(got5);
 89:          row4.add(got6Label);
 90:          got6.setEditable(false);
 91:          row4.add(got6);
 92:          row4.add(drawingsLabel);
 93:          drawings.setEditable(false);
 94:          row4.add(drawings);
 95:          row4.add(yearsLabel);
 96:          years.setEditable(false);
 97:          row4.add(years);
 98:          add(row4);
 99:
100:          setVisible(true);
101:      }
102:
103:      private void setLookAndFeel() {
104:          try {
105:              UIManager.setLookAndFeel(
106:                  "com.sun.java.swing.plaf.nimbus.NimbusLookAndFeel"
107:              );
108:          } catch (Exception exc) {
109:              // ignore error
110:          }
111:      }
112:
113:      public static void main(String[] arguments) {
114:          LottoMadness frame = new LottoMadness();
115:      }
116: }
```

Even though you haven't added any statements that make the program do anything yet, you can run the application to make sure that the graphical interface is organized correctly and collects the information you need.

This application uses several different layout managers. To get a clearer picture of how the application's user interface is laid out, take a look at Figure 14.7. The interface is divided into four horizontal rows that are separated by horizontal black lines in the figure. Each of these rows is a JPanel object, and the overall layout manager of the application organizes these rows into a GridLayout of four rows and one column.

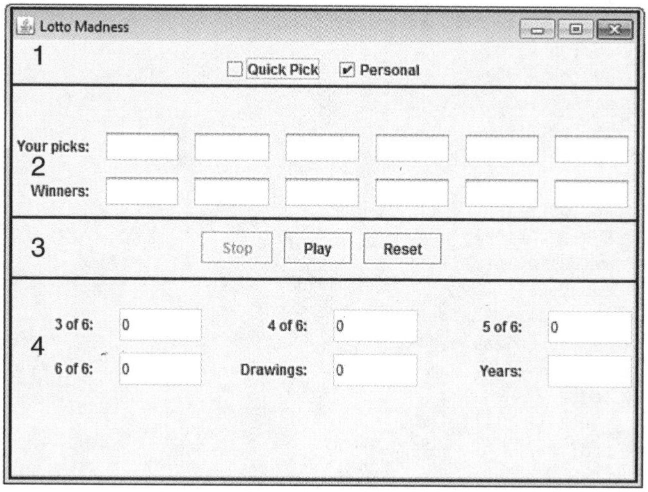

FIGURE 14.7
Dividing the LottoMadness application into panels.

Within the rows, different layout managers are used to determine how the components should appear. Rows 1 and 3 use FlowLayout objects. Lines 45–46 of the program show how these are created:

```
FlowLayout layout1 = new FlowLayout(FlowLayout.CENTER,
    10, 10);
```

Three arguments are used with the FlowLayout() constructor. The first argument, FlowLayout.CENTER, indicates that the components should be centered within their container—the horizontal JPanel on which they are placed. The last two components specify the width and height that each component should be moved away from other components. Using a width of 10 pixels and a height of 10 pixels puts a small amount of extra distance between the components.

Row 2 of the interface is laid out into a grid that is two rows tall and seven columns wide. The GridLayout() constructor also specifies that components should be set apart from other components by 10 pixels in each direction. Lines 54–55 set up this grid:

```
GridLayout layout2 = new GridLayout(2, 7, 10, 10);
row2.setLayout(layout2);
```

Row 4 uses GridLayout to arrange components into a grid that is two rows tall and three columns wide.

The LottoMadness application uses several components described during this hour. Lines 7–35 are used to set up objects for all the components that make up the interface. The statements are organized by row. First, a JPanel object for the row is created, and then each component that goes on the row is set up. This code creates all the components and containers, but they are not displayed unless an add() method is used to add them to the application's main frame.

In Lines 45–98, the components are added. Lines 45–52 are indicative of the entire LottoMadness() constructor:

```
FlowLayout layout1 = new FlowLayout(FlowLayout.CENTER,
    10, 10);
option.add(quickpick);
option.add(personal);
row1.setLayout(layout1);
row1.add(quickpick);
row1.add(personal);
add(row1);
```

After a layout manager object is created, it is used with the setLayout() method of the row's JPanel object—row1 in this case. When the layout has been specified, components are added to the JPanel by using its add() method. After all the components have been placed, the entire row1 object is added to the frame by calling its own add() method.

Summary

When you design a Java program's GUI for the first time, you might have trouble believing that it's an advantage for components to move around. Layout managers provide a way to develop an attractive GUI that is flexible enough to handle differences in presentation.

During the next hour, you learn more about the function of a GUI. You get a chance to see the LottoMadness interface in use as it churns through lottery drawings and tallies up winners.

Q&A

Q. **Why are some of the text fields in the** `LottoMadness` **application shaded in gray while others are white?**

A. The `setEditable()` method has been used on the gray fields to make them impossible to edit. The default behavior of a text field is to enable users to change the value of the text field by clicking within its borders and typing any desired changes. However, some fields are intended to display information rather than take input from the user. The `setEditable()` method prevents users from changing a field they should not modify.

Q. **Was there a Willy Wonka golden ticket winner in** *Willy Wonka and the Chocolate Factory* **whose death was too horrible for the movie?**

A. The fate of Miranda Piker was so gruesome that she was dropped from the final draft of Roald Dahl's book *Charlie and the Chocolate* Factory, which inspired the 1971 movie and its 2005 remake. Piker was a smug child who believed children should never play so they could attend school all the time. Her father was a school headmaster.

Piker and the other kids at Wonka's factory are introduced to Spotty Powder, a sugary concoction that causes the eater to break out in red spots so they can feign illness and miss school. Piker and her father become outraged and decide to destroy the machine that makes it.

As their screams are heard from the adjacent room, Wonka explains that they've gone into the place where the candy's ingredients are ground into powder. "That's part of the recipe," he tells Miranda's mother. "We've got to use one or two schoolmasters occasionally or it doesn't work."

The Oompa-Loompas celebrate her demise with song: "Oh, Miranda Mary Piker,/How could anybody like her,/Such a priggish and revolting little kid./So we said, 'Why don't we fix her/In the Spotty-Powder mixer/Then we're bound to like her better than we did.'/Soon this child who is so vicious/Will have gotten quite delicious,/And her classmates will have surely understood/That instead of saying, 'Miranda!/Oh, the beast! We cannot stand her!'/They'll be saying, 'Oh, how useful and how good!'"

Workshop

To see whether your brain cells are laid out properly, test your Java layout management skills by answering the following questions.

Quiz

1. What container is often used when subdividing an interface into different layout managers?

    A. JWindow

    B. JPanel

    C. Container

2. What is the default layout manager for a panel?

    A. FlowLayout

    B. GridLayout

    B. No default

3. The BorderLayout class gets its name from where?

    A. The border of each component

    B. The way components are organized along the borders of a container

    C. Sheer capriciousness on the part of Java's developers

Answers

1. **B.** JPanel, which is the simplest of the containers.

2. **A.** Panels use flow layout, but the default manager for frames and windows is grid layout.

3. **B.** You must specify the border position of components with the use of directional variables such as BorderLayout.WEST and BorderLayout.EAST as you add them to a container.

Activities

If you'd like to keep going with the flow (and the grid and the border), undertake the following activities:

▶ Create a modified version of the `Crisis` application with the `panic` and `dontPanic` objects organized under one layout manager and the remaining three buttons under another.

▶ Make a copy of the `LottoMadness.java` file that you can rename to `NewMadness.java`. Make changes to this program so the quick pick or personal choice is a combo box and the start, stop, and reset buttons are check boxes.

To see Java programs that implement these activities, visit the book's website at www.java24hours.com.

Responding to User Input

The graphical user interface (GUI) you developed during the past two hours can run on its own. Users can click buttons, fill text fields with text, and resize the window. Sooner or later, even the least discriminating user is going to be left wanting more. The GUI that a program offers has to cause things to happen when a mouse-click or keyboard entry occurs.

These things become possible when your Java program can respond to user events, which is called *event handling*, the activity you learn about during this hour.

Getting Your Programs to Listen

A *user event* in Java is something that happens when a user performs an action with the mouse, keyboard, or another input device.

Before you can receive events, you must learn how to make an object listen. Responding to user events requires the use of one or more EventListener interfaces. *Interfaces* are a feature of object-oriented programming in Java that enable a class to inherit behavior it would not be able to employ otherwise. They're like a contract agreement with other classes that guarantee the class will contain specific methods.

An EventListener interface contains methods that receive user input of a specific type.

Adding an EventListener interface requires two things. First, because the listening classes are part of the java.awt.event package, you must make them available with the following statement:

```
import java.awt.event.*;
```

Second, the class must use the `implements` keyword to declare that it supports one or more listening interfaces. The following statement creates a class that uses `ActionListener`, an interface for responding to button and menu clicks:

```
public class Graph implements ActionListener {
```

[handwritten: needed so busy respond]

`EventListener` interfaces enable a component of a GUI to generate user events. Without one of the listeners in place, a component cannot do anything that can be heard by other parts of a program. A program must include a listener interface for each type of component to which it listens. To have the program respond to a mouse-click on a button or the Enter key being pressed in a text field, you must include the `ActionListener` interface. To respond to the use of a choice list or check boxes, you need the `ItemListener` interface.

When you require more than one interface in the same class, separate their names with commas after the `implements` keyword, as in this code:

```
public class Graph3D implements ActionListener, MouseListener {
    // ...
}
```

[handwritten: how to implement more than one thing]

Setting Up Components to Be Heard

After you have implemented the interface needed for a particular component, you must set that component to generate user events. The `ActionListener` interface listens for action events, such as a button-click or the press of the Enter key. To make a `JButton` object generate an event, employ the `addActionListener()` method, as in the following:

```
JButton fireTorpedos = new JButton("Fire torpedos");
fireTorpedos.addActionListener(this);
```

[handwritten: add action   object]

This code creates the `fireTorpedos` button and calls the button's `addActionListener()` method. The `this` keyword used as an argument to the `addActionListener()` method indicates the current object receives the user event and handles it as needed.

Handling User Events

When a user event is generated by a component that has a listener, a method is called automatically. The method must be found in the class specified when the listener was attached to the component.

Each listener has different methods that are called to receive their events. The `ActionListener` interface sends events to a method called `actionPerformed()`. The following is a short example of an `actionPerformed()` method:

```
public void actionPerformed(ActionEvent event) {
    // method goes here
}
```

[handwritten: default method of actionListener, can be overridden to actually do something]

All action events sent in the program go to this method. If only one component in a program can possibly send action events, you can put statements in this method to handle the event. If more than one component can send these events, you need to check the object sent to the method.

An `ActionEvent` object is sent to the `actionPerformed()` method. Several different classes of objects represent the user events that can be sent in a program. These classes have methods to determine which component caused the event to happen. In the `actionPerformed()` method, if the `ActionEvent` object is named `event`, you can identify the component with the following statement:

```
String cmd = event.getActionCommand();
```

The `getActionCommand()` method sends back a string. If the component is a button, the string is the label on the button. If it's a text field, the string is the text entered in the field. The `getSource()` method sends back the object that caused the event.

You could use the following `actionPerformed()` method to receive events from three components: a `JButton` object called `start`, a `JTextField` called `speed`, and another `JTextField` called `viscosity`:

```
public void actionPerformed(ActionEvent event) {
    Object source = event.getSource();
    if (source == speed) {
        // speed field caused event
    } else if (source == viscosity) {
        // viscosity caused event
    } else {
        // start caused event
    }
}
```

You can call the `getSource()` method on all user events to identify the specific object that caused the event.

[handwritten: how to identify getSource();]

Check Box and Combo Box Events

Combo boxes and check boxes require the `ItemListener` interface. Call the component's `addItemListener()` method to make it generate these events. The following statements create a check box called `superSize` that sends out user events when selected or deselected:

```
JCheckBox superSize = new JCheckBox("Super Size", true);
superSize.addItemListener(this);
```

These events are received by the `itemStateChanged()` method, which takes an `ItemEvent` object as an argument. To see which object caused the event, you can call the event object's `getItem()` method.

To determine whether a check box is selected or deselected, compare the value returned by the `getStateChange()` method to the constants `ItemEvent.SELECTED` and `ItemEvent.DESELECTED`. The following code is an example for an `ItemEvent` object called `item`:

```
int status = item.getStateChange();
if (status == ItemEvent.SELECTED) {
    // item was selected
}
```

To determine the value selected in a `JComboBox` object, use `getItem()` and convert that value to a string, as in the following:

```
Object which = item.getItem();    most likely oels
String answer = which.toString();    the selected one
                                    converts
                                    to a string
```

Keyboard Events

When a program must react immediately once a key is pressed, it uses keyboard events and the `KeyListener` interface.

The first step is to register the component that receives key presses by calling its `addKeyListener()` method. The argument of the method should be the object that implements the `KeyListener` interface. If it is the current class, use `this` as the argument.

An object that handles keyboard events must implement three methods:

▶ `void keyPressed(KeyEvent)` — A method called the moment a key is pressed

▶ `void keyReleased(KeyEvent)` — A method called the moment a key is released

keyboard method {

▶ void keyTyped(*KeyEvent*)—A method called after a key has been pressed and released

Each of these has a KeyEvent object as an argument, which has methods to call to find out more about the event. Call the getKeyChar() method to find out which key was pressed. This key is returned as a char value, and it only can be used with letters, numbers, and punctuation.

To monitor any key on the keyboard, including Enter, Home, Page Up, and Page Down, you can call getKeyCode() instead. This method returns an integer value representing the key. You then can call getKeyText() with that integer as an argument to receive a String object containing the name of the key (such as Home, F1, and so on).

Listing 15.1 contains a Java application that draws the most recently pressed key in a label by using the getKeyChar() method. The application implements the KeyListener interface, so there are keyTyped(), keyPressed(), and keyReleased() methods in the class. The only one of these that does anything is keyTyped() in Lines 22–25. Create a new Java file called KeyViewer, enter the listing in NetBeans' source editor, and save the file.

LISTING 15.1   The Full Text of KeyViewer.java

```
1: import javax.swing.*;
2: import java.awt.event.*;
3: import java.awt.*;
4:
5: public class KeyViewer extends JFrame implements KeyListener {
6:     JTextField keyText = new JTextField(80);
7:     JLabel keyLabel = new JLabel("Press any key in the text field.");
8:
9:     KeyViewer() {
10:         super("KeyViewer");
11:         setLookAndFeel();
12:         setSize(350, 100);
13:         setDefaultCloseOperation(JFrame.EXIT_ON_CLOSE);
14:         keyText.addKeyListener(this);
15:         BorderLayout bord = new BorderLayout();
16:         setLayout(bord);
17:         add(keyLabel, BorderLayout.NORTH);
18:         add(keyText, BorderLayout.CENTER);
19:         setVisible(true);
20:     }
21:
22:     public void keyTyped(KeyEvent input) {
23:         char key = input.getKeyChar();
24:         keyLabel.setText("You pressed " + key);
25:     }
```

LISTING 15.1   Continued

```
26:
27:     public void keyPressed(KeyEvent txt) {
28:         // do nothing
29:     }
30:
31:     public void keyReleased(KeyEvent txt) {
32:         // do nothing
33:     }
34:
35:     private void setLookAndFeel() {
36:         try {
37:             UIManager.setLookAndFeel(
38:                 "com.sun.java.swing.plaf.nimbus.NimbusLookAndFeel"
39:             );
40:         } catch (Exception exc) {
41:             // ignore error
42:         }
43:     }
44:
45:     public static void main(String[] arguments) {
46:         KeyViewer frame = new KeyViewer();
47:     }
48: }
```

When you run the application, it should resemble Figure 15.1.

FIGURE 15.1
Handling keyboard events in a program.

Enabling and Disabling Components

You might have seen a component in a program that appears shaded instead of its normal appearance.

Shading indicates that users cannot do anything to the component because it is disabled. Disabling and enabling components is accomplished with the setEnabled() method of the component. A Boolean value is sent as an argument to the method, so setEnabled(true) enables a component for use, and setEnabled(false) disables it.

The following statements create buttons with the labels Previous, Next, and Finish and disable the first button:

```
JButton previousButton = new JButton("Previous");
JButton nextButton = new JButton("Next");
```

```
JButton finishButton = new JButton("Finish");
previousButton.setEnabled(false);
```

This method is an effective way to prevent a component from sending a user event when it shouldn't. For example, if you're writing a Java application that collects a user's address using text fields, you could disable a Save Address button until the user provided a street address, city, state and ZIP code.

great example on when to use

Completing a Graphical Application

To see how Swing's event-handling classes work in a Java program, you finish LottoMadness, the lottery simulation begun during Hour 14, "Laying Out a User Interface."

At this point, LottoMadness is just a GUI. You can click buttons and enter text into text boxes, but nothing happens in response. In this workshop, you create LottoEvent, a new class that receives user input, conducts lotto drawings, and keeps track of the number of times you win. When the class is complete, you add a few lines to LottoMadness so that it makes use of LottoEvent. It often is convenient to divide Swing projects in this manner, with the GUI in one class and the event-handling methods in another.

The purpose of this application is to assess the user's chance of winning a six-number lotto drawing in a lifetime. Figure 15.2 shows a screen capture of the program as it runs.

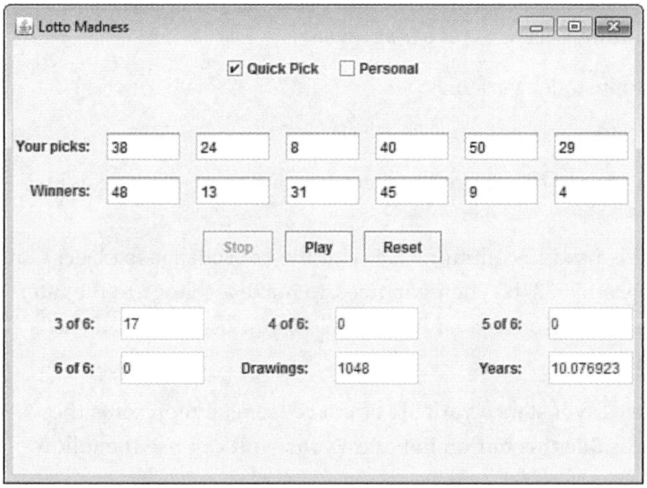

FIGURE 15.2
Running the LottoMadness application.

Instead of using probability to figure this problem out, the computer conducts drawings in rapid succession and doesn't stop until there's a winner. Because the 6-out-of-6 win is extremely unlikely, the program also reports on any combination of three, four, or five winning numbers.

The interface includes 12 text fields for lotto numbers and two check boxes labeled Quick Pick and Personal. Six text fields, disabled for input, are used to display the winning numbers of each drawing. The other six text fields are for the user's choice of numbers. Selecting the Quick Pick box chooses six random numbers for a user. Selecting Personal enables the user to select desired numbers.

Three buttons control the activity of the program: Stop, Play, and Reset. When the Play button is pressed, the program starts a thread called `playing` and generates Lotto drawings.

Pressing the Stop button stops the thread, and pressing Reset clears all fields so the user can start over. You learn about threads in Hour 19, "Creating a Threaded Program."

The `LottoEvent` class implements three interfaces: `ActionListener`, `ItemListener`, and `Runnable`. The Runnable interface relates to threads and is covered in Hour 19. The listeners are needed to listen to user events generated by the application's buttons and check boxes. The program does not need to listen to any events related to the text fields because they are used strictly to store the user's choice of numbers. The user interface handles this storage automatically.

The class requires the use of the main Swing package, `javax.swing`, and Java's event-handling package, `java.awt.event`.

The class has two instance variables:

- `gui`, a LottoMadness object
- `playing`, a Thread object used to conduct continuous lotto drawings

The `gui` variable is used to communicate with the `LottoMadness` object that contains the program's GUI. When you need to make a change to the interface or retrieve a value from one of its text fields, you use the `gui` object's instance variables.

For example, the `play` instance variable of `LottoMadness` represents the Play button. To disable this button in `LottoEvent`, you can use the following statement:

```
gui.play.setEnabled(false);
```

You can use the next statement to retrieve the value of the JTextField object got3:

```
String got3value = gui.got3.getText();
```

Listing 15.2 contains the full text of the LottoEvent class. Create a new empty Java file called LottoEvent in NetBeans to hold the source code.

LISTING 15.2   The Full Text of LottoEvent.java

```
 1: import javax.swing.*;
 2: import java.awt.event.*;
 3:
 4: public class LottoEvent implements ItemListener, ActionListener,
 5:     Runnable {
 6:
 7:     LottoMadness gui;
 8:     Thread playing;
 9:
10:     public LottoEvent(LottoMadness in) {
11:         gui = in;
12:     }
13:
14:     public void actionPerformed(ActionEvent event) {
15:         String command = event.getActionCommand();
16:         if (command.equals("Play")) {
17:             startPlaying();
18:         }
19:         if (command.equals("Stop")) {
20:             stopPlaying();
21:         }
22:         if (command.equals("Reset")) {
23:             clearAllFields();
24:         }
25:     }
26:
27:     void startPlaying() {
28:         playing = new Thread(this);
29:         playing.start();
30:         gui.play.setEnabled(false);
31:         gui.stop.setEnabled(true);
32:         gui.reset.setEnabled(false);
33:         gui.quickpick.setEnabled(false);
34:         gui.personal.setEnabled(false);
35:     }
36:
37:     void stopPlaying() {
38:         gui.stop.setEnabled(false);
39:         gui.play.setEnabled(true);
40:         gui.reset.setEnabled(true);
41:         gui.quickpick.setEnabled(true);
42:         gui.personal.setEnabled(true);
```

LISTING 15.2   Continued

```
43:           playing = null;
44:       }
45:
46:       void clearAllFields() {
47:           for (int i = 0; i < 6; i++) {
48:               gui.numbers[i].setText(null);
49:               gui.winners[i].setText(null);
50:           }
51:           gui.got3.setText("0");
52:           gui.got4.setText("0");
53:           gui.got5.setText("0");
54:           gui.got6.setText("0");
55:           gui.drawings.setText("0");
56:           gui.years.setText("0");
57:       }
58:
59:       public void itemStateChanged(ItemEvent event) {
60:           Object item = event.getItem();
61:           if (item == gui.quickpick) {
62:               for (int i = 0; i < 6; i++) {
63:                   int pick;
64:                   do {
65:                       pick = (int) Math.floor(Math.random() * 50 + 1);
66:                   } while (numberGone(pick, gui.numbers, i));
67:                   gui.numbers[i].setText("" + pick);
68:               }
69:           } else {
70:               for (int i = 0; i < 6; i++) {
71:                   gui.numbers[i].setText(null);
72:               }
73:           }
74:       }
75:
76:       void addOneToField(JTextField field) {
77:           int num = Integer.parseInt("0" + field.getText());
78:           num++;
79:           field.setText("" + num);
80:       }
81:
82:       boolean numberGone(int num, JTextField[] pastNums, int count) {
83:           for (int i = 0; i < count; i++) {
84:               if (Integer.parseInt(pastNums[i].getText()) == num) {
85:                   return true;
86:               }
87:           }
88:           return false;
89:       }
90:
91:       boolean matchedOne(JTextField win, JTextField[] allPicks) {
92:           for (int i = 0; i < 6; i++) {
93:               String winText = win.getText();
```

LISTING 15.2   Continued

```
 94:               if ( winText.equals( allPicks[i].getText() ) ) {
 95:                   return true;
 96:               }
 97:           }
 98:           return false;
 99:       }
100:
101:       public void run() {
102:           Thread thisThread = Thread.currentThread();
103:           while (playing == thisThread) {
104:               addOneToField(gui.drawings);
105:               int draw = Integer.parseInt(gui.drawings.getText());
106:               float numYears = (float)draw / 104;
107:               gui.years.setText("" + numYears);
108:
109:               int matches = 0;
110:               for (int i = 0; i < 6; i++) {
111:                   int ball;
112:                   do {
113:                       ball = (int) Math.floor(Math.random() * 50 + 1);
114:                   } while (numberGone(ball, gui.winners, i));
115:                   gui.winners[i].setText("" + ball);
116:                   if (matchedOne(gui.winners[i], gui.numbers)) {
117:                       matches++;
118:                   }
119:               }
120:               switch (matches) {
121:                   case 3:
122:                       addOneToField(gui.got3);
123:                       break;
124:                   case 4:
125:                       addOneToField(gui.got4);
126:                       break;
127:                   case 5:
128:                       addOneToField(gui.got5);
129:                       break;
130:                   case 6:
131:                       addOneToField(gui.got6);
132:                       gui.stop.setEnabled(false);
133:                       gui.play.setEnabled(true);
134:                       playing = null;
135:               }
136:               try {
137:                   Thread.sleep(100);
138:               } catch (InterruptedException e) {
139:                   // do nothing
140:               }
141:           }
142:       }
143: }
```

The LottoEvent class has one constructor: LottoEvent(*LottoMadness*). The LottoMadness object specified as an argument identifies the object that is relying on LottoEvent to handle user events and conduct drawings.

The following methods are used in the class:

▶ The clearAllFields() method causes all text fields in the application to be emptied out. This method is handled when the user clicks the Reset button.

▶ The addOneToField() method converts a text field to an integer, increments it by one, and converts it back into a text field. Because all text fields are stored as strings, you have to take special steps to use them in expressions.

▶ The numberGone() method takes three arguments—a single number from a lotto drawing, an array that holds several JTextField objects, and a count integer. This method makes sure that each number in a drawing hasn't been selected already in the same drawing.

▶ The matchedOne() method takes two arguments—a JTextField object and an array of six JTextField objects. This method checks to see whether one of the user's numbers matches the numbers from the current lotto drawing.

The application's actionPerformed() method receives the action events when the user clicks a button. The getActionCommand() method retrieves the label of the button to determine which component was clicked.

Clicking the Play button causes the startPlaying() method to be called. This method disables four components. Clicking Stop causes the stopPlaying() method to be called, which enables every component except for the Stop button.

The itemStateChanged() method receives user events triggered by the selection of the Quick Pick or Personal check boxes. The getItem() method sends back an Object that represents the check box that was clicked. If it's the Quick Pick check box, six random numbers from 1 to 50 are assigned to the user's lotto numbers. Otherwise, the text fields that hold the user's numbers are cleared out.

The LottoEvent class uses numbers from 1 to 50 for each ball in the lotto drawings. This is established in Line 113, which multiplies the Math.random() method by 50, adds 1 to the total, and uses this as an argument to the Math.floor() method. The end result is a random integer from 1 to 50. If you replace 50 with a different number here and on Line 65, you could use LottoMadness for lottery contests that generate a wider or smaller range of values.

The LottoMadness project lacks variables used to keep track of things such as the number of drawings, winning counts, and lotto number text fields. Instead, the interface stores values and displays them automatically.

To finish the project, reopen LottoMadness.java in NetBeans. You only need to add six lines to make it work with the LottoEvent class.

First, add a new instance variable to hold a LottoEvent object:

```
LottoEvent lotto = new LottoEvent(this);
```

Next, in the LottoMadness() constructor, call the addItemListener() and addActionListener() methods of each user interface component that can receive user input:

```
// Add listeners
quickpick.addItemListener(lotto);
personal.addItemListener(lotto);
stop.addActionListener(lotto);
play.addActionListener(lotto);
reset.addActionListener(lotto);
```

Listing 15.3 contains the full text of LottoMadness.java after you have made the changes. The lines you added are shaded—the rest is unchanged from the previous hour.

LISTING 15.3   The Full Text of LottoMadness.java

```
 1: import java.awt.*;
 2: import javax.swing.*;
 3:
 4: public class LottoMadness extends JFrame {
 5:     LottoEvent lotto = new LottoEvent(this);
 6:
 7:     // set up row 1
 8:     JPanel row1 = new JPanel();
 9:     ButtonGroup option = new ButtonGroup();
10:     JCheckBox quickpick = new JCheckBox("Quick Pick", false);
11:     JCheckBox personal = new JCheckBox("Personal", true);
12:     // set up row 2
13:     JPanel row2 = new JPanel();
14:     JLabel numbersLabel = new JLabel("Your picks: ", JLabel.RIGHT);
15:     JTextField[] numbers = new JTextField[6];
16:     JLabel winnersLabel = new JLabel("Winners: ", JLabel.RIGHT);
17:     JTextField[] winners = new JTextField[6];
18:     // set up row 3
19:     JPanel row3 = new JPanel();
20:     JButton stop = new JButton("Stop");
```

LISTING 15.3   Continued

```
21:    JButton play = new JButton("Play");
22:    JButton reset = new JButton("Reset");
23:    // set up row 4
24:    JPanel row4 = new JPanel();
25:    JLabel got3Label = new JLabel("3 of 6: ", JLabel.RIGHT);
26:    JTextField got3 = new JTextField("0");
27:    JLabel got4Label = new JLabel("4 of 6: ", JLabel.RIGHT);
28:    JTextField got4 = new JTextField("0");
29:    JLabel got5Label = new JLabel("5 of 6: ", JLabel.RIGHT);
30:    JTextField got5 = new JTextField("0");
31:    JLabel got6Label = new JLabel("6 of 6: ", JLabel.RIGHT);
32:    JTextField got6 = new JTextField("0", 10);
33:    JLabel drawingsLabel = new JLabel("Drawings: ", JLabel.RIGHT);
34:    JTextField drawings = new JTextField("0");
35:    JLabel yearsLabel = new JLabel("Years: ", JLabel.RIGHT);
36:    JTextField years = new JTextField("0");
37:
38:    public LottoMadness() {
39:        super("Lotto Madness");
40:        setLookAndFeel();
41:        setSize(550, 270);
42:        setDefaultCloseOperation(JFrame.EXIT_ON_CLOSE);
43:        GridLayout layout = new GridLayout(5, 1, 10, 10);
44:        setLayout(layout);
45:
46:        // Add listeners
47:        quickpick.addItemListener(lotto);
48:        personal.addItemListener(lotto);
49:        stop.addActionListener(lotto);
50:        play.addActionListener(lotto);
51:        reset.addActionListener(lotto);
52:
53:        FlowLayout layout1 = new FlowLayout(FlowLayout.CENTER,
54:            10, 10);
55:        option.add(quickpick);
56:        option.add(personal);
57:        row1.setLayout(layout1);
58:        row1.add(quickpick);
59:        row1.add(personal);
60:        add(row1);
61:
62:        GridLayout layout2 = new GridLayout(2, 7, 10, 10);
63:        row2.setLayout(layout2);
64:        row2.add(numbersLabel);
65:        for (int i = 0; i < 6; i++) {
66:            numbers[i] = new JTextField();
67:            row2.add(numbers[i]);
68:        }
69:        row2.add(winnersLabel);
70:        for (int i = 0; i < 6; i++) {
71:            winners[i] = new JTextField();
72:            winners[i].setEditable(false);
```

LISTING 15.3   Continued

```
 73:               row2.add(winners[i]);
 74:           }
 75:           add(row2);
 76:
 77:           FlowLayout layout3 = new FlowLayout(FlowLayout.CENTER,
 78:               10, 10);
 79:           row3.setLayout(layout3);
 80:           stop.setEnabled(false);
 81:           row3.add(stop);
 82:           row3.add(play);
 83:           row3.add(reset);
 84:           add(row3);
 85:
 86:           GridLayout layout4 = new GridLayout(2, 3, 20, 10);
 87:           row4.setLayout(layout4);
 88:           row4.add(got3Label);
 89:           got3.setEditable(false);
 90:           row4.add(got3);
 91:           row4.add(got4Label);
 92:           got4.setEditable(false);
 93:           row4.add(got4);
 94:           row4.add(got5Label);
 95:           got5.setEditable(false);
 96:           row4.add(got5);
 97:           row4.add(got6Label);
 98:           got6.setEditable(false);
 99:           row4.add(got6);
100:           row4.add(drawingsLabel);
101:           drawings.setEditable(false);
102:           row4.add(drawings);
103:           row4.add(yearsLabel);
104:           years.setEditable(false);
105:           row4.add(years);
106:           add(row4);
107:
108:           setVisible(true);
109:       }
110:
111:       private void setLookAndFeel() {
112:           try {
113:               UIManager.setLookAndFeel(
114:                   "com.sun.java.swing.plaf.nimbus.NimbusLookAndFeel"
115:               );
116:           } catch (Exception exc) {
117:               // ignore error
118:           }
119:       }
120:
121:       public static void main(String[] arguments) {
122:           LottoMadness frame = new LottoMadness();
123:       }
124: }
```

NOTE

The book's website at www.java24hours.com contains a link to an applet version of the LottoMadness program. At the time of this printing, 410,732,244 drawings have been conducted, which equals 3.9 million years of twice-weekly drawings. There have been 6,364,880 3-out-of-6 winners, 337,285 4-out-of-6 winners, 6,476 5-out-of-6 winners, and 51 6-out-of-6 winners (roughly one out of every 8 million drawings). The first person to win this fictional lottery was Bill Teer on August. 14, 2000, more than four years after the applet went online. His numbers were 3, 7, 1, 15, 34, and 43, and it only took him 241,225 drawings (2,319.47 years) to win.

After you add the shaded lines, you can run the application, which is capable of testing your lotto skills for thousands of years. As you might expect, these lotteries are an exercise in futility. The chance of winning a 6-out-of-6 lotto drawing in a lifetime is extremely slim, even if you live as long as a biblical figure.

Summary

You can create a professional-looking program with a modest amount of programming by using Swing. Although the LottoMadness application is longer than many of the examples you have worked in during the last 14 hours, half of the program was comprised of statements to build the interface.

If you spend some time running the application, you become even more bitter and envious about the good fortune of the people who win these six-number lottery drawings.

My most recent run of the program indicates that I could blow $27,000 and the best 266 years of my life buying tickets, only to win a handful of 4-out-of-6 and 3-out-of-6 prizes. In comparison to those odds, the chance to make your Java programming skills pay off is practically a sure thing.

Q&A

Q. Do you need to do anything with the `paint()` method or `repaint()` to indicate that a text field has been changed?

A. After the `setText()` method of a text component is used to change its value, you don't need to do anything else. Swing handles the updating necessary to show the new value.

Q. Why do you often import a class and also one of its subclasses, as in Listing 15.1 when you import `java.awt.*` and `java.awt.event.*`? Could the first of these statements include the second?

A. Though the names of the `java.awt` and `java.awt.event` packages look like they are related, there's no such thing as inheritance for packages in Java. One package cannot be a subpackage of another.

When you use an asterisk in an `import` statement, you are making all the classes in a package available in a program.

The asterisk only works on classes, not packages. The most a single `import` statement can load is the classes of a single package.

Q. Why is the actor Michael J. Fox identified by his middle initial?

A. There already was a Michael Fox in the Screen Actor's Guild, forcing the future *Family Ties* and *Back to the Future* star to choose another name for his professional work. Michael Andrew Fox is his real name, but he didn't like the sound of Andrew or Andy Fox and Michael A. Fox sounded like he was admiring his own good looks.

He settled on Michael J. Fox as an homage to the character actor Michael J. Pollard.

The other Michael Fox was an actor who appeared on episodes of *Perry Mason*, *Burke's Law*, and numerous other TV shows and movies until his death in 1996.

Workshop

After the `LottoMadness` program has soured you on games of chance, play a game of skill by answering the following questions.

Quiz

1. Why are action events called by that name?

    A. They occur in reaction to something else.

    B. They indicate that some kind of action should be taken in response.

    C. They honor cinematic adventurer Action Jackson.

2. What does `this` signify as the argument to an `addActionListener()` method?

    A. `this` listener should be used when an event occurs.

    B. `this` event takes precedence over others.

    C. `this` object handles the events.

3. Which component stores user input as integers?

    A. `JButton`

    B. `JTextField` or `JTextArea`

    C. Neither A nor B

Answers

1. **B.** Action events include the click of a button and the selection of an item from a pull-down menu.

2. **C.** The `this` keyword refers to the current object. If the name of an object is used as an argument instead of the `this` statement, that object would receive the events and be expected to handle them.

3. **B.** `JTextField` and `JTextArea` components store their values as text, so you must convert their values before you can use them as integers, floating-point numbers, or other nontext values.

Activities

If the main event of this hour didn't provide enough action for your tastes, interface with the following activities:

▶ Add a text field to the `LottoMadness` application that works in conjunction with the `Thread.sleep()` statement in the `LottoEvent` class to slow down the rate that drawings are conducted.

▶ Modify the `LottoMadness` project so it draws five numbers from 1 to 90.

To see Java programs that implement these activities, visit the book's website at www.java24hours.com.

Building a Complex User Interface

Creating a graphical user interface (GUI) with Swing involves more than learning how to use the different interface components, layout managers, and event-handling methods. You also have to familiarize yourself with everything that Swing offers.

More than 400 different classes make Swing one of the most extensive class libraries in Java. Many of these classes can be implemented using the same techniques you have learned during the preceding three hours—Swing containers and components share superclasses with each other, which gives them common behavior.

During this hour, you learn about additional components that you can use in your Swing programs.

Scroll Panes

Components in a GUI are often bigger than the area available to display them. To move from one part of the component to another, vertical and horizontal scrollbars are used.

In Swing, you offer scrolling by adding a component to a scroll pane, a container that is represented by the JScrollPane class.

You can create a scroll pane with the following constructors:

- ▶ JScrollPane()—Create a scroll pane with a horizontal and vertical scrollbar that appear as needed.

- ▶ JScrollPane(*int*, *int*)—Create a scroll pane with the specified vertical scrollbar and horizontal scrollbars.

WHAT YOU'LL LEARN IN THIS HOUR:

- ▶ Scrolling components horizontally and vertically
- ▶ Accepting a range of numeric input with sliders
- ▶ Monitoring user input on sliders
- ▶ Creating image icons and toolbars

> ▶ JScrollPane(*Component*)—Create a scroll pane that contains the specified user interface component.

> ▶ JScrollPane(*Component*, *int*, *int*)—Create a scroll pane with the specified component, vertical scrollbar, and horizontal scrollbar.

The integer arguments to these constructors determine how scrollbars are used in the pane. Use the following class variables as these arguments:

> ▶ JScrollPane.VERTICAL_SCROLLBAR_AS_NEEDED or
> JScrollPane.HORIZONTAL_SCROLLBAR_AS_NEEDED

> ▶ JScrollPane.VERTICAL_SCROLLBAR_NEVER or
> JScrollPane.HORIZONTAL_SCROLLBAR_NEVER

> ▶ JScrollPane.VERTICAL_SCROLLBAR_ALWAYS or
> JScrollPane.HORIZONTAL_SCROLLBAR_ALWAYS

If you have created a scroll pane without a component in it, you can use the pane's add(*Component*) method to add components. After you have finished setting up a scroll pane, it should be added to a container in place of the component.

To see an application that includes a scroll pane, enter Listing 16.1 into a new empty Java file named MailWriter and save the file.

LISTING 16.1   The Full Text of MailWriter.java

```
 1: import javax.swing.*;
 2: import java.awt.*;
 3:
 4: public class MailWriter extends JFrame {
 5:
 6:     public MailWriter() {
 7:         super("Write an E-Mail");
 8:         setLookAndFeel();
 9:         setSize(370, 270);
10:         setDefaultCloseOperation(JFrame.EXIT_ON_CLOSE);
11:         FlowLayout flow = new FlowLayout(FlowLayout.RIGHT);
12:         setLayout(flow);
13:
14:         JPanel row1 = new JPanel();
15:         JLabel toLabel = new JLabel("To:");
16:         row1.add(toLabel);
17:         JTextField to = new JTextField(24);
18:         row1.add(to);
19:         add(row1);
20:
21:         JPanel row2 = new JPanel();
```

LISTING 16.1   Continued

```
22:            JLabel subjectLabel = new JLabel("Subject:");
23:            row2.add(subjectLabel);
24:            JTextField subject = new JTextField(24);
25:            row2.add(subject);
26:            add(row2);
27:
28:            JPanel row3 = new JPanel();
29:            JLabel messageLabel = new JLabel("Message:");
30:            row3.add(messageLabel);
31:            JTextArea message = new JTextArea(4, 22);
32:            message.setLineWrap(true);
33:            message.setWrapStyleWord(true);
34:            JScrollPane scroll = new JScrollPane(message,
35:                JScrollPane.VERTICAL_SCROLLBAR_ALWAYS,
36:                JScrollPane.HORIZONTAL_SCROLLBAR_NEVER);
37:            row3.add(scroll);
38:            add(row3);
39:
40:            JPanel row4 = new JPanel();
41:            JButton send = new JButton("Send");
42:            row4.add(send);
43:            add(row4);
44:
45:            setVisible(true);
46:        }
47:
48:        private void setLookAndFeel() {
49:            try {
50:                UIManager.setLookAndFeel(
51:                    "com.sun.java.swing.plaf.nimbus.NimbusLookAndFeel"
52:                );
53:            } catch (Exception exc) {
54:                // ignore error
55:            }
56:        }
57:
58:        public static void main(String[] arguments) {
59:            MailWriter mail = new MailWriter();
60:        }
61: }
```

When you run the application, you should see a window like the one in Figure 16.1.

The MailWriter application is a GUI used to compose an email. There's no event-handling code in the program, so you can't do anything with the data entered in the form.

FIGURE 16.1
Displaying a scrolling text area in an application.

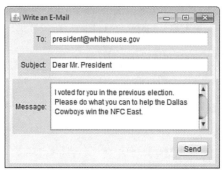

The text of an email is entered in a scrolling text area, which is implemented by creating a text area and adding it to a scroll pane with the following statements:

```
JTextArea message = new JTextArea(4, 22);
message.setLineWrap(true);
message.setWrapStyleWord(true);
JScrollPane scroll = new JScrollPane(message,
    JScrollPane.VERTICAL_SCROLLBAR_ALWAYS,
    JScrollPane.HORIZONTAL_SCROLLBAR_NEVER);
row3.add(scroll);
```

Sliders

The easiest way to collect numeric input from a user is with a *slider*, a component that can be dragged from side to side or up and down. Sliders are represented in Swing by the JSlider class.

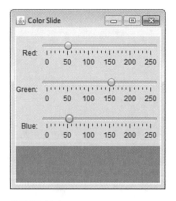

FIGURE 16.2
Choosing a color using three slider components.

Sliders enable a number to be chosen between minimum and maximum values. These values can be displayed on a label that includes the minimum value, maximum value, and intermediate values. An example you create later is shown in Figure 16.2.

You can create a horizontal slider with one of the following constructors:

▶ JSlider()—Create a slider with a minimum of 0, maximum of 100, and starting value of 50.

▶ JSlider(*int*, *int*)—Create a slider with the specified minimum and maximum values.

▶ JSlider(*int*, *int*, *int*)—Create a slider with the specified minimum, maximum, and starting values.

To create a vertical slider, use a constructor with an additional first argument: the orientation of the slider. This argument should be the class variable JSlider.VERTICAL or JSlider.HORIZONTAL.

The following statement creates a vertical slider for a number from 1 to 1,000:

```
JSlider guess = new JSlider(JSlider.VERTICAL, 1, 1000, 500);
```

This slider starts with the *caret*—the part of the component that selects a number—at the 500 position.

To display a label for a slider, you must set up the information the label will contain. Call the slider's setMajorTickSpacing(*int*) and setMinorTickSpacing(*int*) methods to determine how often a tick mark is displayed on the label. Major ticks are displayed as a thicker line than minor ticks.

After you have set up how often tick marks appear, call the slider's setPaintTicks(*boolean*) method with true as the argument. You also can display the numeric value of each major tick by calling the slider's setPaintLabels(*boolean*) method with true.

Change Listeners

To monitor slider input, you must have a class that implements the ChangeListener interface in the javax.swing.event package. This interface includes only one method:

```
public void stateChanged(ChangeEvent event); {
    // statements to handle the event
}
```

To register an object as a change listener, call the addChangeListener(*Object*) method of the container that holds the slider. When the slider is moved, the listening object's stateChanged() method is called.

This method is called with a ChangeEvent object that can identify the slider component that changed in value. Call the object's getSource() method and cast the object to a JSlider, as in the following statement:

```
JSlider changedSlider = (JSlider) event.getSource();
```

In this example, event is the ChangeEvent object that is an argument to the stateChanged() method.

Change events occur throughout a slider's movement. They begin when the slider is first moved, and they don't stop occurring until the slider has been released. For this reason, you might not want to do anything in the stateChanged() method until the slider has stopped moving.

To see if a slider is currently being moved around, call its getValueIsAdjusting() method. This method returns true while movement is taking place and false otherwise.

This technique is demonstrated in your next project, a Java application that uses three sliders to choose a color. Colors are created in Java by using the Color class in the java.awt package.

One way to create a Color object is to specify the amount of red, green, and blue in the color. Each of these can be an integer from 0 to 255 with 255 representing the maximum amount of that color.

The following statement creates a Color object that represents the color butterscotch:

```
Color butterscotch = new Color(255, 204, 128);
```

The red value used to create this Color object is 255, so it contains the maximum amount of red. It also contains a large amount of green and some blue.

Listing 16.2 contains the ColorSliders application, which has three sliders, three labels for the sliders, and a panel where the color is displayed. Create a new empty Java file called ColorSliders, enter the text of the listing in the source editor, and save the file.

LISTING 16.2   The Full Text of ColorSliders.java

```
 1: import javax.swing.*;
 2: import javax.swing.event.*;
 3: import java.awt.*;
 4:
 5: public class ColorSliders extends JFrame implements ChangeListener {
 6:     ColorPanel canvas;
 7:     JSlider red;
 8:     JSlider green;
 9:     JSlider blue;
10:
11:     public ColorSliders() {
12:         super("Color Slide");
13:         setLookAndFeel();
14:         setSize(270, 300);
15:         setDefaultCloseOperation(JFrame.EXIT_ON_CLOSE);
```

LISTING 16.2   Continued

```
16:            setVisible(true);
17:
18:            canvas = new ColorPanel();
19:            red = new JSlider(0, 255, 255);
20:            green = new JSlider(0, 255, 0);
21:            blue = new JSlider(0, 255, 0);
22:
23:            red.setMajorTickSpacing(50);
24:            red.setMinorTickSpacing(10);
25:            red.setPaintTicks(true);
26:            red.setPaintLabels(true);
27:            red.addChangeListener(this);
28:
29:            green.setMajorTickSpacing(50);
30:            green.setMinorTickSpacing(10);
31:            green.setPaintTicks(true);
32:            green.setPaintLabels(true);
33:            green.addChangeListener(this);
34:
35:            blue.setMajorTickSpacing(50);
36:            blue.setMinorTickSpacing(10);
37:            blue.setPaintTicks(true);
38:            blue.setPaintLabels(true);
39:            blue.addChangeListener(this);
40:
41:            JLabel redLabel = new JLabel("Red: ");
42:            JLabel greenLabel = new JLabel("Green: ");
43:            JLabel blueLabel = new JLabel("Blue: ");
44:            GridLayout grid = new GridLayout(4, 1);
45:            FlowLayout right = new FlowLayout(FlowLayout.RIGHT);
46:            setLayout(grid);
47:
48:            JPanel redPanel = new JPanel();
49:            redPanel.setLayout(right);
50:            redPanel.add(redLabel);
51:            redPanel.add(red);
52:            add(redPanel);
53:
54:            JPanel greenPanel = new JPanel();
55:            greenPanel.setLayout(right);
56:            greenPanel.add(greenLabel);
57:            greenPanel.add(green);
58:            add(greenPanel);
59:
60:            JPanel bluePanel = new JPanel();
61:            bluePanel.setLayout(right);
62:            bluePanel.add(blueLabel);
63:            bluePanel.add(blue);
64:            add(bluePanel);
65:            add(canvas);
66:
```

LISTING 16.2   Continued

```
67:            setVisible(true);
68:        }
69:
70:        public void stateChanged(ChangeEvent event) {
71:            JSlider source = (JSlider) event.getSource();
72:            if (source.getValueIsAdjusting() != true) {
73:                Color current = new Color(red.getValue(),
                    ➥green.getValue(),
74:                    blue.getValue());
75:                canvas.changeColor(current);
76:                canvas.repaint();
77:            }
78:        }
79:
80:        public Insets getInsets() {
81:            Insets border = new Insets(45, 10, 10, 10);
82:            return border;
83:        }
84:
85:        private void setLookAndFeel() {
86:            try {
87:                UIManager.setLookAndFeel(
88:                    "com.sun.java.swing.plaf.nimbus.NimbusLookAndFeel"
89:                );
90:            } catch (Exception exc) {
91:                // ignore error
92:            }
93:        }
94:
95:        public static void main(String[] arguments) {
96:            ColorSliders cs = new ColorSliders();
97:        }
98: }
99:
100: class ColorPanel extends JPanel {
101:     Color background;
102:
103:     ColorPanel() {
104:         background = Color.red;
105:     }
106:
107:     public void paintComponent(Graphics comp) {
108:         Graphics2D comp2D = (Graphics2D) comp;
109:         comp2D.setColor(background);
110:         comp2D.fillRect(0, 0, getSize().width, getSize().height);
111:     }
112:
113:     void changeColor(Color newBackground) {
114:         background = newBackground;
115:     }
116: }
```

When you run the application, as shown earlier in Figure 16.2, a frame contains three sliders that represent the amount of red, green, and blue in a panel along the bottom edge of the frame.

Adjust the values of each slider to change the color that is displayed. In Figure 16.2, the application is used to create North Texas Mean Green (red 50, green 150, and blue 50). This shade inspires alumni of the University of North Texas to leap to our feet at sporting events and make ferocious eagle-claw hand gestures that turn visiting teams yellow (red 255, green 255, orange 0).

Using Image Icons and Toolbars

One of the easiest ways to improve the visual appeal of a GUI is to use *icons*, small images used to identify buttons and other parts of an interface.

With many of the components in the Swing class library, you can label a component with an image instead of text by using the ImageIcon class in the javax.swing package.

You can create an ImageIcon from a file on your computer by calling the ImageIcon(*String*) constructor method. The argument to the method is either the name of the file or its location and name, as in these examples:

```
ImageIcon stopSign = new ImageIcon("stopsign.gif");
ImageIcon saveFile = new ImageIcon("images/savefile.gif");
```

The graphics file used to create the image icon must be in GIF, JPEG, or PNG format. Most are in GIF format which is well suited to displaying small graphics with a limited number of colors.

The ImageIcon constructor loads the entire image from the file immediately.

You can use image icons as labels and buttons by using the JLabel(*ImageIcon*) and JButton(*ImageIcon*) constructor methods, as in the following example:

```
ImageIcon siteLogo = new ImageIcon("siteLogo.gif");
JLabel logoLabel = new JLabel(siteLogo);
ImageIcon searchWeb = new ImageIcon("searchGraphic.gif");
JButton search = new JTextField(searchWeb);
```

Several components can have an icon and a text label. The following statement creates a button with both:

```
JButton refresh = new JButton("Refresh",
    "images/refreshIcon.gif");
```

CAUTION

Although some operating systems use the \ character to separate folders and filenames, the ImageIcon constructor requires the / character as a separator.

Image icons often are used in toolbars, containers that group several components together into a row or column.

Toolbars, which are created by using the JToolBar class, can be designed so that a user can move them from one part of a GUI to another. This process is called *docking,* and these components are also called *dockable toolbars.*

You can create a toolbar with one of the following constructor methods:

- ▶ JToolBar()—Create a toolbar that lines up components in a horizontal direction

- ▶ JToolBar(*int*)—Create a toolbar that lines up components in the specified direction, which is either SwingConstants.HORIZONTAL or SwingConstants.VERTICAL.

Components are added to a toolbar in the same way they are added to other containers—the add(*Component*) method is called with the component to be added.

For a toolbar to be dockable, it must be placed in a container that uses BorderLayout as its layout manager. This layout arranges a container into north, south, east, west, and center areas. When you are using a dockable toolbar, however, the container only should use two of these: the center and one directional area.

The toolbar should be added to the directional area. The following statements create a vertical, dockable toolbar with three icon buttons:

```
BorderLayout border = new BorderLayout();
pane.setLayout(border);
JToolBar bar = new JToolBar(SwingConstants.VERTICAL);
ImageIcon play = new ImageIcon("play.gif");
JButton playButton = new JButton(play);
ImageIcon stop = new ImageIcon("stop.gif");
JButton stopButton = new JButton(stop);
ImageIcon pause = new ImageIcon("pause.gif");
JButton pauseButton = new JButton(pause);
bar.add(playButton);
bar.add(stopButton);
bar.add(pauseButton);
add(bar, BorderLayout.WEST);
```

The next project you undertake during this hour is Tool, a Java application that includes image icons and a dockable toolbar around. Create an empty Java file called Tool, enter Listing 16.3 in the file, and save the file.

LISTING 16.3   The Full Text of `Tool.java`

```
 1: import java.awt.*;
 2: import java.awt.event.*;
 3: import javax.swing.*;
 4:
 5: public class Tool extends JFrame {
 6:     public Tool() {
 7:         super("Tool");
 8:         setLookAndFeel();
 9:         setSize(370, 200);
10:         setDefaultCloseOperation(JFrame.EXIT_ON_CLOSE);
11:
12:         // build toolbar buttons
13:         ImageIcon image1 = new ImageIcon("newfile.gif");
14:         JButton button1 = new JButton(image1);
15:         ImageIcon image2 = new ImageIcon("openfile.gif");
16:         JButton button2 = new JButton(image2);
17:         ImageIcon image3 = new ImageIcon("savefile.gif");
18:         JButton button3 = new JButton(image3);
19:
20:         // build toolbar
21:         JToolBar bar = new JToolBar();
22:         bar.add(button1);
23:         bar.add(button2);
24:         bar.add(button3);
25:
26:         // build text area
27:         JTextArea edit = new JTextArea(8, 40);
28:         JScrollPane scroll = new JScrollPane(edit);
29:
30:         // create frame
31:         BorderLayout border = new BorderLayout();
32:         setLayout(border);
33:         add("North", bar);
34:         add("Center", scroll);
35:         setVisible(true);
36:     }
37:
38:     private void setLookAndFeel() {
39:         try {
40:             UIManager.setLookAndFeel(
41:                 "com.sun.java.swing.plaf.nimbus.NimbusLookAndFeel"
42:             );
43:         } catch (Exception exc) {
44:             // ignore error
45:         }
46:     }
47:
48:     public static void main(String[] arguments) {
49:         Tool frame = new Tool();
50:     }
51: }
```

The `Tool` application requires three graphics files that are used to create the icons on the toolbar: `newfile.gif`, `openfile.gif`, and `savefile.gif`. Download these files from the Hour 16 page on the book's website at www.java24hours.com and save them in the `Java24` project folder (or the folder you designated for your Java projects in NetBeans).

Figure 16.3 and Figure 16.4 show two different screenshots of this application as it runs. The toolbar has been moved from its original location (see Figure 16.3) to another edge of the interface (see Figure 16.4).

FIGURE 16.3
Using an application with a toolbar.

FIGURE 16.4
Docking a toolbar at a new location.

Compile the application and try it out by moving the toolbar around. You can move a toolbar by clicking its handle and dragging the toolbar to a different edge of the text area. When you release the toolbar, it is placed along that edge and the text area moves over to make room for it.

Oracle offers a repository of icon graphics that you can use in your own programs. The three icons used in this hour's workshop are from that collection. To view the graphics, visit http://java.sun.com/developer/techDocs/hi/repository.

Summary

This is the last of four hours devoted to Swing, the part of the Java language that supports GUI software.

Although Swing is by far the largest part of the Java class library, most of the classes are used in similar ways. After you know how to create a component, add a component to a container, apply a layout manager to a container, and respond to user input, you can make use of many new Swing classes as you explore the language.

Q&A

Q. How can I find out about the rest of the Swing classes in the Java class library?

A. On Oracle's official Java site, the full documentation for the Java class library is published at http://download.oracle.com/javase/7/docs/api. You can see the classes that are included in `javax.swing`, `java.awt`, and `java.awt.event`, the packages that are covered during the preceding four hours. All Swing classes and interfaces are documented, including their constructors, class variables, and instance variables.

Q. Why is a videogame about a barrel-tossing, princess-kidnapping ape and an Italian plumber called Donkey Kong?

A. Donkey Kong was named by Shigeru Miyamoto, who created the game for Nintendo as a coin-operated arcade game in 1981. Miyamoto was under the mistaken impression that the word "donkey" meant "stupid" in English, but by the time Nintendo's American division learned of it the name had stuck.

Miyamoto's gorilla/princess/plumber love triangle was inspired by Nintendo's failed attempt to license *Popeye* for a videogame. Later videogames established that the original Donkey Kong has become Cranky Kong, an elderly bad-tempered ape who believes that an excessive amount of processing power is devoted to current games compared to his 8-bit heyday.

Workshop

No pane, no gain: Exercise some brain muscle by answering the following questions about scroll panes, image icons, and other Swing features.

Quiz

1. What graphics file formats are supported by the `ImageIcon` class?

    A. GIF

    B. GIF and JPEG

    C. GIF, PNG, and JPEG

2. What does a `JSlider` object's `getValueIsAdjusting()` method accomplish?

    A. It determines whether the slider has been changed from its original value.

    B. It determines whether the slider is currently being changed in value.

    C. Not a lot; this method is a major disappointment to its parent superclass.

3. The Swing library was named after a style of dance band jazz that was popularized in the 1930s and revived in the 1990s. Which of the following is not a real title of a song performed by a Swing musician?

    A. "Cement Mixer (Put-ti, Put-ti)"

    B. "Sussudio"

    C. "Flat Foot Floogie (with the Floy Floy)"

Answers

1. **C.** PNG support in `ImageIcon` was added in Java 1.3.

2. **B.** The `getValueIsAdjusting()` method returns `true` while the slider is being moved and `false` otherwise.

3. **B.** "Sussudio," a hit song by Phil Collins in 1985, was five decades too late for Swing. The other two songs are Swing hits by Slim Gaillard, whose gift for gibberish also was evident in the songs "Boot-Ta-La-Za," "Ra-Da-Da-Da," "Bingie-Bingie-Scootie," and "Vout Oreenie."

Activities

To see if you have got the swing of things, try the following activities:

▶ Create a GUI that includes a combo box in a scroll pane.

▶ Add event-handling to the `MailWriter` application that displays the contents of the `to`, `subject`, and `message` components using `System.out.println()` when the Send button is clicked.

To see Java programs that implement these activities, visit the book's website at www.java24hours.com.

HOUR 17
Creating Interactive Web Programs

Java has become successful as a general-purpose language that runs on many distinct platforms, including cell phones, web servers, and Internet appliances. When the language was introduced in the mid-1990s, it was the first programming language that could run inside a web browser.

Applets are Java programs designed to run as part of a web page. When a Java applet is encountered on a page, it is downloaded to the user's computer and begins running.

Programming applets is different than creating applications with the language. Because applets must be downloaded from a page each time they are run, they're smaller than most applications to reduce download time. Also, because applets run on the computer of the person using the applet, they have security restrictions in place to prevent malicious or damaging code from being run.

Standard Applet Methods

The first step in the creation of an applet is to make it a subclass of JApplet, a class in the Swing package javax.swing. An applet is treated as a visual window inside a web page, so JApplet is part of Swing alongside buttons, scrollbars, and other components of a program's user interface.

The applets you write inherit all the behavior and attributes they need to be run as part of a web page. Before you begin writing any other statements in your applets, they are able to interact with a web browser, load and unload themselves, redraw their windows in response to changes in the browser window, and handle other necessary tasks.

WHAT YOU'LL LEARN IN THIS HOUR:

▶ Stopping and starting an applet
▶ Putting an applet on a web page
▶ Customizing an applet with parameters on a web page
▶ Displaying web pages in an application

Applications begin running with the first statement inside the `main()` block. There is no `main()` method in a Java applet, so there's no set starting place for the program. Instead, an applet has a group of standard methods that are handled in response to specific events as the applet runs.

The following are the events that could prompt one of the applet methods to be handled:

- ▶ The program is loaded for the first time, which causes the applet's `init()` and `start()` methods to be called.

- ▶ Something happens that requires the applet window to be redisplayed, which causes the applet's `paint()` method to be called.

- ▶ The program is stopped by the browser, which calls the applet's `stop()` method.

- ▶ The program restarts after a stop, which calls `start()`.

- ▶ The program is unloaded as it finishes running, which calls `destroy()`.

The following is an example of a bare-bones applet:

```
public class Skeleton extends javax.swing.JApplet {
    // program will go here
}
```

Applet class files must be `public` because the `JApplet` class also is public. (If your applet uses other class files of your own creation, they do not have to be declared `public`.)

Your applet's class inherits all the methods that are handled automatically when needed: `init()`, `paint()`, `start()`, `stop()`, and `destroy()`. However, none of these methods do anything. If you want something to happen, you must override these methods with new versions in your applet.

Painting an Applet Window

The `paint()` method is used to display text and graphics within the applet window. Whenever something needs to be displayed or redisplayed in the applet, the `paint()` method handles the task. You also can force `paint()` to be called by using the following statement in an applet:

```
repaint();
```

The main time the paint() method is called is when something changes in the browser or the operating system running the browser. For example, if a user closes a window of another program that was in front of the browser, the paint() method is called to redisplay everything in the applet.

The paint() method takes a single argument, a Graphics object from the java.awt package:

```
public void paint(Graphics screen) {
    Graphics2D screen2D = (Graphics2D) screen;
    // display statements go here
}
```

The Graphics class represents a *graphical context*, an environment in which something can be displayed. As you did with Swing applications, you should cast this to a Graphics2D object from the java.awt package to use Swing's graphical capabilities.

Later this hour, you learn about drawString(), a method for displaying text in the Graphics2D classes.

If you are using a Graphics or Graphics2D object in your applet, you should add the following import statements before the class statement at the beginning of the source file:

```
import java.awt.Graphics;
import java.awt.Graphics2D;
```

Alternatively, you can make all java.awt classes available by using the wildcard character "*":

```
import java.awt.*;
```

Initializing an Applet

The init() method is called once—and only once—when an applet is run. It's an ideal place to set up values for objects and variables that are needed for the applet to run successfully. This method also is a good place to set up fonts, colors, and the applet window's background color. Here's an example:

```
public void init() {
    FlowLayout flo = new FlowLayout();
    setLayout(flo);
    JButton run = new JButton("Run");
    add(run);
}
```

If you are going to use a variable in other methods, it should not be created inside an init() method because it only exists within the scope of that method. Create any variables you need to use throughout a class as instance variables.

Starting and Stopping an Applet

When the applet program starts running, the start() method is called. When a program first begins, the init() method is followed by the start() method. After that, the start() method only is called again if the applet stops execution at some point and is later restarted.

The stop() method is called when an applet stops execution. This event can occur when a user leaves the web page containing the applet and continues to another page. It also can occur when the stop() method is called directly in a program.

Destroying an Applet

The destroy() method is the opposite of the init() method. It is handled just before an applet completely closes down and completes running.

Putting an Applet on a Web Page

Applets are placed on a web page by using HTML, the markup language used to create web pages. HTML is a way to combine formatted text, images, sound, and other elements together and present them in a web browser. HTML uses markup commands called tags that are surrounded by < and > marks, including <img> for the display of images, <p> for the insertion of a paragraph mark, and <h1> and </h1> to indicate the text that they surround is a heading.

The performance of HTML tags can be affected by attributes that determine how they function. The src attribute of an img tag provides the name of the image file that should be displayed, as in this example of HTML markup:

```
<img src="graduation.jpg">
```

This markup causes a web page to display the image stored in the file graduation.jpg. One way to place applets on a web page is to use applet tag and several attributes. The following HTML markup runs an applet on a page:

```
<applet code="StripYahtzee.class" codebase="javadir" height="300"
width="400">
<p>Sorry, no dice ... this requires a Java-enabled browser.</p>
</applet>
```

The `code` attribute identifies the name of the applet's class file. If more than one class file is being used with an applet, `code` should refer to the class that's a subclass of the `JApplet` class.

The `codebase` applet contains the path of the folder or subfolder where the applet and related files can be found. If there is no `codebase` attribute, all files associated with the applet must be in the same folder as the web page that contains the applet. In the preceding example, `codebase` indicates that the `StripYahtzee` applet can be found in the `javadir` subfolder.

The `height` and `width` attributes designate the size of the applet window on the web page in pixels. It must be big enough to handle the things you are displaying in your applet.

In between the opening `<applet>` tag and the closing `</applet>` tag, you can provide some HTML markup to display to web users whose browsers either do not support Java or have Java turned off.

In the preceding example, the paragraph "Sorry, no dice…this requires a Java-enabled browser" is displayed in place of the applet in browsers that don't run Java. You can put instructions here on how to download a Java-enabled browser from Oracle at www.java.com. You also can include hyperlinks and other HTML elements.

Another useful attribute, `align`, designates how an applet is displayed in relation to the surrounding material on the page, including text and graphics. The value `align="left"` lines up an applet to the left of adjacent page elements and `align="right"` to the right.

Creating an Applet

This hour's first project is an applet that displays the string "Saluton mondo!", the traditional Esperanto greeting that is becoming more traditional by the hour. You get a feel for how applets are structured by re-creating the `Saluton` application from Hour 2, "Writing Your First Program," as a program that can run on a web page.

Create a new empty Java file called `SalutonApplet`, enter the text from Listing 17.1 into the file, and save the file.

LISTING 17.1   The Full Text of SalutonApplet.java

```
1: import java.awt.*;
2:
3: public class SalutonApplet extends javax.swing.JApplet {
4:     String greeting;
5:
6:     public void init() {
7:         greeting = "Saluton mondo!";
8:     }
9:
10:     public void paint(Graphics screen) {
11:         Graphics2D screen2D = (Graphics2D) screen;
12:         screen2D.drawString(greeting, 25, 50);
13:     }
14: }
```

The SalutonApplet program stores the string "Saluton mondo!" inside the init() method in lines 6–8 and displays it in the applet window in line 12. The applet does not need to use the start(), stop(), or destroy() methods, so they are not included in the program. You run the applet after learning more about how it was coded.

Drawing in an Applet Window

Text is displayed in an applet window by using the drawString() method of the Graphics2D class, which draws text in a user interface component. The drawString() method is similar to the System.out.println() method that you've been using to display text in applications.

The following three arguments are sent to drawString():

▶ The text to display, which can be several different strings and variables strung together with the + operator

▶ The x position in an (x,y) coordinate system, where the string should be displayed

▶ The y position in an (x,y) coordinate system, where the string should be displayed

The (x,y) coordinate system in an applet is used with several methods. It begins with the (0,0) point in the upper-left corner of the applet window. The x values count up as you move to the right and y values count up as you move down.

Testing the `SalutonApplet` Program

Java applets can't be run like applications because they lack a `main()` method.

Instead, to run an applet, you must add markup to a web page that contains the applet. To create an example web page for `SalutonApplet`, create a new web page in NetBeans by following these steps:

1. Choose File, New File. The New File dialog opens.

2. Choose Other from the Categories pane and HTML File from File Types, then click Next. The New HTML File dialog opens.

3. Give the file the name `SalutonApplet` and click Finish.

NetBeans opens the source code editor with some default HTML markup. Delete all the markup that's been provided for you, enter Listing 17.2 into the editor, and save the file.

LISTING 17.2   The Full Text of `SalutonApplet.html`

```
 1: <html>
 2: <head>
 3: <title>Saluton Mondo!</title>
 4: </head>
 5: <body bgcolor="#000000" text="#FF00FF">
 6: <p>This is a Java applet.</p>
 7: <applet
 8:     code="SalutonApplet.class"
 9:     codebase="..\\..\\build\\classes"
10:     height="150"
11:     width="300"
12: >
13: <p>You need a Java-enabled browser to see this.</p>
14: </applet>
15: </body>
16: </html>
```

The `<applet>` tag is defined in lines 7–14, but line 13 will be ignored in any browser equipped to run Java.

After saving the file, you can view it in a web browser: In the Project pane to the left of the source code editor, right-click the filename `SalutonApplet.html`, and then choose `View`. The web page opens in your computer's default web browser, as shown in Figure 17.1.

FIGURE 17.1
The SalutonApplet applet loaded with Microsoft Internet Explorer.

When you run the applet in a browser, you might be asked whether it's OK to run the program. Many web browsers must be configured to enable Java programs before they run Java applets.

Java applets are run in current browsers by the Java Plug-in, an interpreter from Oracle that supports the most up-to-date version of the language.

A *plug-in* is a program that works in conjunction with a web browser to expand its functionality. Plug-ins handle a type of data that the browser normally could not handle. Apple offers a plug-in to display QuickTime movies, Macromedia distributes a plug-in to run Flash animation files, and many other kinds of special content are supported in this manner.

The plug-in can be downloaded from Sun's Java site at www.java.com.

Sending Parameters from a Web Page

The functionality of an applet can be customized with the use of parameters, settings stored in HTML markup that serve the same purpose as command-line arguments in applications.

Parameters are stored as part of the web page that contains an applet. They're created using the HTML tag param and its two attributes: name and value. You can have more than one param tag with an applet, but all must be placed between the opening <applet> and closing </applet> tags. Here's an applet tag that includes several parameters:

```
<applet code="ScrollingHeadline" height="50" width="400">
    <param name="headline1" value="Dewey defeats Truman">
    <param name="headline2" value="Stix nix hix pix">
    <param name="headline3" value="Man bites dog">
</applet>
```

This markup could be used with an applet that scrolls news headlines across a web page. Because news changes all the time, the only way to design a program like that is through the use of parameters.

The name attribute give a parameter a name and value assigns it a value.

Receiving Parameters in the Applet

You access parameters in an applet by. calling the getParameter(*String*) method of the applet—inherited from JApplet—with its name as the argument, as in this statement:

```
String display1 = getParameter("headline1");
```

The getParameter() method returns parameter values as strings, so they must be converted to other types as needed. If you want to use a parameter as an integer, you could use statements such as the following:

```
int speed;
String speedParam = getParameter("speed");
if (speedParam != null) {
    speed = Integer.parseInt(speedParam);
}
```

This example sets the speed integer variable by using the speedParam string. When you try to retrieve a parameter with getParameter() that was not included on a web page with the param tag, it is sent as null, which is the value of an empty string.

Handling Parameters in an Applet

The workshop for this hour takes a person's weight and displays it under several different units. The applet takes two parameters: a weight in pounds and the name of the person who weighs that amount. The weight is used to figure out the person's weight in ounces, kilograms, and metric tons, which are all displayed.

Create a new empty Java file called WeightScale, enter the text of Listing 17.3 into the file, and save the file.

LISTING 17.3   The Full Text of `WeightScale.java`

```
1: import java.awt.*;
2:
3: public class WeightScale extends javax.swing.JApplet {
4:     float lbs = 0F;
5:     float ozs;
6:     float kgs;
7:     float metricTons;
8:     String name = "somebody";
9:
10:     public void init() {
11:         String lbsValue = getParameter("weight");
12:         if (lbsValue != null) {
13:             lbs = Float.valueOf(lbsValue);
14:         }
15:         String personValue = getParameter("person");
16:         if (personValue != null) {
17:             name = personValue;
18:         }
19:         ozs = (float) (lbs * 16);
20:         kgs = (float) (lbs / 2.204623);
21:         metricTons = (float) (lbs / 2204.623);
22:     }
23:
24:     public void paint(Graphics screen) {
25:         Graphics2D screen2D = (Graphics2D) screen;
26:         screen2D.drawString("Studying the weight of " + name, 5, 30);
27:         screen2D.drawString("In pounds: " + lbs, 55, 50);
28:         screen2D.drawString("In ounces: " + ozs, 55, 70);
29:         screen2D.drawString("In kilograms: " + kgs, 55, 90);
30:         screen2D.drawString("In metric tons: " + metricTons, 55, 110);
31:     }
32: }
```

The `init()` method is where the two parameters are loaded into the applet. Because parameters come from the web page as strings, the `weight` parameter must be converted to a floating-point number to use it in mathematical expressions. The `Float` object class includes a `valueOf(String)` that returns a string's value as a `Float`. This value is automatically unboxed to the `float` variable type in Line 13.

Lines 19–21 are used to convert the `lbs` variable into different units of measure. Each statement has `(float)` in front of the conversion equation. This is used to cast the result of the equation into a floating-point number.

The `paint()` method of the applet uses `drawString()` to display a line of text. The `paint()` method has three arguments: the text to display, the x position, and the y position where the text should be shown.

Before you can test the `WeightScale` applet, you must create a web page that contains the applet. Create a new HTML file in NetBeans called `WeightScale`. Enter Listing 17.4 into the file, and then open the newly created web page in a browser—right-click `WeightScale.html` in the Project pane and choose View.

LISTING 17.4   The Full Text of `WeightScale.html`

```
1: <applet code="WeightScale.class" codebase="..\\..\\build\\classes"
2:     height="170" width="210">
3:     <param name="person" value="Konishiki">
4:     <param name="weight" value="605">
5: </applet>
```

This demonstration uses Konishiki, an American-born sumo wrestling champion who weighed 605 pounds when he competed, making him the largest of the immodest, bikini-wearing behemoths. You can substitute anyone whose weight is either exemplary or well-known. Figure 17.2 shows an example of output from the applet.

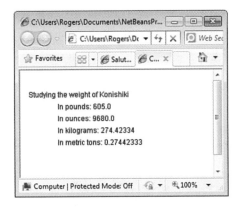

FIGURE 17.2
The *WeightScale* applet loaded with Internet Explorer.

To make the applet display a different name along with a different value for the `weight` parameter, you have to change the `WeightScale.html` file. The applet itself continues to work correctly.

Using the Object Tag

The newest version of HTML, HTML5, has replaced the `<applet>` tag with an `<object>` tag for loading Java applets, Flash programs, and other forms of interactive content. This tag has `height` and `width` attributes just like

`<applet>`. There's also a `type` attribute that must be `"application/x-java-applet"`, the designated MIME type of Java applets. (MIME types categorize file formats that can be delivered over the Internet.) Here's the start to the formatting of an object:

```
<object type="application/x-java-applet" height="300" width="400">
</object>
```

The `code` and `codebase` of an applet are not designated as attributes. Instead, parameters named `code` and `codebase` are placed within the opening `<object>` tag and closing `</object>` tag.

The following HTML5 markup displays an applet:

```
<object type="application/x-java-applet" height="300" width="400">
  <param name="code" value="StripYahtzee" />
  <param name="codebase" value="javadir" />
  <p>Sorry, no dice ... this requires a Java-enabled browser.</p>
</object>
```

Summary

Most of the hours in this book focus on applications, primarily because most Java programmers today don't do a lot of work designing applets for the Web.

Applets are limited by a set of default security restrictions that make them safe to be executed on user computers in a web browser. They can't save files to the computer, read files from the computer, list file folders, or create pop-up windows that are not identified as Java applets, among other safeguards.

These restrictions can be overcome by signing an applet with a digital signature and asking a user to approve the applet. An alternative to deploying Java programs as applets is to use Java Web Start, a technology for launching Java applications from a web browser.

Q&A

Q. Is there a reason why the `codebase` attribute should be used in an `applet` tag?

A. If all Java programs are grouped into their own subfolder using `codebase`, this structure might improve the way a website is organized, but there's no other reason why using `codebase` is better than omitting it. The choice is a matter of personal preference.

Q. Why don't applets have a `main()` method?

A. Applets don't use `main()` because they have a more complicated life cycle than applications. An application starts, runs until its work is complete, and exits. An applet can be started and stopped multiple times in a browser as the page on which it is contained is displayed.

If a user uses the back button to leave the page and then the forwards button to return, the applet's `start()` method is called again. If a pop-up window that obscures the applet is closed, the applet's `paint()` method is called.

The `JApplet` class was designed to make these more complex interactions work inside a browser.

Q. Have the Washington Generals ever beaten the Harlem Globetrotters?

A. The Generals have beaten the Globetrotters seven times over the decades, most recently in 1971. Playing in Martin, Tennessee, the Generals won 100–99 on a shot by team owner Louis "Red" Klotz.

Although the Generals are known today for being patsies, they began in 1921 as the Philadelphia Sphas, a legitimate team that played in the Eastern and American basketball leagues. The Sphas—an acronym for South Philadelphia Hebrew Association—won 10 championships. Klotz was a former Sphas player who bought the team and changed their name to the Generals in 1952 when they became the permanent touring partner of Harlem's famous team.

The 1971 victory ended a 2,495-game winning streak for the Globetrotters.

Workshop

The following questions test your knowledge of applets.

Quiz

1. What type of argument is used with the `paint()` method?

    A. A `Graphics` object

    B. A `Graphics2D` object

    C. None

2. Which method is handled right before an applet finishes running?

    A. `decline()`

    B. `destroy()`

    C. `defenestrate()`

3. Why can't all variables needed in an applet be created inside the `init()` method?

    A. The scope of the variables would be limited to the method only.

    B. Federal legislation prohibits it.

    C. They can be created there without any problems.

Answers

1. **A.** The `Graphics` object keeps track of the behavior and attributes needed to display things on-screen in the applet window. You might create a `Graphics2D` object inside the method, but it isn't sent as an argument.

2. **B.** The `destroy()` method can be used to free up resources used by the applet.

3. **A.** Variables that are used in more than one method of a class should be created right after the class statement but before any methods begin.

Activities

You can apply your applet programming knowledge with the following activities:

- ▶ Write an applet in which the text that is displayed moves each time the applet window is repainted.

- ▶ Install the Java Plug-in with your preferred browser and try the applets at www.javaonthebrain.com.

To see Java programs that implement these activities, visit the book's website at www.java24hours.com.

Handling Errors in a Program

Errors, the bugs, blunders, and typos that prevent a program from running correctly, are a natural part of the software development process. "Natural" is probably the kindest word that's ever been used to describe them. In my own programming, when I can't find the cause of an elusive error, I use words that would make a gangsta rapper blush.

Some errors are flagged by the compiler and prevent you from creating a class. Others are noted by the interpreter in response to a problem that keeps it from running successfully. Java divided errors into two categories:

- **Exceptions**—Events that signal an unusual circumstance has taken place as a program runs
- **Errors**—Events that signal the interpreter is having problems that might be unrelated to your program

Errors normally aren't something a Java program can recover from, so they're not the focus of this hour. You might have encountered an `OutOfMemoryError` as you worked on Java programs; nothing can be done to handle that kind of error. The program exits with the error.

Exceptions often can be dealt with in a way that keeps a program running properly.

Exceptions

Although you are just learning about them now, you have probably become well-acquainted with exceptions during the last 17 previous hours. These errors turn up when you write a Java program that compiles successfully but encounters a problem as it runs.

WHAT YOU'LL LEARN IN THIS HOUR:

- How to respond to exceptions in your Java programs
- How to create methods that ignore an exception, leaving it for another class to handle
- How to use methods that cause exceptions
- How to create your own exceptions

For example, a common programming mistake is to refer to an element of an array that doesn't exist, as in the following statements:

```
String[] greek = { "Alpha", "Beta", "Gamma" };
System.out.println(greek[3]);
```

The String array greek has three elements. Because the first element of an array is numbered 0 rather than 1, the first element is greek[0], the second greek[1], and the third greek[2]. So the statement attempting to display greek[3] is erroneous. The preceding statements compile successfully, but when you run the program, the Java interpreter halts with a message such as the following:

Output ▼

```
Exception in thread "main" java.lang.ArrayIndexOutBoundsException: 3
    at SampleProgram.main(SampleProgram.java:4)
```

This message indicates that the application has generated an exception, which the interpreter noted by displaying an error message and stopping the program.

The error message refers to a class called ArrayIndexOutOfBoundsException in the java.lang package. This class is an *exception*, an object that represents an exceptional circumstance that has taken place in a Java program.

When a Java class encounters an exception, it alerts users of the class to the error. In this example, the user of the class is the Java interpreter.

NOTE

Two terms are used to describe this process: *throw* and *catch*. Objects throw exceptions to alert others that they have occurred. These exceptions are caught by other objects or the Java interpreter.

All exceptions are subclasses of Exception in the java.lang package. The ArrayIndexOutOfBoundsException does what you would expect—it reports that an array element has been accessed outside the array's boundaries.

There are hundreds of exceptions in Java. Many such as the array exception indicate a problem that can be fixed with a programming change. These are comparable to compiler errors—after you correct the situation, you don't have to concern yourself with the exception any longer.

Other exceptions must be dealt with every time a program runs by using five new keywords: try, catch, finally, throw, and throws.

Catching Exceptions in a try-catch Block

Up to this point, you have dealt with exceptions by fixing the problem that caused them. There are times you can't deal with an exception in that manner and must handle the issue within a Java class.

As an introduction to why this is useful, enter the short Java application in Listing 18.1 in a new empty Java file called `Calculator` and save the file.

LISTING 18.1   The Full Text of `Calculator.java`

```
1: public class Calculator {
2:     public static void main(String[] arguments) {
3:         float sum = 0;
4:         for (int i = 0; i < arguments.length; i++) {
5:             sum = sum + Float.parseFloat(arguments[i]);
6:         }
7:         System.out.println("Those numbers add up to " + sum);
8:     }
9: }
```

The `Calculator` application takes one or more numbers as command-line arguments, adds them up, and displays the total.

Because all command-line arguments are represented by strings in a Java application, the program must convert them into floating-point numbers before adding them together. The `Float.parseFloat()` class method in Line 5 takes care of this, adding the converted number to a variable named `sum`.

Before running the application with the following command-line arguments, which can be set in NetBeans with the Run, Set Project Configuration, Customize command: 8 6 7 5 3 0 9. Choose Run, Run Main Project to run the application and see the output in Figure 18.1.

```
Output - Java24 (run)
run:
Those numbers add up to 38.0
BUILD SUCCESSFUL (total time: 0 seconds)
```

FIGURE 18.1
The output of the `Calculator` application.

Run the program several times with different numbers as arguments. It should handle them successfully, which might make you wonder what this has to do with exceptions.

To see the relevance, change the `Calculator` application's command-line arguments to 1 3 5x.

The third argument contains a typo—there shouldn't be an x after the number 5. The `Calculator` application has no way to know this is a mistake, so it tries to add 5x to the other numbers, causing the following exception to be displayed:

Output ▼

```
Exception in thread "main" java.lang.NumberFormatException: For input
string: "5x" at sun.misc.FloatingDecimal.readJavaFormatString
(FloatingDecimal.java:1224)
    at java.lang.Float.parseFloat(Float.java:422)
    at Calculator.main(Calculator.java:5)
```

This message can be informative to a programmer, but it's not something you'd want a user to see. Java programs can take care of their own exceptions by using a try-catch block statement, which takes the following form:

```
try {
    // statements that might cause the exception
} catch (Exception e) {
    // what to do when the exception occurs
}
```

A try-catch block must be used on any exception that you want a method of a class to handle. The Exception object that appears in the catch statement should be one of three things:

▶ The class of the exception that might occur

▶ More than one class of exception, separated by | characters

▶ A superclass of several different exceptions that might occur

The try section of the try-catch block contains the statement (or statements) that might throw an exception. In the Calculator application, the call to the Float.parseFloat(*String*) method in Line 5 of Listing 18.1 throws a NumberFormatException whenever it is used with a string argument that can't be converted to a floating-point value.

To improve the Calculator application so that it never stops running with this kind of error, you can use a try-catch block.

Create a new empty Java file called NewCalculator and enter the text of Listing 18.2.

LISTING 18.2   The Full Text of NewCalculator.java

```
1: public class NewCalculator {
2:     public static void main(String[] arguments) {
3:         float sum = 0;
4:         for (int i = 0; i < arguments.length; i++) {
5:             try {
6:                 sum = sum + Float.parseFloat(arguments[i]);
7:             } catch (NumberFormatException e) {
8:                 System.out.println(arguments[i] + " is not a
                    ➥number.");
```

Listing 18.2   Continued

```
 9:            }
10:         }
11:         System.out.println("Those numbers add up to " + sum);
12:      }
13: }
```

After you save the application, run it with the command-line argument 1 3 5x and you see the output shown in Figure 18.2.

FIGURE 18.2
The output of the NewCalculator application.

The try-catch block in Lines 5–9 deals with NumberFormatException errors thrown by Float.parseFloat(). These exceptions are caught within the NewCalculator class, which displays an error message for any argument that is not a number. Because the exception is handled within the class, the Java interpreter does not display an error. You can often deal with problems related to user input and other unexpected data by using try-catch blocks.

Catching Several Different Exceptions

A try-catch block can be used to handle several different kinds of exceptions, even if they are thrown by different statements.

One way to handle multiple classes of exceptions is to devote a catch block to each one, as in this code:

```
String textValue = "35";
int value;
try {
    value = Integer.parseInt(textValue);
catch (NumberFormatException exc) {
    // code to handle exception
} catch (Arithmetic Exception exc) {
    // code to handle exception
}
```

As of Java 7, you also can handle multiple exceptions in the same catch block by separating them with pipe (|) characters and ending the list with a name for the exception variable. Here's an example:

```
try {
    value = Integer.parseInt(textValue);
catch (NumberFormatException | Arithmetic Exception exc) {
    // code to handle exceptions
}
```

If a NumberFormatException or ArithmeticException is caught, it will be assigned to the exc variable.

Listing 18.3 contains an application called NumberDivider that takes two integer arguments from the command-line and uses them in a division expression.

This application must be able to deal with two potential problems in user input:

▶ Nonnumeric arguments

▶ Division by zero

Create a new empty Java file for NumberDivider and enter the text of Listing 18.3 into the source editor.

LISTING 18.3   The Full Text of NumberDivider.java

```
 1: public class NumberDivider {
 2:     public static void main(String[] arguments) {
 3:         if (arguments.length == 2) {
 4:             int result = 0;
 5:             try {
 6:                 result = Integer.parseInt(arguments[0]) /
 7:                     Integer.parseInt(arguments[1]);
 8:                 System.out.println(arguments[0] + " divided by " +
 9:                     arguments[1] + " equals " + result);
10:             } catch (NumberFormatException e) {
11:                 System.out.println("Both arguments must be numbers.");
12:             } catch (ArithmeticException e) {
13:                 System.out.println("You cannot divide by zero.");
14:             }
15:         }
16:     }
17: }
```

Using command-line arguments to specify two arguments, you can run it with integers, floating-point numbers, and nonnumeric arguments.

The if statement in Line 3 checks to make sure that two arguments are sent to the application. If not, the program exits without displaying anything.

The NumberDivider application performs integer division, so the result is an integer. In integer division, 5 divided by 2 equals 2, not 2.5.

If you use a floating-point or nonnumeric argument, a NumberFormat Exception is thrown by Lines 6–7 and caught by Lines 10–11.

If you use an integer as the first argument and a zero as the second argument, a ArithmeticExpression is thrown in Lines 6–7 and caught by Lines 12–13.

Handling Something After an Exception

When you are dealing with multiple exceptions by using try and catch, there are times when you want the program to do something at the end of the block whether an exception occurred or not.

You can handle this by using a try-catch-finally block, which takes the following form:

```
try {
    // statements that might cause the exception
} catch (Exception e) {
    // what to do when the exception occurs
} finally {
    // statements to execute no matter what
}
```

The statement or statements within the finally section of the block is executed after everything else in the block, even if an exception occurs.

One place this is useful is in a program that reads data from a file on disk, which you do in Hour 20, "Reading and Writing Files." There are several ways an exception can occur when you are accessing data—the file might not exist, a disk error could occur, and so on. If the statements to read the disk are in a try section and errors are handled in a catch section, you can close the file in the finally section. This makes sure that the file is closed whether or not an exception is thrown as it is read.

Throwing Exceptions

When you call a method of another class, that class can control how the method is used by throwing exceptions.

As you make use of the classes in the Java class library, the compiler often displays a message such as the following:

Output ▼

```
NetReader.java:14: unreported exception java.net.MalformedURLException;
must be caught or declared to be thrown
```

Whenever you see an error stating that an exception "must be caught or declared to be thrown," it indicates the method you are trying to use throws an exception.

Any class that calls these methods, such as an application that you write, must do one of the following things:

- ▶ Handle the exception with a try-catch block.
- ▶ Throw the exception.
- ▶ Handle the exception with a try-catch block and then throw it.

Up to this point in the hour, you have seen how to handle exceptions. If you would like to throw an exception after handling it, you can use a throw statement followed by the exception object to throw.

The following statements handle a NumberFormatException error in a catch block, and then throw the exception:

```
try {
    principal = Float.parseFloat(loanText) * 1.1F;
} catch (NumberFormatException e) {
    System.out.println(arguments[i] + " is not a number.");
    throw e;
}
```

This rewritten code handles all exceptions that could be generated in the try block and throws them:

```
try {
    principal = Float.parseFloat(loanText) * 1.1F;
} catch (Exception e) {
    System.out.println("Error " + e.getMessage());
    throw e;
}
```

`Exception` is the parent of all exception subclasses. A `catch` statement will catch the class and any subclass below it in the class hierarchy.

When you throw an exception with `throw`, it generally means you have not done everything that needs to be done to take care of the exception.

An example of where this might be useful: Consider a hypothetical program called `CreditCardChecker`, an application that verifies credit card purchases. This application uses a class called `CheckDatabase`, which has the following job:

1. Make a connection to the credit card lender's computer.

2. Ask that computer if the customer's credit card number is valid.

3. Ask the computer if the customer has enough credit to make the purchase.

As the `CheckDatabase` class is doing its job, what happens if the credit card lender's computer doesn't answer the phone at all? This kind of error is exactly the kind of thing that the `try-catch` block was designed for, and it is used within `CheckDatabase` to handle connection errors.

If the `CheckDatabase` class handles this error by itself, the `CreditCardChecker` application doesn't know that the exception took place at all. This isn't a good idea—the application should know when a connection cannot be made so it can report this to the person using the application.

One way to notify the `CreditCardChecker` application is for `CheckDatabase` to catch the exception in a `catch` block, and then throw it again with a `throw` statement. The exception is thrown in `CheckDatabase`, which must then deal with it like any other exception.

Exception handling is a way that classes can communicate with each other in the event of an error or other unusual circumstance.

When using `throw` in a `catch` block that catches a parent class, such as `Exception`, throwing the exception throws that class. This loses some detail of what kind of error occurred, because a subclass such as `NumberFormatException` tells you a lot more about the problem than simply the `Exception` class.

Java 7 offers a new way to keep this detail: the `final` keyword in a `catch` statement.

```
try {
    principal = Float.parseFloat(loanText) * 1.1F;
} catch (final Exception e) {
    System.out.println("Error " + e.getMessage());
    throw e;
}
```

That `final` keyword in `catch` causes `throw` to behave differently. The specific class that was caught is thrown.

Ignoring Exceptions

The last technique that is covered this hour is how to ignore an exception completely. A method in a class can ignore exceptions by using a `throws` clause as part of the method definition.

The following method throws a `MalformedURLException`, an error that can occur when you are working with web addresses in a Java program:

```
public loadURL(String address) throws MalformedURLException {
    URL page = new URL(address);
    loadWebPage(page);
}
```

The second statement in this example creates a `URL` object, which represents an address on the Web. The constructor method of the `URL` class throws a `MalformedURLException` to indicate that an invalid address is used, so no object can be constructed. The following statement causes one of these exceptions to be thrown:

```
URL source = new URL("http:www.java24hours.com");
```

The string `http:www.java24hours.com` is not a valid URL. It's missing some punctuation—two slash characters (`//`) after the colon.

Because the `loadURL()` method has been declared to throw `MalformedURLException` errors, it does not have to deal with them inside the method. The responsibility for catching this exception falls to any method that calls the `loadURL()` method.

Throwing and Catching Exceptions

For the next project, you create a class that uses exceptions to tell another class about an error that has taken place.

The classes in this project are HomePage, a class that represents a personal home page on the Web, and PageCatalog, an application that catalogs these pages.

Enter the text of Listing 18.4 in a new empty Java file called HomePage.

LISTING 18.4   The Full Text of HomePage.java

```
 1: import java.net.*;
 2:
 3: public class HomePage {
 4:     String owner;
 5:     URL address;
 6:     String category = "none";
 7:
 8:     public HomePage(String inOwner, String inAddress)
 9:         throws MalformedURLException {
10:
11:         owner = inOwner;
12:         address = new URL(inAddress);
13:     }
14:
15:     public HomePage(String inOwner, String inAddress, String inCategory)
16:         throws MalformedURLException {
17:
18:         this(inOwner, inAddress);
19:         category = inCategory;
20:     }
21: }
```

You can use the compiled HomePage class in other programs. This class represents personal web pages on the Web. It has three instance variables: address, a URL object representing the address of the page; owner, the person who owns the page; and category, a short comment describing the page's primary subject matter.

Like any class that creates URL objects, HomePage must either deal with MalformedURLException errors in a try-catch block or declare that it is ignoring these errors.

The class takes the latter course, as shown in Lines 8–9 and Lines 15–16. By using throws in the two constructor methods, HomePage removes the need to deal with MalformedURLException errors in any way.

To create an application that uses the HomePage class, return to NetBeans and create an empty Java file called PageCatalog that contains the text of Listing 18.5.

LISTING 18.5   The Full Text of `PageCatalog.java`

```
 1: import java.net.*;
 2:
 3: public class PageCatalog {
 4:     public static void main(String[] arguments) {
 5:         HomePage[] catalog = new HomePage[5];
 6:         try {
 7:             catalog[0] = new HomePage("Mark Evanier",
 8:                 "http://www.newsfromme.com", "comic books");
 9:             catalog[1] = new HomePage("Todd Smith",
10:                 "http://www.sharkbitten.com", "music");
11:             catalog[2] = new HomePage("Rogers Cadenhead",
12:                 "http://workbench.cadenhead.org", "programming");
13:             catalog[3] = new HomePage("Juan Cole",
14:                 "http://www.juancole.com", "politics");
15:             catalog[4] = new HomePage("Rafe Colburn",
16:                 "www.rc3.org");
17:             for (int i = 0; i < catalog.length; i++) {
18:                 System.out.println(catalog[i].owner + ": " +
19:                     catalog[i].address + " — " +
20:                     catalog[i].category);
21:             }
22:         } catch (MalformedURLException e) {
23:             System.out.println("Error: " + e.getMessage());
24:         }
25:     }
26: }
```

When you run the compiled application, the following output is displayed:

Output ▼

```
Error: no protocol: www.rc3.org
```

The `PageCatalog` application creates an array of `HomePage` objects and then displays the contents of the array. Each `HomePage` object is created using up to three arguments:

- ▸ The name of the page's owner
- ▸ The address of the page (as a `String`, not a `URL`)
- ▸ The category of the page

The third argument is optional, and it is not used in Lines 15–16.

The constructor methods of the `HomePage` class throw `MalformedURLException` errors when they receive a string that cannot be converted into a valid `URL` object. These exceptions are handled in the `PageCatalog` application by using a try-catch block.

To correct the problem causing the "no protocol" error, edit Line 16 so the string begins with the text http:// like the other web addresses in Lines 7–14. When you run the program again, you see the output shown in Figure 18.3.

FIGURE 18.3
The output of the PageCatalog application.

Summary

Now that you have put Java's exception handling techniques to use, the subject of errors ought to be a bit more popular than it was at the beginning of the hour.

You can do a lot with these techniques:

▶ Catch an exception and deal with it.

▶ Ignore an exception, leaving it for another class or the Java interpreter to take care of.

▶ Catch several different exceptions in the same try-catch block.

▶ Throw your own exception.

Managing exceptions in your Java programs makes them more reliable, more versatile, and easier to use because you don't display any cryptic error messages to people who are running your software.

Q&A

Q. Is it possible to create your own exceptions?

A. You can create your own exceptions easily by making them a subclass of an existing exception, such as `Exception`, the superclass of all exceptions. In a subclass of `Exception`, there are only two methods you might want to override: `Exception()` with no arguments and `Exception()` with a `String` as an argument. In the latter, the string should be a message describing the error that has occurred.

Q. Why doesn't this hour cover how to throw and catch errors in addition to exceptions?

A. Java divides problems into `Errors` and `Exceptions` because they differ in severity. Exceptions are less severe, so they are something that should be dealt with in your programs using `try-catch` or `throws` in the method declaration. Errors, on the other hand, are more serious and can't be dealt with adequately in a program.

Two examples of these errors are stack overflows and out-of-memory errors. These can cause the Java interpreter to crash, and there's no way you can fix them in your own program as the interpreter runs it.

Q. What is the oldest comic strip that's still running in newspapers?

A. *Katzenjammer Kids*, which was created by Rudolph Dirks in 1897 and is still offered today by King Features Syndicate. The strip was started only two years after the first comic strip, *The Yellow Kid*, and is the first to use speech balloons.

Dirks, a German immigrant to the United States, was inspired to create the rebellious kids Hans and Fritz by a children's story from his native country. He quit the strip in 1912 in a contractual dispute and was succeeded by Harold Knerr, who wrote and drew it until 1949. There have been five subsequent cartoonists working on it. Hy Eisman has been doing it since 1986.

The word *katzenjammer* literally means "the wailing of cats" in German, but it's more often used to describe a hangover.

Workshop

Although this hour is literally filled with errors, see if you can answer the following questions about them without making any errors of your own.

Quiz

1. How many exceptions can a single `catch` statement handle?

    A. Only one.

    B. Several different exceptions.

    C. This answer intentionally left blank.

2. When are the statements inside a `finally` section be run?

    A. After a `try-catch` block has ended with an exception

    B. After a `try-catch` block has ended without an exception

    C. Both

3. With all this talk about throwing and catching, what do the Texas Rangers need to do in the off season?

    A. Get more starting pitching.

    B. Sign a left-handed power-hitting outfielder who can reach the short porch in right.

    C. Bring in new middle relievers.

Answers

1. **B.** An `Exception` object in the `catch` statement can handle all exceptions of its own class and its superclasses.

2. **C.** The statement (or statements) in a `finally` section always are executed after the rest of a `try-catch` block, whether an exception has occurred.

3. **A.** Every answer is correct, but A is more correct than the others and will probably be correct for the next 30 years.

Activities

To see whether you are an exceptional Java programmer, try to make as few errors as possible in the following activities:

▶ Modify the `NumberDivider` application so that it throws any exceptions that it catches and run the program to see what happens.

▶ There's a `try-catch` block in the `LottoEvent` class you created in Hour 15, "Responding to User Input." Use this block as a guide to create your own `Sleep` class, which handles `InterruptedException` so other classes such as `LottoEvent` don't need to deal with them.

To see Java programs that implement these activities, visit the book's website at www.java24hours.com.

Creating a Threaded Program

A computer term used often to describe the hectic pace of daily life is *multitasking*, which means to do more than one thing at once—such as browsing the Web at your desk while participating in a conference call and doing butt crunch exercises. A multitasking computer is one that can run more than one program at a time.

One sophisticated feature of the Java language is the ability to write programs that can multitask, which is made possible through a class of objects called *threads*.

Threads

In a Java program, each of the simultaneous tasks the computer handles is called a *thread* and the overall process is called *multithreading*. Threading is useful in animation and many other programs.

Threads are a way to organize a program so that it does more than one thing at a time. Each task that must occur simultaneously is placed in its own thread, and this often is accomplished by implementing each task as a separate class.

Threads are represented by the Thread class and the Runnable interface, which are both part of the java.lang package of classes. Because they belong to this package, you don't have to use an import statement to make them available in your programs.

One of the simplest uses of the Thread class is to slow down how fast a program does something.

WHAT YOU'LL LEARN IN THIS HOUR:

▶ Using an interface with a program
▶ Creating threads
▶ Starting, stopping, and pausing threads
▶ Catching errors

Slowing Down a Program

The Thread class has a sleep() method that you can call in any program that should stop running for a short period of time. You often see this technique used in a program that features animation because it prevents images from being displayed faster than the Java interpreter can handle them.

To use the sleep() method, call Thread.sleep() with the number of milliseconds to pause, as in the following statement:

```
Thread.sleep(5000);
```

The preceding statement causes the Java interpreter to pause for five seconds before doing anything else. If for some reason the interpreter can't pause that long, an InterruptedException is thrown by the sleep() method.

Because this exception might be thrown, you must deal with it in some manner when using the sleep() method. One way to do this is to place the Thread.sleep() statement inside a try-catch block:

```
try {
    Thread.sleep(5000);
} catch (InterruptedException e) {
    // wake up early
}
```

When you want a Java program to handle more than one thing at a time, you must organize the program into threads. Your program can have as many threads as needed, and they all can run simultaneously without affecting each other.

Creating a Thread

A Java class that can be run as a thread is referred to as a *runnable* (or *threaded*) class. Although you can use threads to pause a program's execution for a few seconds, programmers often use them for the opposite reason—to speed up a program. If you put time-consuming tasks in their own threads, the rest of the program runs more quickly. This often is used to prevent a task from slowing down the responsiveness of a program's graphical user interface (GUI).

For example, if you have written an application that loads stock market price data from disk and compiles statistics, the most time-consuming task is to load the data from disk. If threads are not used in the application, the program's interface might respond sluggishly as the data is being loaded. This can be extremely frustrating to a user.

Two ways to place a task in its own thread include

▶ Putting the task in a class that implements the Runnable interface

▶ Putting the task in a class that is a subclass of Thread

To support the Runnable interface, the implements keyword is used when the class is created, as in this example:

```java
public class LoadStocks implements Runnable {
    // body of the class
}
```

When a class implements an interface, it indicates that the class contains some extra behavior in addition to its own methods.

Classes that implement the Runnable interface must include the run() method, which has the following structure:

```java
public void run() {
    // body of the method
}
```

The run() method should take care of the task that the thread was created to accomplish. In the stock-analysis example, the run() method could contain statements to load data from disk and compile statistics based on that data.

When a threaded application is run, the statements in its run() method are not executed automatically. Threads can be started and stopped in Java, and a thread doesn't begin running until you do two things:

▶ Create an object of the threaded class by calling the Thread constructor

▶ Start the thread by calling its start() method

The Thread constructor takes a single argument—the object that contains the thread's run() method. Often, you use the this keyword as the argument, which indicates the current class includes the run() method.

Listing 19.1 contains a Java application that displays a sequence of prime numbers in a text area. Create a new empty Java file named PrimeFinder, enter the text from the listing in the file, and save the file.

LISTING 19.1   The Full Text of `PrimeFinder.java`

```
 1: import java.awt.*;
 2: import javax.swing.*;
 3: import java.awt.event.*;
 4:
 5: class PrimeFinder extends JFrame implements Runnable, ActionListener {
 6:     Thread go;
 7:     JLabel howManyLabel;
 8:     JTextField howMany;
 9:     JButton display;
10:     JTextArea primes;
11:
12:     PrimeFinder() {
13:         super("Find Prime Numbers");
14:         setLookAndFeel();
15:         setSize(400, 300);
16:         setDefaultCloseOperation(JFrame.EXIT_ON_CLOSE);
17:         BorderLayout bord = new BorderLayout();
18:         setLayout(bord);
19:
20:         howManyLabel = new JLabel("Quantity: ");
21:         howMany = new JTextField("400", 10);
22:         display = new JButton("Display primes");
23:         primes = new JTextArea(8, 40);
24:
25:         display.addActionListener(this);
26:         JPanel topPanel = new JPanel();
27:         topPanel.add(howManyLabel);
28:         topPanel.add(howMany);
29:         topPanel.add(display);
30:         add(topPanel, BorderLayout.NORTH);
31:
32:         primes.setLineWrap(true);
33:         JScrollPane textPane = new JScrollPane(primes);
34:         add(textPane, BorderLayout.CENTER);
35:
36:         setVisible(true);
37:     }
38:
39:     public void actionPerformed(ActionEvent event) {
40:         display.setEnabled(false);
41:         if (go == null) {
42:             go = new Thread(this);
43:             go.start();
44:         }
45:     }
46:
47:     public void run() {
48:         int quantity = Integer.parseInt(howMany.getText());
49:         int numPrimes = 0;
50:         // candidate: the number that might be prime
51:         int candidate = 2;
```

LISTING 19.1   Continued

```
52:            primes.append("First " + quantity + " primes:");
53:            while (numPrimes < quantity) {
54:                if (isPrime(candidate)) {
55:                    primes.append(candidate + " ");
56:                    numPrimes++;
57:                }
58:                candidate++;
59:            }
60:        }
61:
62:    public static boolean isPrime(int checkNumber) {
63:        double root = Math.sqrt(checkNumber);
64:        for (int i = 2; i <= root; i++) {
65:            if (checkNumber % i == 0) {
66:                return false;
67:            }
68:        }
69:        return true;
70:    }
71:
72:    private void setLookAndFeel() {
73:        try {
74:            UIManager.setLookAndFeel(
75:                "com.sun.java.swing.plaf.nimbus.NimbusLookAndFeel"
76:            );
77:        } catch (Exception exc) {
78:            // ignore error
79:        }
80:    }
81:    public static void main(String[] arguments) {
82:        PrimeFinder fp = new PrimeFinder();
83:    }
84: }
```

The `PrimeFinder` application displays a text field, a Display Primes button, and a text area, as shown in Figure 19.1.

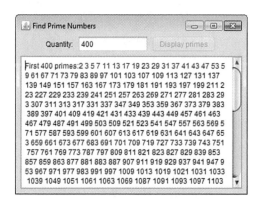

FIGURE 19.1
Running the `PrimeFinder` application.

Most statements in the application are used to create the GUI or display a sequence of prime numbers. The following statements are used to implement threads in this program:

▶ Line 5: The `Runnable` interface is applied to the `PrimeFinder` class.

▶ Line 6: A `Thread` object variable is created with the name `go` but isn't assigned a value.

▶ Lines 41–44: If the `go` object variable has a value of `null`, which indicates the thread hasn't been created yet, a new `Thread` object is created and stored in the variable. The thread is started by calling the thread's `start()` method, which causes the `run()` method of the `PrimeFinder` class to be called.

▶ Lines 47–60: The `run()` method looks for a sequence of prime numbers beginning with 2, displaying each one in the `primes` text area component by calling its `append()` method. The number of primes in the sequence is determined by the value in the `howMany` text field.

Working with Threads

CAUTION

It's a good idea to heed this deprecation warning. Oracle has deprecated the `stop()` method because it can cause problems for other threads running in the Java interpreter. The `resume()` and `suspend()` methods of the class also are deprecated.

You can start a thread by calling its `start()` method, which might lead you to believe there's also a `stop()` method to bring it to a halt.

Although Java includes a `stop()` method in the `Thread` class, it has been deprecated. In Java, a *deprecated* element is a class, interface, method, or variable that has been replaced with something that works better.

The next project you undertake shows how you can stop a thread. The program you are writing rotates through a list of website titles and the addresses used to visit them.

The title of each page and the web address is displayed in a continuous cycle. Users are able to visit the currently displayed site by clicking a button on the applet window. This program operates over a period of time, displaying information about each website in sequence. Because of this time element, threads are the best way to control the program.

Instead of entering this program into the NetBeans source editor first and learning about it afterward, you get a chance to enter the full text of the `LinkRotator` applet at the end of the hour. Before then, each section of the program is described.

The class Declaration

The first thing you need to do in this applet is to use import for classes in the packages java.awt, java.net, java.applet, java.awt.event, and javax.swing.

After you have used import to make some classes available, you're ready to begin the applet with the following statement:

```
public class LinkRotator extends JApplet
    implements Runnable, ActionListener {
```

This statement creates the LinkRotator class as a subclass of the JApplet class. It also indicates that two interfaces are supported by this class—Runnable and ActionListener. By implementing the Runnable class, you are able to use a run() method in this applet to make a thread begin running. The ActionListener interface enables the applet to respond to mouse clicks.

Setting Up Variables

The first thing to do in LinkRotator is create the variables and objects of the class. Create a six-element array of String objects called pageTitle and a six-element array of URL objects called pageLink:

```
String[] pageTitle = new String[6];
URL[] pageLink = new URL[6];
```

The pageTitle array holds the titles of the six websites that are displayed. The URL class of objects stores the value of a website address. URL has all the behavior and attributes needed to keep track of a web address and use it to load the page with a web browser.

The last three things to create are a Color object named butterscotch, an integer variable called current, and a Thread object called runner:

```
Color butterscotch = new Color(255, 204, 158);
int current = 0;
Thread runner;
```

Color objects represent colors you can use on fonts, user interface components, and other visual aspects of Swing. You find out how to use them during Hour 23, "Creating Java2D Graphics."

The current variable keeps track of which site is being displayed so you can cycle through the sites. The Thread object runner represents the thread this program runs. You call methods of the runner object when you start, stop, and pause the operation of the applet.

Starting with init()

The init() method of an applet automatically is handled once when the applet first starts to run. This method is used to assign values to the arrays pageTitle and pageLink. It also is used to create a clickable button that appears on the applet. The method consists of the following statements:

```
public void init() {
    pageTitle = new String[] {
        "Sun's Java site",
        "Cafe au Lait",
        "JavaWorld",
        "Java in 24 Hours",
        "Sams Publishing",
        "Workbench"
        };
    pageLink[0] = getURL("http://java.sun.com");
    pageLink[1] = getURL("http://www.ibiblio.org/javafaq");
    pageLink[2] = getURL("http://www.javaworld.com");
    pageLink[3] = getURL("http://www.java24hours.com");
    pageLink[4] = getURL("http://www.samspublishing.com");
    pageLink[5] = getURL("http://workbench.cadenhead.org");
    Button goButton = new Button("Go");
    goButton.addActionListener(this);
    FlowLayout flow = new FlowLayout();
    setLayout(flow);
    add(goButton);
}
```

The title of each page is stored in the six elements of the pageTitle array, which is initialized using six strings. The elements of the pageLink array are assigned a value returned by the getURL() method, yet to be created.

The last seven statements of the init() method create and lay out a button labeled "Go" in the applet window.

Catching Errors as You Set Up URLs

When you set up a URL object, you must make sure the text used to set up the address is in a valid format. http://workbench.cadenhead.org and http://www.samspublishing.com are valid, but http:www.javaworld.com would not be because of missing "/" marks.

The getURL(String) method takes a web address as an argument, returning a URL object representing that address. If the string is not a valid address, the method returns null instead:

```
URL getURL(String urlText) {
    URL pageURL = null;
    try {
        pageURL = new URL(getDocumentBase(), urlText);
    } catch (MalformedURLException m) {
        // do nothing
    }
    return pageURL;
}
```

The `try-catch` block deals with any `MalformedURLException` errors that occur when URL objects are created. Because nothing needs to happen if this exception is thrown, the `catch` block only contains a comment.

Handling Screen Updates in the paint() Method

An applet's `paint()` method is executed when the applet window needs to be updated. You can also manually call the `paint()` method within an applet.

Calling `repaint()` forces the `paint()` method to be called. This statement tells the GUI that something has happened to make a display update necessary.

The `LinkRotator` applet has a short `paint()` method:

```
public void paint(Graphics screen) {
    Graphics2D screen2D = (Graphics2D) screen;
    screen2D.setColor(butterscotch);
    screen2D.fillRect(0, 0, getSize().width, getSize().height);
    screen2D.setColor(Color.black);
    screen2D.drawString(pageTitle[current], 5, 60);
    screen2D.drawString("" + pageLink[current], 5, 80);
}
```

The first statement in this method creates a `screen2D` object that represents the drawable area of the applet window. All drawing is done by calling the methods of this object.

The `setColor()` method of `Graphics2D` selects the color used for subsequent drawing. The color is set to butterscotch before a rectangle that fills the entire applet window is drawn. Next, the color is set to black and lines of text are displayed on the screen at the (x,y) positions of (5,60) and (5,80). The first line displayed is an element of the `pageTitle` array. The second line displayed is the address of the URL object, which is stored in the `pageLink` array. The `current` variable determines the element of the arrays to display.

Starting the Thread

In this applet, the runner thread starts when the applet's start() method is called and stop when its stop() method is called.

The start() method is called right after the init() method and every time the program is restarted. Here's the method:

```
public void start() {
    if (runner == null) {
        runner = new Thread(this);
        runner.start();
    }
}
```

This method starts the runner thread if it is not already started.

The statement runner = new Thread(this) creates a new Thread object with one argument—the this keyword. The this keyword refers to the applet itself, designating it as the class that runs within the thread.

The call to runner.start() causes the thread to begin running. When a thread begins, the run() method of that thread is called. Because the runner thread is the applet itself, the run() method of the applet is called.

Running the Thread

The run() method is where the main work of a thread takes place. In the LinkRotator applet, the following represents the run() method:

```
public void run() {
    Thread thisThread = Thread.currentThread();
    while (runner == thisThread) {
        current++;
        if (current > 5) {
            current = 0;
        }
        repaint();
        try {
            Thread.sleep(10000);
        } catch (InterruptedException e) {
            // do nothing
        }
    }
}
```

The first thing that takes place in the run() method is the creation of a Thread object called thisThread. A class method of the Thread class,

currentThread(), sets up the value for the thisThread object. The
currentThread() method keeps track of the thread that's currently running.

All statements in this method are part of a while loop that compares the
runner object to the thisThread object. Both objects are threads, and as
long as they refer to the same object, the while loop continues looping.
There's no statement inside this loop that causes the runner and
thisThread objects to have different values, so it loops indefinitely unless
something outside of the loop changes one of the Thread objects.

The run() method calls repaint(). Next, the value of the current variable
increases by one, and if current exceeds 5, it is set to 0 again. The current
variable is used in the paint() method to determine which website's information to display. Changing current causes a different site to be displayed
the next time paint() is handled.

This method includes another try-catch block that handles errors. The
Thread.sleep(10000) statement causes a thread to pause 10 seconds, long
enough for users to read the name of the website and its address. The
catch statement takes care of any InterruptedException errors that might
occur while the Thread.sleep() statement is being handled. These errors
would occur if something interrupted the thread as it slept.

Stopping the Thread

The stop() method is called any time the applet is stopped because the
applet's page is exited, which makes it an ideal place to stop a running
thread. The stop() method for the LinkRotator applet contains the following statements:

```
public void stop() {
    if (runner != null) {
        runner = null;
    }
}
```

The if statement tests whether the runner object is equal to null. If it is,
there isn't an active thread that needs to be stopped. Otherwise, the statement sets runner equal to null.

Setting the runner object to a null value causes it to have a different value
than the thisThread object. When this happens, the while loop inside the
run() method stops running.

Handling Mouse Clicks

The last thing to take care of in the `LinkRotator` applet is event handling. Whenever a user clicks the Go button, the web browser should open the website shown. This is done with a method called `actionPerformed()`, which is called whenever the button is clicked.

The following is the `actionPerformed()` method of the `LinkRotator` applet:

```
public void actionPerformed(ActionEvent event) {
    if (runner != null) {
        runner = null;
    }
    AppletContext browser = getAppletContext();
    if (pageLink[current] != null) {
        browser.showDocument(pageLink[current]);
    }
}
```

The first thing that happens in this method is that the `runner` thread is stopped. The next statement creates a new `AppletContext` object called `browser`.

An `AppletContext` object represents the environment in which the applet is being presented—in other words, the page it's located on and the web browser that loaded the page.

The `showDocument(URL)` method loads the specified web address in a browser. If `pageLink[current]` is a valid address, `showDocument()` requests that the browser load the page.

Displaying Revolving Links

You're now ready to create the program and test it. Create a new empty Java file named `LinkRotator` and type in the text from Listing 19.2.

LISTING 19.2   The Full Text of `LinkRotator.java`

```
1: import java.applet.*;
2: import java.awt.*;
3: import java.awt.event.*;
4: import javax.swing.*;
5: import java.net.*;
6:
7: public class LinkRotator extends JApplet
8:     implements Runnable, ActionListener {
```

LISTING 19.2   Continued

```
 9:
10:     String[] pageTitle = new String[6];
11:     URL[] pageLink = new URL[6];
12:     Color butterscotch = new Color(255, 204, 158);
13:     int current = 0;
14:     Thread runner;
15:
16:     public void init() {
17:         pageTitle = new String[] {
18:             "Sun's Java site",
19:             "Cafe au Lait",
20:             "JavaWorld",
21:             "Java in 24 Hours",
22:             "Sams Publishing",
23:             "Workbench"
24:         };
25:         pageLink[0] = getURL("http://java.sun.com");
26:         pageLink[1] = getURL("http://www.ibiblio.org/javafaq");
27:         pageLink[2] = getURL("http://www.javaworld.com");
28:         pageLink[3] = getURL("http://www.java24hours.com");
29:         pageLink[4] = getURL("http://www.samspublishing.com");
30:         pageLink[5] = getURL("http:// workbench.cadenhead.org");
31:         Button goButton = new Button("Go");
32:         goButton.addActionListener(this);
33:         FlowLayout flow = new FlowLayout();
34:         setLayout(flow);
35:         add(goButton);
36:     }
37:
38:     URL getURL(String urlText) {
39:         URL pageURL = null;
40:         try {
41:             pageURL = new URL(getDocumentBase(), urlText);
42:         } catch (MalformedURLException m) { }
43:         return pageURL;
44:     }
45:
46:     public void paint(Graphics screen) {
47:         Graphics2D screen2D = (Graphics2D) screen;
48:         screen2D.setColor(butterscotch);
49:         screen2D.fillRect(0, 0, getSize().width, getSize().height);
50:         screen2D.setColor(Color.black);
51:         screen2D.drawString(pageTitle[current], 5, 60);
52:         screen2D.drawString("" + pageLink[current], 5, 80);
53:     }
54:
55:     public void start() {
56:         if (runner == null) {
57:             runner = new Thread(this);
58:             runner.start();
59:         }
```

LISTING 19.2   Continued

```
60:     }
61:
62:     public void run() {
63:         Thread thisThread = Thread.currentThread();
64:         while (runner == thisThread) {
65:             current++;
66:             if (current > 5) {
67:                 current = 0;
68:             }
69:             repaint();
70:             try {
71:                 Thread.sleep(10000);
72:             } catch (InterruptedException e) {
73:                 // do nothing
74:             }
75:         }
76:     }
77:
78:     public void stop() {
79:         if (runner != null) {
80:             runner = null;
81:         }
82:     }
83:
84:     public void actionPerformed(ActionEvent event) {
85:         if (runner != null) {
86:             runner = null;
87:         }
88:         AppletContext browser = getAppletContext();
89:         if (pageLink[current] != null) {
90:             browser.showDocument(pageLink[current]);
91:         }
92:     }
93: }
```

After you save the program, you need to create a web page in which to put the applet—it won't work correctly if you use Run, Run File to test it in NetBeans because links can't be opened that way. Create a new web page—choose File, New File, and then click Other to find the HTML File option in the File Types pane of the Choose File Type dialog. Name the web page LinkRotator, which NetBeans saves as NetBeans.html, and then enter Listing 19.3 as the web page's markup.

LISTING 19.3   The Full Text of `LinkRotator.html`

```
1: <applet
2:     code="LinkRotator.class"
3:     codebase="..\\build\\classes"
4:     width="300"
5:     height="100"
6: >
7: </applet>
```

When you're done, right-click the name `LinkRotator.html` in the Project pane and choose View. The page opens in a web browser, and the applet displays each of the links in rotation. Click the Go button to visit a site. Figure 19.2 shows what the applet looks like in Internet Explorer.

Summary

Threads are a powerful concept implemented with a small number of classes and interfaces in Java. By supporting multithreading in your programs, you make them more responsive and can speed up how quickly they perform tasks.

Even if you learned nothing else from this hour, you now have a new term to describe your frenzied lifestyle. Use it in a few sentences to see if it grabs you:

▶ "Boy, I was really multithreading yesterday after we held up that string of liquor stores."

▶ "I multithreaded all through lunch, and it gave me gas."

▶ "Not tonight, dear, I'm multithreading."

FIGURE 19.2
Displaying revolving links in an applet window.

Q&A

Q. **Are there any reasons to do nothing within a** `catch` **statement, as the** `LinkRotator` **applet does?**

A. It depends on the type of error or exception being caught. In the `LinkRotator` applet, you know with both `catch` statements what the cause of an exception would be, so you can be assured that doing nothing is always appropriate. In the `getURL()` method, the `MalformedURLException` would be caused only if the URL sent to the method is invalid.

Q. **Whatever happened to the band that sang "My Future's So Bright, I Gotta Wear Shades"?**

A. Their future was not bright. Timbuk3, a band formed by husband and wife Pat and Barbara K. MacDonald, never had another hit after the song that became a top 20 single in 1986. They produced six albums from 1986 to 1995, when they broke up the band and divorced.

Pat MacDonald continues to perform and release albums under his own name. He's also written songs for Cher, Peter Frampton, Night Ranger, Aerosmith, and other musicians.

Barbara Kooyman performs as Barbara K and has several albums, one that reinterprets Timbuk3 songs. She also formed the artist's free speech charity Artists for Media Diversity.

Their best known song, widely taken to be a positive message about the future, was supposed to be ironic. The MacDonalds said the bright future was actually an impending nuclear holocaust.

Workshop

Set aside your threads (in the Java sense, not the nudity sense) and answer the following questions about multithreading in Java.

Quiz

1. What interface must be implemented for a program to use threads?

   A. `Runnable`

   B. `Thread`

   C. `JApplet`

2. If an interface contains three different methods, how many of them must be included in a class that implements the interface?

    A. None of them.

    B. All of them.

    C. I know, but I'm not telling.

3. You're admiring the work of another programmer who has created a program that handles four simultaneous tasks. What should you tell him?

    A. "That's not half as exciting as the Anna Kournikova screensaver I downloaded off the Web."

    B. "You're the wind beneath my wings."

    C. "Nice threads!"

Answers

1. **A.** `Runnable` must be used with the `implements` statement. `Thread` is used inside a multithreaded program, but it is not needed in the class statement that begins a program.

2. **B.** An interface is a guarantee that the class includes all the interface's methods.

3. **C.** This compliment could be confusing if the programmer is well dressed, but let's be honest, what are the chances of that?

Activities

If this long workshop hasn't left you feeling threadbare, expand your skills with the following activities:

▶ If you are comfortable with HTML, create your own home page that includes the `LinkRotator` applet and six of your own favorite websites. Use the applet along with other graphics and text on the page.

▶ Add a button to the `PrimeFinder` application that can stop the thread while the sequence of prime numbers is still being calculated.

To see Java programs that implement these activities, visit the book's website at www.java24hours.com.

Reading and Writing Files

There are numerous ways to represent data on a computer. You already have worked with one by creating objects. An *object* includes data in the form of variables and references to objects. It also includes methods that use the data to accomplish tasks.

To work with other kinds of data, such as files on your hard drive and documents on a web server, you can use the classes of the java.io package. The "io" part of its name stands for "input/output" and the classes are used to access a source of data, such as a hard drive, CD-ROM, or the computer's memory.

You can bring data into a program and send data out by using a communications system called *streams*, or objects that take information from one place to another.

Streams

To save data permanently within a Java program, or to retrieve that data later, you must use at least one stream.

A *stream* is an object that takes information from one source and sends it somewhere else, taking its name from water streams that take fish, boats, and industrial pollutants from one place to another.

Streams connect a diverse variety of sources, including computer programs, hard drives, Internet servers, computer memory, and DVD-ROMs. After you learn how to work with one kind of data using streams, you are able to work with others in the same manner.

During this hour, you use streams to read and write data stored in files on your computer.

WHAT YOU'LL LEARN IN THIS HOUR:

▶ Reading bytes from a file into a program

▶ Creating a new file on your computer

▶ Saving an array of bytes to a file

▶ Making changes to the data stored in a file

Java class files are stored as bytes in a form called *bytecode*. The Java interpreter runs bytecode, which doesn't actually have to be produced by the Java language. It can run compiled bytecode produced by other languages, including NetRexx and Jython. You also hear the Java interpreter referred to as the bytecode interpreter.

There are two kinds of streams:

- ▶ Input streams, which read data from a source
- ▶ Output streams, which write data to a source

All input and output streams are made up of bytes, individual integers with values ranging from 0 to 255. You can use this format to represent data, such as executable programs, word-processing documents, and MP3 music files, but those are only a small sampling of what bytes can represent. A *byte stream* is used to read and write this kind of data.

A more specialized way to work with data is in the form of characters—individual letters, numbers, punctuation, and the like. You can use a character stream when you are reading and writing a text source.

Whether you work with a stream of bytes, characters, or other kinds of information, the overall process is the same:

- ▶ Create a stream object associated with the data.
- ▶ Call methods of the stream to either put information in the stream or take information out of it.
- ▶ Close the stream by calling the object's `close()` method.

Files

In Java, files are represented by the `File` class, which also is part of the `java.io` package. Files can be read from hard drives, CD-ROMs, and other storage devices.

This example works on a Windows system, which uses the backslash (\\) character as a separator in path and filenames. Linux and other Unix-based systems use a forward slash (/) character instead. To write a Java program that refers to files in a way that works regardless of the operating system, use the class variable `File.pathSeparator` instead of a forward or backslash, as in this statement:

```
File bookName = new
File("data" +
File.pathSeparator
    + "address.dat");
```

A `File` object can represent files that already exist or files you want to create. To create a `File` object, use the name of the file as the constructor, as in this example:

```
File bookName = new File("address.dat");
```

This creates an object for a file named `address.dat` in the current folder. You also can include a path in the filename:

```
File bookName = new File("data\\address.dat");
```

When you have a `File` object, you can call several useful methods on that object:

- ▶ `exists()`—true if the file exists, `false` otherwise
- ▶ `getName()`—The name of the file, as a `String`

- ▶ length()—The size of the file, as a long value
- ▶ createNewFile()—Creates a file of the same name, if one does not exist already
- ▶ delete()—Deletes the file, if it exists
- ▶ renameTo(*File*)—Renames the file, using the name of the File object specified as an argument

You also can use a File object to represent a folder on your system rather than a file. Specify the folder name in the File constructor, which can be absolute (such as "C:\\MyDocuments\\") or relative (such as "java\\ database").

After you have an object representing a folder, you can call its listFiles() method to see what's inside the folder. This method returns an array of File objects representing every file and subfolder it contains.

Reading Data from a Stream

The first project of the hour is to read data from a file using an input stream. You can do this using the FileInputStream class, which represents input streams that are read as bytes from a file.

You can create a file input stream by specifying a filename or a File object as the argument to the FileInputStream() constructor method.

The file must exist before the file input stream is created. If it doesn't, an IOException is generated when you try to create the stream. Many of the methods associated with reading and writing files generate this exception, so it's often convenient to put all statements involving the file in their own try-catch block, as in this example:

```
try {
    File cookie = new File("cookie.web");
    FileInputStream stream = new FileInputStream(cookie);
    System.out.println("Length of file: " + cookie.length());
} catch (IOException e) {
    System.out.println("Could not read file.");
}
```

File input streams read data in bytes. You can read a single byte by calling the stream's read() method without an argument. If no more bytes are available in the stream because you have reached the end of the file, a byte value of –1 is returned.

When you read an input stream, it begins with the first byte in the stream, such as the first byte in a file. You can skip some bytes in a stream by calling its skip() method with one argument: an int representing the number of bytes to skip. The following statement skips the next 1024 bytes in a stream named scanData:

```
scanData.skip(1024);
```

If you want to read more than one byte at a time, do the following:

- ▶ Create a byte array that is exactly the size of the number of bytes you want to read.

- ▶ Call the stream's read() method with that array as an argument. The array is filled with bytes read from the stream.

You create an application that reads ID3 data from an MP3 audio file. Because MP3 is such a popular format for music files, 128 bytes are often added to the end of an ID3 file to hold information about the song, such as the title, artist, and album.

The ID3Reader application reads an MP3 file using a file input stream, skipping everything but the last 128 bytes. The remaining bytes are examined to see if they contain ID3 data. If they do, the first three bytes are the numbers 84, 65, and 71.

Create a new empty Java file called ID3Reader and fill it with the text from Listing 20.1.

NOTE

On the ASCII character set, which is included in the Unicode Standard character set supported by Java, those three numbers represent the capital letters "T," "A," and "G," respectively.

LISTING 20.1   The Full Text of ID3Reader.java

```
 1: import java.io.*;
 2:
 3: public class ID3Reader {
 4:     public static void main(String[] arguments) {
 5:         try {
 6:             File song = new File(arguments[0]);
 7:             FileInputStream file = new FileInputStream(song);
 8:             int size = (int) song.length();
 9:             file.skip(size - 128);
10:             byte[] last128 = new byte[128];
11:             file.read(last128);
12:             String id3 = new String(last128);
13:             String tag = id3.substring(0, 3);
14:             if (tag.equals("TAG")) {
15:                 System.out.println("Title: " + id3.substring(3, 32));
16:                 System.out.println("Artist: " + id3.substring(33, 62));
17:                 System.out.println("Album: " + id3.substring(63, 91));
```

LISTING 20.1   Continued

```
18:                    System.out.println("Year: " + id3.substring(93, 97));
19:                } else {
20:                    System.out.println(arguments[0] + " does not contain"
21:                        + " ID3 info.");
22:                }
23:                file.close();
24:            } catch (Exception e) {
25:                System.out.println("Error — " + e.toString());
26:            }
27:        }
28: }
```

Before running this class as an application, you must specify an MP3 file as a command-line argument. The program can be run with any MP3, such as Come On and Gettit.mp3, the unjustly forgotten 1973 soul classic by Marion Black. If you have the song Come On and Gettit.mp3 on your system (and you really should), Figure 20.1 shows what the ID3Reader application displays.

```
: Output - Java24 (run)
 run:
 Title: Come On and Gettit
 Artist: Marion Black
 Album: Eccentric Soul: The Prix Lab
 Year: 2007
 BUILD SUCCESSFUL (total time: 0 seconds)
```

FIGURE 20.1
Running the ID3Reader application.

The application reads the last 128 bytes from the MP3 in Lines 10–11 of Listing 20.1, storing them in a byte array. This array is used in Line 12 to create a String object that contains the characters represented by those bytes.

If the first three characters in the string are "TAG," the MP3 file being examined contains ID3 information in a format the application understands.

In Lines 15–18, the string's substring() method is called to display portions of the string. The characters to display are from the ID3 format, which always puts the artist, song, title, and year information in the same positions in the last 128 bytes of an MP3 file.

TIP

If you don't have Come On and Gettit.mp3 on your computer (a big mistake, in my opinion), you can look for MP3 songs to examine using the Creative Commons license using Yahoo! Search at http://search.yahoo.com/cc.

Creative Commons is a set of copyright licenses that stipulate how a work such as a song or book can be distributed, edited, or republished. The website Rock Proper, at www.rockproper.com, offers a collection of MP3 albums that are licensed for sharing under Creative Commons.

NOTE

You might be tempted to find a copy of Come On and Gettit.mp3 on a service such as BitTorrent, one of the most popular file-sharing services. I can understand this temptation perfectly where "Come On and Gettit" is concerned. However, according to the Recording Industry Association of America, anyone who downloads MP3 files for music CDs you do not own will immediately burst into flame. *Eccentric Soul* is available from Amazon.com, eBay, Apple iTunes, and other leading retailers.

Some MP3 files either don't contain ID3 information at all or contain ID3 information in a different format than the application can read.

The file Come On and Gettit.mp3 contains readable ID3 information if you created it from a copy of the *Eccentric Soul* CD that you purchased because programs that create MP3 files from audio CDs read song information from a music industry database called CDDB.

After everything related to the ID3 information has been read from the MP3's file input stream, the stream is closed in Line 23. You should always close streams when you are finished with them to conserve resources in the Java interpreter.

Buffered Input Streams

One of the ways to improve the performance of a program that reads input streams is to buffer the input. Buffering is the process of saving data in memory for use later when a program needs it. When a Java program needs data from a buffered input stream, it looks in the buffer first, which is faster than reading from a source such as a file.

To use a buffered input stream, you create an input stream such as a FileInputStream object, and then use that object to create a buffered stream. Call the BufferedInputStream(*InputStream*) constructor with the input stream as the only argument. Data is buffered as it is read from the input stream.

To read from a buffered stream, call its read() method with no arguments. An integer from 0 to 255 is returned and represents the next byte of data in the stream. If no more bytes are available, –1 is returned instead.

As a demonstration of buffered streams, the next program you create adds a feature to Java that many programmers miss from other languages they have used: console input.

Console input is the ability to read characters from the console (also known as the command-line) while running an application.

The System class, which contains the out variable used in the System.out.print() and System.out.println() statements, has a class variable called in that represents an InputStream object. This object receives input from the keyboard and makes it available as a stream.

You can work with this input stream like any other. The following statement creates a buffered input stream associated with the System.in input stream:

```
BufferedInputStream bin = new BufferedInputStream(System.in);
```

The next project, the Console class, contains a class method you can use to receive console input in any of your Java applications. Enter the text from Listing 20.2 in a new empty Java file named Console.

LISTING 20.2   The Full Text of Console.java

```
 1: import java.io.*;
 2:
 3: public class Console {
 4:     public static String readLine() {
 5:         StringBuffer response = new StringBuffer();
 6:         try {
 7:             BufferedInputStream bin = new
 8:                 BufferedInputStream(System.in);
 9:             int in = 0;
10:             char inChar;
11:             do {
12:                 in = bin.read();
13:                 inChar = (char) in;
14:                 if (in != -1) {
15:                     response.append(inChar);
16:                 }
17:             } while ((in != -1) & (inChar != '\n'));
18:             bin.close();
19:             return response.toString();
20:         } catch (IOException e) {
21:             System.out.println("Exception: " + e.getMessage());
22:             return null;
23:         }
24:     }
25:
26:     public static void main(String[] arguments) {
27:         System.out.print("You are standing at the end of the road ");
28:         System.out.print("before a small brick building. Around you ");
29:         System.out.print("is a forest. A small stream flows out of ");
30:         System.out.println("the building and down a gully.\n");
31:         System.out.print("> ");
32:         String input = Console.readLine();
33:         System.out.println("That's not a verb I recognize.");
34:     }
35: }
```

The `Console` class includes a `main()` method that demonstrates how it can be used. When you run the application, the output should resemble Figure 20.2.

FIGURE 20.2
Running the `Console` application.

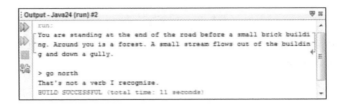

NOTE

The `Console` class is also the world's least satisfying text adventure game. You can't enter the building, wade in the stream, or even wander off. For a more full-featured version of this game, which is called Adventure, visit the Interactive Fiction archive at www.wurb.com/if/game/1.

The `Console` class contains one class method, `readLine()`, which receives characters from the console. When the Enter key is hit, `readLine()` returns a `String` object that contains all the characters that are received.

If you save the `Console` class in a folder that is listed in your CLASSPATH environment variable (on Windows), you can call `Console.readLine()` from any Java program that you write.

Writing Data to a Stream

In the `java.io` package, the classes for working with streams come in matched sets. There are `FileInputStream` and `FileOutputStreams` classes for working with byte streams, `FileReader` and `FileWriter` classes for working with character streams, and many other sets for working with other kinds of stream data.

To begin writing data, you first create a `File` object that is associated with an output stream. This file doesn't have to exist on your system.

You can create a `FileOutputStream` in two ways. If you want to append bytes onto an existing file, call the `FileOutputStream()` constructor method with two arguments: a `File` object representing the file and the `boolean` of `true`. The bytes you write to the stream are tacked onto the end of the file.

If you want to write bytes into a new file, call the `FileOutputStream()` constructor method with a `File` object as its only object.

After you have an output stream, you can call different `write()` methods to write bytes to it:

> ▶ Call `write()` with a byte as its only argument to write that byte to the stream.

▶ Call write() with a byte array as its only argument to write all the array's bytes to the stream.

▶ Specify three arguments to the write(byte[], int, int) method: a byte array, an integer representing the first element of the array to write to the stream, and the number of bytes to write.

The following statement creates a byte array with 10 bytes and writes the last 5 to an output stream:

```
File dat = new File("data.dat");
FileOutputStream datStream = new FileOutputStream(dat);
byte[] data = new byte[] { 5, 12, 4, 13, 3, 15, 2, 17, 1, 18 };
datStream.write(data, 5, 5);
```

When writing bytes to a stream, you can convert text to an array of bytes by calling the String object's getBytes() method, as in this example:

```
String name = "Puddin N. Tane";
byte[] nameBytes = name.getBytes();
```

After you have finished writing bytes to a stream, you close it by calling the stream's close() method.

The next project you write is a simple application, ConfigWriter, that saves several lines of text to a file by writing bytes to a file output stream. Create an empty Java file of that name and enter the text from Listing 20.3 into the source editor.

LISTING 20.3   The Full Text of ConfigWriter.java

```
 1: import java.io.*;
 2:
 3: class ConfigWriter {
 4:     String newline = System.getProperty("line.separator");
 5:
 6:     ConfigWriter() {
 7:         try {
 8:             File file = new File("program.properties");
 9:             FileOutputStream fileStream = new FileOutputStream(file);
10:             write(fileStream, "username=max");
11:             write(fileStream, "score=12550");
12:             write(fileStream, "level=5");
13:         } catch (IOException ioe) {
14:             System.out.println("Could not write file");
15:         }
16:     }
17:
18:     void write(FileOutputStream stream, String output)
19:         throws IOException {
```

LISTING 20.3   Continued

```
20:
21:          output = output + newline;
22:          byte[] data = output.getBytes();
23:          stream.write(data, 0, data.length);
24:      }
25:
26:      public static void main(String[] arguments) {
27:          ConfigWriter cw = new ConfigWriter();
28:      }
29: }
```

When this application is run, it creates a file called `program.properties` that contains the following three lines of text:

Output ▼

```
username=max
score=12550
level=5
```

Reading and Writing Configuration Properties

Java programs are more versatile when they can be configured using command-line arguments, as you have demonstrated in several applications created in preceding hours. The `java.util` package includes a class, `Properties`, that enables configuration settings to be loaded from another source: a text file.

The file can be read like other file sources in Java:

- ▶ Create a `File` object that represents the file.
- ▶ Create a `FileInputStream` object from that File object.
- ▶ Call `load()` to retrieve the properties from that input stream.

A properties file has a set of property names followed by an equal sign (=) and their values. Here's an example:

```
username=lepton
lastCommand=open database
windowSize=32
```
variable some values

Each property has its own line, so this sets up properties named `username`, `lastCommand`, and `windowSize` with the values "lepton", "open database", and "32", respectively. (The same format was used by the `ConfigWriter` class.)

The following code loads a properties file called `config.dat`:

```
File configFile = new File("config.dat");
FileInputStream inStream = new FileInputStream(configFile);
Properties config = new Properties();
config.load(inStream);
```

Configuration settings, which are called *properties*, are stored as strings in the `Properties` object. Each property is identified by a key that's like an applet parameter. The `getProperty()` method retrieves a property using its key, as in this statement:

```
String username = config.getProperty("username");
```

Because properties are stored as strings, you must convert them in some manner to use a numerical value, as in this code:

```
String windowProp = config.getProperty("windowSize");
int windowSize = 24;
try {
    windowSize = Integer.parseInt(windowProp);
} catch (NumberFormatException exception) {
    // do nothing
}
```

Properties can be stored by calling the `setProperty()` method with two arguments—the key and value:

```
config.setProperty("username", "max");
```

You can display all properties by calling the `list(PrintStream)` method of the `Properties` object. `PrintStream` is the class of the out variable of the `System` class, which you've been using throughout the book to display output in `System.out.println()` statements. The following code calls `list()` to display all properties:

```
config.list(System.out);
```

After you have made changes to the properties, you can store them back to the file:

▶ Create a `File` object that represents the file.

▶ Create a `FileOutputStream` object from that File object.

▶ Call store(*OutputStream*, *String*) to save the properties to the designated output stream with a description of the properties file as the string.

For the next project, you build on the ConfigWriter application, which wrote several program settings to a file. The Configurator application reads those settings into a Java properties file, adds a new property named runtime with the current date and time, and saves the altered file.

Create a new empty Java file to hold the Configurator class and enter the text from Listing 20.4.

LISTING 20.4   The Full Text of Configurator.java

```
 1: import java.io.*;
 2: import java.util.*;
 3:
 4: class Configurator {
 5:
 6:     Configurator() {
 7:         try {
 8:             // load the properties file
 9:             File configFile = new File("program.properties");
10:             FileInputStream inStream = new
               ➥FileInputStream(configFile);
11:             Properties config = new Properties();
12:             config.load(inStream);
13:             // create a new property
14:             Date current = new Date();
15:             config.setProperty("runtime", current.toString());
16:             // save the properties file
17:             FileOutputStream outStream = new
               ➥FileOutputStream(configFile);
18:             config.store(outStream, "Properties settings");
19:             inStream.close();
20:             config.list(System.out);
21:         } catch (IOException ioe) {
22:             System.out.println("IO error " + ioe.getMessage());
23:         }
24:     }
25:
26:     public static void main(String[] arguments) {
27:         Configurator con = new Configurator();
28:     }
29: }
```

The output of the Configurator application is shown in Figure 20.3.

FIGURE 20.3
Running the Configurator
application.

The program.properties file now contains the following text:

Output ▼

```
#Properties settings
#Tue May 12 22:51:26 EDT 2009
runtime=Tue May 12 22\:51\:26 EDT 2009
score=12550
level=5
username=max
```

The backslash character's (\) formatting, which differs from the output of the application, ensures the properties file is stored properly.

Summary

During this hour, you worked with input streams and output streams that wrote bytes, the simplest way to represent data over a stream.

There are many more classes in the java.io package to work with streams in other ways. There's also a package of classes called java.net that enables you to read and write streams over an Internet connection.

Byte streams can be adapted to many uses because you can easily convert bytes into other data types, such as integers, characters, and strings.

The first project of this hour, the ID3Reader application, read bytes from a stream and converted them into a string because it was easier to read the ID3 data in this format from a song such as "Come On and Gettit" by Marian Black off the album *Eccentric Soul*.

Have I mentioned yet that you should buy the song?

Q&A

Q. Why do some of the byte stream methods in this hour use integers as arguments? Should they be using `byte` arguments?

A. There's a difference between the bytes in a stream and the bytes represented by the `byte` class. A `byte` in Java has a value ranging from –128 to 127, while a byte in a stream has a value from 0 to 255. You often have to use `int` when working with bytes for this reason—it can hold the values 128 to 255, whereas `byte` cannot.

Q. What is Mumblety-Peg?

A. It's a schoolyard game played by children with pocketknives.

In the simplest form, players stand and throw knives at their own feet. The one whose knife lands closest wins. Other versions involve throwing the knife at each other so the opponent has to stretch a foot to where it lands. The player who stretches too far and falls down loses.

The name comes from a rule that the winner could pound a peg into the ground with three blows of the knife. The loser had to "mumble the peg," removing it solely with his teeth.

The game faded from popularity in the early 20th century when the world reached the collective realization that children throwing knives at each other might not be the greatest idea in the world.

Workshop

To see whether you took a big enough byte from the tree of knowledge during this hour, answer the following questions about streams in Java.

Quiz

1. Which of the following techniques can be used to convert an array of bytes into a string?

A. Call the array's `toString()` method.

B. Convert each byte to a character and then assign each one to an element in a `String` array.

C. Call the `String()` constructor method with the array as an argument.

2. What kind of stream is used to read from a file in a Java program?

    A. An input stream

    B. An output stream

    C. Either

3. What method of the `File` class can be used to determine the size of a file?

    A. `getSize()`

    B. `read()`

    C. `length()`

Answers

1. **C.** You can deal with each byte individually, as suggested in answer B, but you can easily create strings from other data types.

2. **A.** An input stream is created from a `File` object or by providing a filename to the input stream's constructor method.

3. **C.** This method returns a `long`, representing the number of bytes in the stream.

Activities

To experience the refreshing feeling of wading through another stream, test the waters with the following activities:

▶ Write an application that reads the ID3 tags of all MP3 files in a folder and renames the files using the artist, song, and album information (when it is provided).

▶ Write a program that reads a Java source file and writes it back without any changes under a new name.

▶ Buy a copy of the song "Come on and Gettit" by Marian Black.

To see Java programs that implement these activities, visit the book's website at www.java24hours.com.

Reading and Writing XML Data

The rise to prominence of Java in the 1990s coincided with another dramatic change in the development of computer software: the introduction of Extensible Markup Language (XML). *XML*, a format for organizing and storing data so that it can be read by any program, has become ginormous, to borrow my kids' favorite adjective.

Thanks to XML, data can be read and written independently of the software used to create it. This is a welcome change from the bad old days when every program seemed to have its own proprietary and idiosyncratic format.

XML data can be read with a *parser*, a program that recognizes the format and can extract portions of the data as needed.

During this hour, you read and write XML data using the *XML Object Model* (XOM), a Java class library that makes it easy to work with XML data in Java programs.

Creating an XML File

Before exploring XOM, you should learn some things about XML and how it stores data. XML data turns up in countless places—it can be stored to a file, transmitted over an Internet network, and held in a program's memory.

Several classes in the Java class library can read and write XML, including the `Properties` class in the `java.util` package, which was covered in Hour 20, "Reading and Writing Files."

A `Properties` object can be stored as XML rather than in the *name=value* format covered in the preceding hour.

WHAT YOU'LL LEARN IN THIS HOUR:

▶ Reading XML from a file
▶ Extracting XML elements
▶ Collecting a set of child elements
▶ Reading attribute values for an XML element
▶ Writing an XML file

After the object has been filled with configuration properties, its storeToXML() method saves it to an XML file. This method takes two arguments:

▶ A FileOutputStream over which the file should be saved

▶ A comment, which can be the empty string " " if the data requires no comment

This hour's first project is a simple application, PropertyFileCreator, that stores configuration properties in XML format. Fire up NetBeans, enter the text from Listing 21.1 in a new empty Java file named PropertyFileCreator, and save the file.

LISTING 21.1   The Full Text of PropertyFileCreator.java

```
 1: import java.io.*;
 2: import java.util.*;
 3:
 4: public class PropertyFileCreator {
 5:     public PropertyFileCreator() {
 6:         Properties prop = new Properties();
 7:         prop.setProperty("username", "rcade");
 8:         prop.setProperty("browser", "Mozilla Firefox");
 9:         prop.setProperty("showEmail", "no");
10:         try {
11:             File propFile = new File("properties.xml");
12:             FileOutputStream propStream = new
            ➥FileOutputStream(propFile);
13:             Date now = new Date();
14:             prop.storeToXML(propStream, "Created on " + now);
15:         } catch (IOException exception) {
16:             System.out.println("Error: " + exception.getMessage());
17:         }
18:     }
19:
20:     public static void main(String[] arguments) {
21:         PropertyFileCreator pfc = new PropertyFileCreator();
22:     }
23: }
```

When you run the application, it creates a properties file with three settings: the username "rcade", browser "Mozilla Firefox", and showEmail "no".

If the properties had been saved in the other format, it would look like this:

```
#Created on Wed Jun 15 20:56:33 EDT 2011
# Thu Wed Jun 15 20:56:33 EDT 2011
showEmail=no
browser=Mozilla Firefox
username=rcade
```

When you run the application, it creates the XML file `properties.xml`, which is presented in Listing 21.2.

LISTING 21.2   The Full Text of `properties.xml`

```
1: <?xml version="1.0" encoding="UTF-8"?>
2: <!DOCTYPE properties SYSTEM "http://java.sun.com/dtd/properties.dtd">
3: <properties>
4: <comment>Created on Wed Jun 15 20:56:33 EDT 2011</comment>
5: <entry key="showEmail">no</entry>
6: <entry key="browser">Mozilla Firefox</entry>
7: <entry key="username">rcade</entry>
8: </properties>
```

XML organizes data in a self-documenting manner, making it possible to understand a great deal about the data simply by looking at it.

As you glance over Listing 21.2, you can tell pretty quickly how it stored the configuration properties. The `?xml` and `!DOCTYPE` tags might be tough to follow, but the rest of the file should be reasonably simple.

Data in an XML file is surrounded by tags that look a lot like HTML, the markup language employed on the Web.

Start tags begin with a < character followed by the name of an element and a > character, such as `<properties>` on Line 3 of Listing 21.2.

End tags begin with < followed by the same element name and the /> characters, such as `</properties>` on Line 8.

Everything nested within a start tag and end tag is considered to be the element's value.

XML data must have a single root element that encloses all its data. In Listing 21.2, the root is the `properties` element defined in Lines 3–8.

An element might contain text, a child element, or multiple child elements. The `properties` element holds four children: a `comment` element and three `entry` elements.

Here's the `comment` element:

```
<comment>Created on Wed Jun 15 20:56:33 EDT 2011</comment>
```

This element has the value of the text it encloses: "Created on Wed Jun 15 20:56:33 EDT 2011."

An XML element also can have one or more attributes, which are defined inside its start tag as *name="value"* pairs. Attributes must be separated by spaces. They provide supplemental information about the element.

Each `entry` element has an attribute and a value:

```
<entry key="showEmail">no</entry>
```

This element has the value "no" and a `key` attribute with the value "showEmail".

One kind of XML element isn't present in Listing 21.2: an element defined entirely as a single tag. These elements begin with the < character, followed by the element name and the /> characters.

For instance, this element could be present as a child of the `properties` element:

```
<inactive />
```

Although XML has been described as a format and compared to HTML, it's not actually a language itself. Instead, XML describes how to create data formats specific to the tasks you want to accomplish with a computer program. XML formats are called *dialects*.

The XML dialect created by Java's `Properties` class is an example of this. Oracle has developed this format for the representation of software configuration settings.

Data that follows the rules of XML formatting is described as *well-formed*. Software that reads or writes XML must accept well-formed data.

Data also can follow a more meticulous standard called *validity*. A valid XML file contains the right elements in the right places, requiring some means of defining the valid elements.

Reading an XML File

As you have discovered during the first 20 hours, 13 minutes, and 52 seconds of this book, a wealth of Java code is already written for you to greatly simplify your job. Within the Java class library, you can adopt Swing classes for user interface programming, the `java.io` classes for file access, `java.awt.event` to take user input, and other classes to do as little programming of your own as possible.

A vital skill to develop in your Java programming is to learn where to look for Java classes and packages you can employ in your own projects. Reusing a well-developed class library is considerably easier than coding your own classes from scratch.

The Java team at Oracle isn't the only developer producing terrific Java classes, which you see during the remainder of this hour by using XOM, a class library developed by the computer programmer and book author Elliotte Rusty Harold. Harold, an expert in both the Java language and XML, grew frustrated with how existing XML libraries worked. (You might be sensing a theme here—Java itself was developed by James Gosling as an expression of his frustration with another language.)

Harold created his own class library that represents XML data as a tree holding each element as a node.

You can download the library from www.xom.nu.

Unpack the archive in a folder on your system. I used `C:\\java\\XOM` on my Windows XP system, devoting the top-level folder `C:\\java` to Java libraries I use. After downloading and unpacking a library, you must add it to your current project in NetBeans:

1. Choose File, Project Properties. The Project Properties dialog opens.

2. Click Libraries in the Categories pane, and then click the Add Library button. The Add Library dialog opens.

3. Click the Create button. The Create New Library dialog opens.

4. Enter **XOM** in the Library Name field and click OK. The Customize Library dialog opens.

5. Click Add JAR/Folder. The Browser JAR/Folder dialog opens.

6. Find the folder where you saved XOM and choose the `xom-1.2.1` and `xom-samples` files. (The version number of XOM might be different.) Click Add JAR/Folder.

7. In the Customize Library dialog, click OK.

8. In the Add Library dialog, choose XOM and click Add Library.

9. In the Project Properties dialog, click OK.

The XOM library is now available to your project.

XOM has classes to read and write XML data, saving it to files and other destinations.

CAUTION

XOM has been made available at no cost under an open source license, the GNU Lesser General Public License (LGPL). You can distribute the XOM library without modification with Java applications that rely on it.

You also can make changes to the classes in the library, but you must make these changes available under the LGPL. You can view the full details of the license at www.xom.nu/license.xhtml.

NOTE

The web address
http://tinyurl.com/rd4r72 is a
shortened URL that redirects to
the actual address on the
Weather Underground site,
which is considerably more difficult to type in correctly. Here's
the full address:

http://wunderground.com/auto
/wui/geo/ForecastXML/
index.xml?query=Wasilla,AK

This contains the weather forecast for Wasilla, Alaska.

The next program you create is the WeatherStation application, which
reads forecast information offered in an XML dialect by the Weather
Underground website, which is available at www.wunderground.com.

The core classes of the XOM library are in the nu.xom package, made available in your programs with an import statement:

```
import nu.xom.*;
```

The Builder class can load and parse XML data in any dialect, as long as
it's well formed.

Here's the code to create a builder and load the forecast file with it:

```
File file = new File("forecast.xml");
Builder builder = new Builder();
Document doc = builder.build(propFile);
```

XOM also can load XML data over the Web. Instead of calling build(*File*),
call the method with the web address of the data, as in this code:

```
Builder builder = new Builder();
Document doc = builder.build("http://tinyurl.com/rd4r72");
```

When the builder loads XML data, it makes it available as a Document
object, which holds an entire XML document.

You can retrieve the document's root element with its getRootElement()
method:

```
Element root = doc.getRootElement();
```

The Element class represents a single element. Each element has several
methods that you can use to examine its contents:

▶ The getFirstChildElement() method grabs the first child matching
  a specified name.

▶ The get(*int*) method reads an element matching a specified index,
  numbered in order from 0 up.

▶ The getChildElements() method grabs all its child elements.

▶ The getValue() method reads its text.

▶ The getAttribute() method retrieves one of its attributes.

The following statements retrieve the comment element and its value:

```
Element highF = high.FirstChildElement("fahrenheit");
String highTemp = highF.getValue();
```

This approach doesn't work when several elements share the same name, as the forecastday element does. For those, you can retrieve all the elements and loop through them with a for loop:

```
Elements days = root.getChildElements("simpleday");
for (int current = 0; current < days.size(); current++) {
    Element day = days.get(current);
}
```

This program does not make use of attributes, but an element's attribute can be accessed with the getAttribute() method, which takes the attribute's name as an argument:

```
Attribute key = day.getAttribute("key");
```

When you have the attribute, its getValue() method reveals the matching value:

```
String keyValue = key.getValue();
```

Create a new empty Java file called WeatherStation and enter the text from Listing 21.3 into the file.

LISTING 21.3   The Full Text of WeatherStation.java

```
 1: import java.io.*;
 2: import nu.xom.*;
 3:
 4: public class WeatherStation {
 5:     int[] highTemp = new int[6];
 6:     int[] lowTemp = new int[6];
 7:     String[] conditions = new String[6];
 8:
 9:     public WeatherStation() throws ParsingException, IOException {
10:         // get the XML document
11:         Builder builder = new Builder();
12:         Document doc = builder.build("http://tinyurl.com/rd4r72");
13:         // get the root element, <forecast>
14:         Element root = doc.getRootElement();
15:         // get the <simpleforecast> element
16:         Element simple = root.getFirstChildElement("simpleforecast");
17:         // get the <forecastday> elements
18:         Elements days = simple.getChildElements("forecastday");
19:         for (int current = 0; current < days.size(); current++) {
20:             // get current <forecastday>
21:             Element day = days.get(current);
22:             // get current <high>
23:             Element high = day.getFirstChildElement("high");
24:             Element highF = high.getFirstChildElement("fahrenheit");
25:             // get current <low>
```

LISTING 21.3   Continued

```
26:                Element low = day.getFirstChildElement("low");
27:                Element lowF = low.getFirstChildElement("fahrenheit");
28:                // get current <icon>
29:                Element icon = day.getFirstChildElement("icon");
30:                // store values in object variables
31:                lowTemp[current] = -1;
32:                highTemp[current] = -1;
33:                try {
34:                    lowTemp[current] = Integer.parseInt(lowF.getValue());
35:                    highTemp[current] =
                        ➥Integer.parseInt(highF.getValue());
36:                } catch (NumberFormatException nfe) {
37:                    // do nothing
38:                }
39:                conditions[current] = icon.getValue();
40:            }
41:        }
42:
43:    public void display() {
44:        for (int i = 0; i < conditions.length; i++) {
45:            System.out.println("Period " + i);
46:            System.out.println("\tConditions: " + conditions[i]);
47:            System.out.println("\tHigh: " + highTemp[i]);
48:            System.out.println("\tLow: " + lowTemp[i]);
49:        }
50:    }
51:
52:    public static void main(String[] arguments) {
53:        try {
54:            WeatherStation station = new WeatherStation();
55:            station.display();
56:        } catch (Exception exception) {
57:            System.out.println("Error: " + exception.getMessage());
58:        }
59:    }
60: }
```

The WeatherStation application, which requires no command-line arguments, produces seven forecasts for Wasilla, Alaska, as in the following output:

Output ▼

```
Period 0
    Conditions: rain
    High: 56
    Low: 40
Period 1
    Conditions: partlycloudy
    High: 59
    Low: 40
```

```
Period 2
    Conditions: partlycloudy
    High: 61
    Low: 41
Period 3
    Conditions: chancerain
    High: 67
    Low: 43
Period 4
    Conditions: chancerain
    High: 67
    Low: 47
Period 5
    Conditions: chancerain
    High: 65
    Low: 49
```

NOTE

The Java class library includes the Java API for XML Processing (JAXP), a set of classes that serve the same purpose as XOM. JAXP can represent XML data as an object or a stream of events, giving a programmer more control over how the data is parsed. XOM is easier to learn and requires properly formatted and valid XML at all times. More information on JAXP can be found on the Web at http://jaxp.java.net.

Reading RSS Syndication Feeds

There are hundreds of XML dialects out there representing data in a platform-independent, software-independent manner. One of the most popular XML dialects is RSS, a format for sharing headlines and links from online news sites, weblogs, and other sources of information.

RSS makes web content available in XML form, perfect for reading in software, in web-accessible files called *feeds*. RSS readers, called *news aggregators*, have been adopted by several million information junkies to track all their favorite websites. There also are web applications that collect and share RSS items.

The hard-working `Builder` class in the `nu.xom` package can load XML over the Internet from any URL:

```
String rssUrl = "http://feeds.drudge.com/retort";
Builder builder = new Builder();
Document doc = builder.build(rssUrl);
```

This hour's workshop employs this technique to read an RSS file, presenting the 15 most recent items.

Open your editor and enter the text from Listing 21.4. Save the result as `Aggregator.java`.

LISTING 21.4   The Full Text of `Aggregator.java`

```
1: import java.io.*;
2: import nu.xom.*;
3:
4: public class Aggregator {
```

LISTING 21.4   Continued

```
 5:     public String[] title = new String[15];
 6:     public String[] link = new String[15];
 7:     public int count = 0;
 8:
 9:     public Aggregator(String rssUrl) {
10:         try {
11:             // retrieve the XML document
12:             Builder builder = new Builder();
13:             Document doc = builder.build(rssUrl);
14:             // retrieve the document's root element
15:             Element root = doc.getRootElement();
16:             // retrieve the root's channel element
17:             Element channel = root.getFirstChildElement("channel");
18:             // retrieve the item elements in the channel
19:             if (channel != null) {
20:                 Elements items = channel.getChildElements("item");
21:                 for (int current = 0; current < items.size(); current++) {
22:                     if (count > 15) {
23:                         break;
24:                     }
25:                     // retrieve the current item
26:                     Element item = items.get(current);
27:                     Element titleElement = item.getFirstChildElement("title");
28:                     Element linkElement = item.getFirstChildElement("link");
29:                     title[current] = titleElement.getValue();
30:                     link[current] = linkElement.getValue();
31:                     count++;
32:                 }
33:             }
34:         } catch (ParsingException exception) {
35:             System.out.println("XML error: " + exception.getMessage());
36:             exception.printStackTrace();
37:         } catch (IOException ioException) {
38:             System.out.println("IO error: " + ioException.getMessage());
39:             ioException.printStackTrace();
40:         }
41:     }
42:
43:     public void listItems() {
44:         for (int i = 0; i < 15; i++) {
45:             if (title[i] != null) {
46:                 System.out.println("\n" + title[i]);
47:                 System.out.println(link[i]);
48:                 i++;
49:             }
50:         }
51:     }
52:
53:     public static void main(String[] arguments) {
54:         if (arguments.length > 0) {
```

LISTING 21.4   Continued

```
55:             Aggregator aggie = new Aggregator(arguments[0]);
56:             aggie.listItems();
57:         } else {
58:             System.out.println("Usage: java Aggregator rssUrl");
59:         }
60:     }
61: }
```

Before running the application, set up a command-line argument for the feed you'd like to read, which can be any RSS feed. If you don't know any, use http://feeds.drudge.com/retort, which contains headlines from the Drudge Retort, an online news site that I publish.

Sample output from the feed is shown in Figure 21.1.

FIGURE 21.1
Running the Aggregator application.

BY THE WAY

You can find out more about the RSS XML dialect from the RSS Advisory Board website at www.rssboard.org. I'm the chairman of the board, which offers guidance on the format and a directory of software that can be used to read RSS feeds.

Summary

The Java language liberates software from dependence on a particular operating system. The program you write with the language on a Windows box creates class files that can be run on a Linux server or a Mac OS X computer.

XML achieves a similar liberation for the data produced by software. If XML data follows the simple rules required to make it well formed, you can read it with any software that parses XML. You don't need to keep the originating program around just to ensure there's always a way to access it.

The XOM library makes it easy to read and write XML data.

When you're using Java and XML, you can declare your independence from two of the major obstacles faced by computer programmers for decades: obsolete data and obsolete operating systems.

Q&A

Q. **What's the purpose of the DOCTYPE statement in the XML file produced by the PropertyFileCreator application?**

A. That's a reference to a *document type definition* (DTD), a file that defines the rules XML data must follow to be considered valid in its dialect.

If you load the web page referred to in that statement, http://java.sun.com/dtd/properties.dtd, you find references to each of the elements and attributes contained in the XML file produced by the Java library's Properties class.

Although Sun provides this DTD, Java's official documentation indicates that it shouldn't be relied upon when evaluating property configuration data. Parsers are supposed to ignore it.

Q. **Are the Hatfields and McCoys still feuding?**

A. The West Virginia and Kentucky families are on good terms 121 years after the last casualty in their infamous 35-year conflict.

In 1979, Hatfields and McCoys got together to play the TV game show *Family Feud* for a week. A pig was kept on stage and awarded to the winning family.

In 2003, a formal peace treaty was reached between the families in Pikeville, KY.

The Hatfield-McCoy Trails, 500 miles of trails for recreational off-road driving, were established in West Virginia in 2000 and expanded over the next decade.

Workshop

To see whether your knowledge of XML processing in Java is well-formed, answer the following questions.

Quiz

1. Which of the following terms should not be used to complement XML data that is properly formatted?

    A. This data is well formed.

    B. This data is valid.

    C. This data is dy-no-mite!

2. What method reads all the elements that are enclosed within a parent element?

    A. `get()`

    B. `getChildElements()`

    C. `getFirstChildElement()`

3. What method of the `Elements` class can be used to determine the number of elements that it contains?

    A. `count()`

    B. `length()`

    C. `size()`

Answers

1. **C.** Well-formed data has properly structured start and end tags, a single root element containing all child elements, and an ?XML declaration at the top. Valid data follows the rules of a particular XML dialect. "Dy-no-mite!" is the catchphrase of the comedian Jimmie "J.J." Walker.

2. **B.** The `getChildElements()` method returns an `Elements` object holding all the elements.

3. **C.** Just like vectors, `Elements` uses a `size()` method that provides a count of the items it holds.

Activities

To extend your knowledge of XML, parse the following activities:

▶ Revise the `WeatherStation` application to display an additional element from the Weather Underground forecast data.

▶ Write a program that displays the data contained in `shortChanges.xml`, an XML document of weblog information available at www.weblogs.com/shortChanges.xml.

To see Java programs that implement these activities, visit the book's website at www.java24hours.com.

Creating Web Services with JAX-WS

Now that the Internet is everywhere, driving millions of desktop computers, web servers, phones, videogame consoles, and other devices, the desire to connect them all together has given rise to *web services*, software that communicates with other software over *HTTP*, the protocol of the Web.

One of the most exciting new features of Java is the Java API for XML Web Services (JAX-WS). *JAX-WS* is a set of packages and classes that create clients that make requests of web services and services that take those requests.

JAX-WS supports web services that are implemented using the Simple Object Access Protocol (SOAP) and Representational State Transfer (REST). JAX-WS greatly simplifies the task of supporting these protocols. As a programmer, you create Java objects and call methods to use web services and the rest is taken care of behind the scenes.

Defining a Service Endpoint Interface

The first step in the creation of a JAX-WS web service is to create a *Service Endpoint Interface*, a Java interface that defines the methods that clients can call when they're using the web service.

The `SquareRootServer` web service you are developing this hour is a service that can handle two simple tasks:

- Calculating the square root of a number
- Displaying the current date and time

WHAT YOU'LL LEARN IN THIS HOUR:

- ▶ Defining a Java interface for a web service
- ▶ Applying this interface to a Java class
- ▶ Deploying a web service on the Internet
- ▶ Viewing a web service contract
- ▶ Creating a web service client

An interface is a set of methods that provides names, arguments, and return types but does not contain code that implements the methods. The interface serves as a contract between objects—if an object implements an interface, other objects know they can call all the interface's methods on that object.

In Hour 15, "Responding to User Input," you had to implement the `ActionListener` interface in any Java class that needed to receive action events when a button was clicked.

For this project, you're handling the other side of the contract. The `SquareRootServer` interface defines two methods that must be present in a class that implements the web service: `squareRoot(double)` and `getTime()`.

The following statements define the interface:

```
public interface SquareRootServer {
    double getSquareRoot(double input);
    String getTime();
}
```

The method definitions in an interface are followed by a semicolon rather than { and } characters around a block statement. Interfaces don't define the behavior of methods; that's handled by classes that implement the interface.

Because these methods can be called as a JAX-WS web service, an extra modifier must be added in front of each one, the annotation @WebMethod:

```
public interface SquareRootServer {
    @WebMethod double getSquareRoot(double input);
    @WebMethod String getTime();
}
```

Using Annotations to Simplify Java Code

Annotations are a smarter form of comments that can be understood by the Java interpreter, compiler, and programming tools. They provide a way to define information about a program that's not part of the program itself but which can trigger actions when the program is compiled or run.

Annotations begin with an @ sign followed by the name of the annotation.

One of the most common annotations is @Override, which indicates a method overrides a superclass method. Here's an example:

```
@Overrides public void paintComponent(Graphics comp) {
    // definition of method here
}
```

If you've made an error and it does not override a method—which would happen if you used the wrong type or number of parameters—the compiler can catch the error.

The @WebMethod annotation indicates that a method can be called as a web service. The SquareRootServer interface also uses an @WebService annotation that indicates the interface defines a service endpoint interface.

Annotations can take parameters that provide further customization. SquareRootServer includes one final annotation:

```
@SOAPBinding(style = Style.RPC)
```

This annotation helps define the contract between the web service and the client programs that call the service. You learn more about this later in the hour.

For now, it's time to begin coding the web service. Create a new empty Java file in NetBeans with the class name SquareRootServer and the package name com.java24hours.ws. Enter the contents of Listing 22.1 into the file.

LISTING 22.1   The Full Text of SquareRootServer.java

```
 1: package com.java24hours.ws;
 2:
 3: import javax.jws.*;
 4: import javax.jws.soap.*;
 5: import javax.jws.soap.SOAPBinding.*;
 6:
 7: @WebService
 8:
 9: @SOAPBinding(style = Style.RPC)
10:
11: public interface SquareRootServer {
12:     // get the square root of a number
13:     @WebMethod double getSquareRoot(double input);
14:
15:     // get the current time and date as a string
16:     @WebMethod String getTime();
17:
18: }
```

This class has been placed in the com.java24hours.ws package, a design decision that makes it easier for the web service to be deployed for other software to access over the Internet.

Now that you've finished defining this interface, you're ready to write the code that implements its two methods: getSquareRoot() and getTime().

Creating a Service Implementation Bean

The Java class that implements the Service Endpoint Interface is called the Service Implementation Bean. Learning odd new bits of jargon is an unavoidable part of JAX-WS.

The `SquareRootServerImpl` class implements the `SquareRootServer` interface, as stated in the class declaration:

```
public class SquareRootServerImpl implements SquareRootServer {
```

This means the class you're creating must contain all the methods in the interface, each with the proper parameters.

The `getSquareRoot(double)` and `getTime()` methods are implemented using techniques you've learned previously.

The only new aspect of the class is the following annotation, which appears before the `class` statement:

```
@WebService(endpointInterface = "com.java24hours.ws.SquareRootServer")
```

This annotation indicates the class is a service implementation bean for a service endpoint interface named `com.java24hours.ws.SquareRootServer`. You must use the full class name, including the name of its package.

Take note of the fact that annotations are not followed by semicolons, unlike statements.

Start coding this class: Create a new empty Java file named `SquareRootServerImpl` in the package `com.java24hours.ws`, and then fill it with the contents of Listing 22.2.

LISTING 22.2   The Full Text of `SquareRootServerImpl.java`

```
 1: package com.java24hours.ws;
 2:
 3: import java.util.*;
 4: import javax.jws.*;
 5:
 6: @WebService(endpointInterface = "com.java24hours.ws.SquareRootServer")
 7:
 8: public class SquareRootServerImpl implements SquareRootServer {
 9:
10:     public double getSquareRoot(double input) {
11:         return Math.sqrt(input);
12:     }
```

LISTING 22.2   Continued

```
13:
14:      public String getTime() {
15:          Date now = new Date();
16:          return now.toString();
17:      }
18: }
```

With the two classes you've created, you're ready to launch the web service so it can be called by other software.

Publishing the Web Service

JAX-WS web services can be deployed by Java application servers such as BEA WebLogic, GlassFish, JBoss, and Jetty. If you had created the SquareRootServer web service in a development environment that supported those servers, you'd be ready at this point to launch it.

You also can write your own Java application that loads a web service and makes it available over the Internet.

The SquareRootServerPublisher application handles this task, which requires only two steps:

▶ Load the class that implements the web service

▶ Publish that object at an address accessible to the Internet

The EndPoint class in the javax.xml.ws package has a class method, publish(String, Object), that deploys a web service.

This method's first argument is the web address where the service can be accessed, which for this project is http://127.0.0.1:5335/service. This web address begins with a host name, 127.0.0.1, that's called the localhost because it's the local computer you're using to create and run your Java programs.

The second part of the address is the port number on the localhost where the web service waits for connections. The port 5335 has been chosen arbitrarily because it's not likely to be in use by other Internet-aware programs on your computer.

CAUTION

The name of Service Implementation Beans refers to JavaBeans, special Java classes designed to function as reusable software components in the Java Enterprise Edition. However, the reference to beans is a bit of a misnomer when it comes to JAX-WS. Any Java object can be a Service Implementation Bean as long as it follows the rules for web service methods and has been created with the proper annotations.

The final part of the address, /service, is the path. Every web service must have a unique path. If you run any other web services on your computer, they can't have the same path as SquareRootServer.

To deploy the web service, create an empty Java file called SquareRootServerPublisher in the com.java24hours.ws package. Enter the text of Listing 22.3 in this file.

LISTING 22.3   The Full Text of SquareRootServerPublisher.java

```
 1: package com.java24hours.ws;
 2:
 3: import javax.xml.ws.*;
 4:
 5: public class SquareRootServerPublisher {
 6:     public static void main(String[] arguments) {
 7:         SquareRootServerImpl srsi = new SquareRootServerImpl();
 8:         Endpoint.publish(
 9:             "http://127.0.0.1:5335/service",
10:             srsi
11:         );
12:     }
13: }
```

When you run the application, it waits for connections on port 5335 of your computer. You can call the methods of the web service from any program that supports SOAP- or REST-based web services, whether the program is written in Java or another language. As long as your web service is on the Internet, any other Internet-connected software can call the methods.

Using Web Service Definition Language Files

Before trying out this web service, you can test the availability of the SquareRootServerPublisher application with any web browser.

Open a browser and load the address http://127.0.0.1:5335/service?wsdl. The browser displays the XML file shown in Listing 22.4. This file is being served by the application that you just created.

This file is a service contract that's written in Web Service Description Language (WSDL), an XML dialect for spelling out exactly how a web service functions so that servers and clients can make full use of it.

You don't have to understand WSDL to create JAX-WS services and clients to access those services. It's worthwhile to take a cursory look at the contents to get a picture for how SOAP- and REST-based web services operate.

LISTING 22.4   A Web Service Description Language Contract

```
1: <?xml version="1.0" encoding="UTF-8"?>
2: <!-- Published by JAX-WS RI at http://jax-ws.dev.java.net. RI's version
3: is JAX-WS RI 2.2.2 in JDK 7. -->
4: <!-- Generated by JAX-WS RI at http://jax-ws.dev.java.net. RI's version
5: is JAX-WS RI 2.2.2 in JDK 7. -->
6: <definitions xmlns:soap="http://schemas.xmlsoap.org/wsdl/soap/"
7: xmlns:tns="http://ws.java24hours.com/"
8: xmlns:xsd="http://www.w3.org/2001/XMLSchema"
9: xmlns="http://schemas.xmlsoap.org/wsdl/"
10: targetNamespace="http://ws.java24hours.com/"
11: name="SquareRootServerImplService">
12: <types></types>
13: <message name="getSquareRoot">
14: <part name="arg0" type="xsd:double"></part>
15: </message>
16: <message name="getSquareRootResponse">
17: <part name="return" type="xsd:double"></part>
18: </message>
19: <message name="getTime"></message>
20: <message name="getTimeResponse">
21: <part name="return" type="xsd:string"></part>
22: </message>
23: <portType name="SquareRootServer">
24: <operation name="getSquareRoot" parameterOrder="arg0">
25: <input message="tns:getSquareRoot"></input>
26: <output message="tns:getSquareRootResponse"></output>
27: </operation>
28: <operation name="getTime" parameterOrder="">
29: <input message="tns:getTime"></input>
30: <output message="tns:getTimeResponse"></output>
31: </operation>
32: </portType>
33: <binding name="SquareRootServerImplPortBinding"
34: type="tns:SquareRootServer">
35: <soap:binding transport="http://schemas.xmlsoap.org/soap/http"
36: style="rpc"></soap:binding>
37: <operation name="getSquareRoot">
38: <soap:operation soapAction=""></soap:operation>
39: <input>
40: <soap:body use="literal"
41: namespace="http://ws.java24hours.com/"></soap:body>
42: </input>
43: <output>
44: <soap:body use="literal"
45: namespace="http://ws.java24hours.com/"></soap:body>
46: </output>
```

LISTING 22.4   Continued

```
47: </operation>
48: <operation name="getTime">
49: <soap:operation soapAction=""></soap:operation>
50: <input>
51: <soap:body use="literal"
52: namespace="http://ws.java24hours.com/"></soap:body>
53: </input>
54: <output>
55: <soap:body use="literal"
56: namespace="http://ws.java24hours.com/"></soap:body>
57: </output>
58: </operation>
59: </binding>
60: <service name="SquareRootServerImplService">
61: <port name="SquareRootServerImplPort"
62: binding="tns:SquareRootServerImplPortBinding">
63: <soap:address location="http://127.0.0.1:5335/service"></soap:address>
64: </port>
65: </service>
66: </definitions>
```

A WSDL file is called a service contract because it stipulates how a web service can be reached, the messages that can be exchanged with the service, and the data types of the information being transferred.

Lines 13–22 of the WSDL contract define the web service's methods, the parameters of those methods, and the data returned in response. Take a look over those lines to see if you can determine where it states that the `getSquareRoot()` method takes a double parameter and returns a double value.

The data types referenced in the contract are not Java data types. They're data types that are generalized for use by any programming language that supports SOAP. (There's nothing about web services that's tailored specifically to Java.)

NOTE

Because a WSDL contract defines a web service in such specific detail, you can use it to automate much of the process of programming web services. The Java Development Kit (JDK) includes a command-line tool, `wsimport`, that takes a WSDL file as input and writes Java classes to access the web service.

Creating a Web Service Client

In this section, you create `SquareRootClient`, a Java application that can call the methods of the web service you just created. The service must, of course, be running for the client to connect to it.

Because web service technology like the JAX-WS library supports standards such as SOAP, REST, HTTP, and XML, you don't have to use a Java program to connect to the square root web service. Perl, Python, Ruby and other languages all have libraries that support web services.

The JAX-WS library offers the `Service` class in the `javax.xml.ws` package, a factory that creates objects that can call a web service.

The class method `Service.create(URL, QName)` creates the factory. The arguments are a `URL` object from `java.net` and a `QName` from `javax.xml.namespace`.

The `URL` must be the address of the web service's WSDL contract:

```
URL url = new URL("http://127.0.0.1:5335/service?wsdl");
```

The `QName` is a qualified name, an XML identifier that's associated with the provider of the web service. A qualified name consists of a namespace URI and a local identifier.

Namespace URIs are similar to URLs but do not necessarily work as a web address. Because the package name of the square root web service is `com.java24hours.ws`, which by convention in Java associates it with the Internet host name `ws.java24hours.com`, the namespace URI for this web service is `http://ws.java24hours.com`.

The local identifier for the web service is the name of the Service Implementation Bean with the word "Service" appended. Here's the statement that creates the qualified name:

```
QName qname = new QName(
    "http://ws.java24hours.com/",
    "SquareRootServerImplService"
);
```

With the URL and qualified name, you can create the web service client factory:

```
Service service = Service.create(url, qname);
```

The factory has a `getPort(Class)` method that creates an object of the specified class. To identify a Java class for use as a method argument, use a class variable of the class named `class`. Confusing? It makes more sense when you see it in a Java statement:

```
SquareRootServer srs = service.getPort(SquareRootServer.class);
```

The call to getPort() with SquareRootServer.class as the argument causes the factory to create a SquareRootServer object. This object is stored in the srs variable.

Call the methods of the SquareRootServer object as you would any other object in Java:

```
System.out.println(srs.getTime());
System.out.println(srs.getSquareRoot(625D));
```

The JAX-WS library packages these method calls as SOAP messages, sends them over the Internet to the web service, and transmits the calls.

When the service responds to the calls, it packages the responses as SOAP messages, sends them back over the Internet, and they're converted back to Java data types.

Put all these together by creating an empty Java file named SquareRootClient and entering the text from Listing 22.5 in the file.

LISTING 22.5   The Full Text of SquareRootClient.java

```
 1: package com.java24hours.ws;
 2:
 3: import java.net.*;
 4: import javax.xml.namespace.*;
 5: import javax.xml.ws.*;
 6:
 7: class SquareRootClient {
 8:     public static void main(String[] arguments) throws Exception {
 9:         URL url = new URL("http://127.0.0.1:5335/service?wsdl");
10:         QName qname = new QName(
11:             "http://ws.java24hours.com/",
12:             "SquareRootServerImplService"
13:         );
14:         Service service = Service.create(url, qname);
15:         SquareRootServer srs = service.getPort(SquareRootServer.class);
16:
17:         System.out.println(srs.getTime());
18:         System.out.println(srs.getSquareRoot(625D));
19:     }
20: }
```

When you run the client application, you see the output shown in Figure 22.1 if the SquareRootPublisher application is running.

FIGURE 22.1
Calling a web service and displaying the response.

Summary

The JAX-WS set of packages and classes is the successor to the Java API for XML-based RPC (JAX-RPC), a technology for making remote procedure calls from one Java object to another over the Internet.

The ability to call other software, regardless of its location and the programming language in which it's written, is one of the building blocks of a software development trend called Web 2.0.

Web 2.0 enables software to take as much advantage of the Internet's ubiquitous connectivity as humans have enjoyed since the Web became popular in the mid-1990s.

This hour's covered all four steps of creating and using a web service using JAX-WS. You can create an interface for the service (a Service Endpoint Interface), implement the service (a Service Implementation Bean), publish the service on the Internet, and create a client to access it.

Many programming tools, including NetBeans and the JDK, make it possible to create code automatically to simplify the job of creating and accessing web services.

Q&A

Q. How does XML-RPC fit in with SOAP web services?

A. XML-RPC is a protocol for calling methods and receiving data in an XML format over HTTP, the protocol of the Web. SOAP is all those things as well, and in fact the two web service protocols share a common origin.

XML-RPC was created from a draft version of the protocol that eventually became SOAP. Because XML-RPC was out first and is simpler to implement, it developed its own following and remains popular today. The Apache XML-RPC Java library, available from http://ws.apache.org/xmlrpc, supports the creation of web services and clients that employ XML-RPC.

SOAP's a more sophisticated web service protocol that supports a wider range of client/service interactions.

Q. I'm not clear on why a package named com.java24hours.ws **is associated with the Internet host** ws.java24hours.com. **How does that work?**

A. Java package names are created by the programmers who developed the package. Oracle starts the names of Java packages from the Java class library with either java or javax, such as java.util and javax.swing. When other programmers create package, they follow a convention that prevents two entities from choosing the same package name and being confused with each other.

The convention is to choose a package name that's based on something the entity owns—a domain name. As the owner of the domain name cadenhead.org, I've created Java classes with package names that begin with org.cadenhead, such as org.cadenhead.web. The Apache Software Foundation, which owns apache.org, calls its XML-RPC package org.apache.xmlrpc.

Q. What was the first website on the Internet?

A. The first site was http://info.cern.ch, which is still online today. Tim Berners-Lee, a physicist at the European Organization for Nuclear Research (CERN), used the site to describe his new invention, the World Wide Web.

The first webpage was at http://info.cern.ch/hypertext/WWW/TheProject.html and was updated daily as the Web attracted users, publishers, and software developers.

The site defined the web as a "a wide-area hypermedia information retrieval initiative aiming to give universal access to a large universe of documents."

Workshop

See how many facts about web services have filled your bean by answering the following questions.

Quiz

1. What is a Service Implementation Bean?

    A. An interface that identifies the methods reachable over a web service

    B. A class that implements a web service

    C. A service contract between a web service and clients that call the service

2. When text such as `@WebMethod` or `@Override` appears in a method declaration, what is it called?

    A. An annotation

    B. An assertion

    C. An aggravation

3. What does WSDL stand for?

    A. Web Services Deployment Language

    B. Web Services Description Language

    C. Lucy in the Sky with Diamonds

Answers

1. **B.** Answer A. refers to a Service Endpoint Interface.

2. **A.** Though I guess answer C. is also potentially true, depending on how much trouble you had in that section of the hour.

3. **B.** It's often mistakenly called Web Services Definition Language.

Activities

To further service your knowledge of this hour's topic, do the following activities:

▶ Add a method to the square root web service that multiplies a number by 10, and modify the `SquareRootClient` application to call that method.

▶ Create a new web service that uses the `WeatherStation` class from Hour 21, "Reading and Writing XML Data," and makes the current high temperature, low temperature, and weather conditions accessible through a web service.

To see Java programs that implement these activities, visit the book's website at www.java24hours.com.

Creating Java2D Graphics

During this hour, you learn how to turn Swing containers—the plain gray panels and frames that hold graphical user interface (GUI) components—into an artistic canvas on which you can draw fonts, colors, shapes, and graphics.

Using the Font Class

Colors and fonts are represented in Java by the Color and Font classes in the java.awt package. With these classes, you can present text in different fonts and sizes and change the color of text and graphics. Fonts are created with the Font(*String*, *int*, *int*) constructor, which takes three arguments:

- ▶ The typeface of the font as either a generic name ("Dialog," "DialogInput," "Monospaced," "SanSerif," or "Serif") or an actual font name ("Arial Black," "Helvetica," or "Courier New")

- ▶ The style as one of three class variables: Font.BOLD, Font.ITALIC, or Font.PLAIN

- ▶ The size of the font in points

The following statement creates a 12-point italic Serif Font object:

```
Font current = new Font("Serif", Font.ITALIC, 12);
```

If you use a specific fonts rather than one of the generic ones, it must be installed on the computer of users running your program. You can combine the font styles by adding them together, as in the following example:

```
Font headline = new Font("Courier New", Font.BOLD + Font.ITALIC, 72);
```

WHAT YOU'LL LEARN IN THIS HOUR:

- ▶ Setting the font and color of text
- ▶ Setting up a container's background color
- ▶ Drawing lines, rectangles, and other shapes
- ▶ Drawing GIF and JPEG graphics
- ▶ Drawing filled and unfilled shapes

When you have a font, you call the `Graphics2D` component's
`setFont(Font)` method to designate it as the current font. All subsequent
drawing operations use that font until another one is set. Statements in the
following example create a "Comic Sans" font object and designate it as
the current font before drawing text:

```
public void paintComponent(Graphics comp) {
    Graphics2D comp2D = (Graphics2D) comp;
    Font font = new Font("Comic Sans", Font.BOLD, 15);
    comp2D.setFont(font);
    comp2D.drawString("Potrzebie!", 5, 50);
}
```

Java supports *antialiasing* to draw fonts and graphics more smoothly and
less blocky in appearance. To enable this functionality, you must set a rendering hint in Swing. A `Graphics2D` object has a `setRenderingHint(int,
int)` method that takes two arguments:

▶ The key of the rendering hint

▶ The value to associate with that key

These values are class variables in the `RenderingHints` class of `java.awt`.
To activate antialiasing, call `setRenderingHint()` with two arguments:

```
comp2D.setRenderingHint(RenderingHints.KEY_ANTIALIASING,
    RenderingHints.VALUE_ANTIALIAS_ON);
```

The `comp2D` object in this example is the `Graphics2D` object that represents
a container's drawing environment.

Using the `Color` Class

Colors in Java are represented by the `Color` class, which includes the following constants as class variables: `black`, `blue`, `cyan`, `darkGray`, `gray`,
`green`, `lightGray`, `magenta`, `orange`, `pink`, `red`, `white`, and `yellow`.

In a container, you can set the background color of the component using
these constants by calling the `setBackground(Color)` method like this:

```
setBackground(Color.orange);
```

The current color, like the current font, must be set before drawing takes
place using the `setColor(Color)` method. The following code includes a
statement to set the current color to orange and draw text in that color:

```
public void paintComponent(Graphics comp) {
    Graphics2D comp2D = (Graphics2D) comp;
    comp2D.setColor(Color.orange);
    comp2D.drawString("Go, Buccaneers!", 5, 50);
}
```

Unlike the setBackground() method, which you can call directly on a container, you must call the setColor() method on a Graphics2D object.

Creating Custom Colors

You can create custom colors in Java by specifying their Standard Red Green Blue (sRGB) value. *sRGB* defines a color by the amount of red, green, and blue present in the color. Each value ranges from 0 (none of that color) to 255 (the maximum amount).

The constructor Color(*int*, *int*, *int*) takes arguments representing the red, green, and blue values. The following code draws a panel that displays light orange text (230 red, 220 green, 0 blue) on a dark red (235 red, 50 green, 50 blue) background:

```
import java.awt.*;
import javax.swing.*;

public class GoBucs extends JPanel {
    Color lightOrange = new Color(230, 220, 0);
    Color darkRed = new Color(235, 50, 50);

    public void paintComponent(Graphics comp) {
        Graphics2D comp2D = (Graphics2D) comp;
        comp2D.setColor(darkRed);
        comp2D.fillRect(0, 0, 200, 100);
        comp2D.setColor(lightOrange);
        comp2D.drawString("Go, Buccaneers!", 5, 50);
    }
}
```

This example calls the fillRect() method of Graphics2D to draw a filled-in rectangle using the current color.

> NOTE
>
> sRGB values enable the creation of 16.5 million possible combinations, though most computer monitors only offer a close approximation for most of them. For guidance on whether burnt-midnight blue goes well with medium-faded-baby green, read *Sams Teach Yourself Color Sense While Waiting in Line at This Bookstore.*

Drawing Lines and Shapes

Drawing shapes such as lines and rectangles is as easy in a Java program as displaying text. All you need is a Graphics2D object to define the drawing surface and objects that represent things to draw.

The Graphics2D object has methods used to draw text with a command such as the following:

```
comp2D.drawString("Draw, pardner!", 15, 40);
```

This draws the text "Draw, pardner!" at the coordinates (15,40). Drawing methods use the same (x,y) coordinate system as text. The (0,0) coordinate is at the upper-left corner of the container, x values increase to the right, and y values increase as you go down. You can determine the maximum (x,y) value you can use in an applet with the following statements:

```
int maxXValue = getSize().width;
int maxYValue = getSize().height;
```

With the exception of lines, shapes you draw can be filled or unfilled. A filled shape is drawn with the current color completely filling the space taken up by the shape. Unfilled shapes draw a border with the current color.

Drawing Lines

A 2D drawing of an object is created and represents the shape that is being drawn.

The objects that define shapes belong to the java.awt.geom package of classes.

The Line2D.Float class creates a line connecting a beginning (x,y) point and an ending (x,y) point. The following statement creates a line from the point (40,200) to the point (70,130):

```
Line2D.Float line = new Line2D.Float(40F, 200F, 70F, 130F);
```

The arguments are followed by the letter F to indicate they are floating-point values. If this was omitted, Java would treat them as integers.

All shapes except for lines are drawn by calling a method of the Graphics2D class—draw() for outlines and fill() for filled shapes.

The following statement draws the line object created in the previous example:

```
comp2D.draw(line);
```

NOTE

Line2D.Float has a period in the middle of its class name, which differs from most classes you've worked with before. That's because Float is an inner class of the Line2D class, a subject covered in Hour 11, "Describing What Your Object Is Like."

Drawing Rectangles

Rectangles can be filled or unfilled and have rounded or square corners. They are created using the `Rectangle2D.Float(int, int, int, int)` constructor with these arguments:

- The x coordinate at the upper left of the rectangle
- The y coordinate at upper left
- The width of the rectangle
- The height

The following statement draws an unfilled rectangle with square corners:

```
Rectangle2D.Float box = new
    Rectangle2D.Float(245F, 65F, 20F, 10F);
```

This statement creates a rectangle with its upper-left corner at the (x,y) coordinate (245,65) with a width of 20 pixels and a height of 10. To draw this rectangle as an outline, you could use the following statement:

```
comp2D.draw(box);
```

If you want to make the rectangle filled in, use the `fill()` method instead:

```
comp.fill(box);
```

You can create rectangles with rounded corners instead of square ones by using the `RoundRectangle2D.Float` class.

The constructor to this class starts with the same four arguments as the `Rectangle2D.Float` class and adds the following two arguments:

- A number of pixels in the x direction away from the corner of the rectangle
- A number of pixels in the y direction away from the corner

These distances are used to determine where the rounding of the rectangle's corner should begin.

The following statement creates a rounded rectangle:

```
RoundRectangle2D.Float ro = new RoundRectangle.Float(
    10F, 10F,
    100F, 80F,
    15F, 15F);
```

This rectangle has its upper-left corner at the (10,10) coordinate. The third and fourth arguments specify how wide and tall the rectangle should be. In this case, it should be 100 pixels wide and 80 pixels tall.

The last two arguments to `drawRoundRect()` specify that all four corners should begin rounding 15 pixels away from the corner at (10,10).

Drawing Ellipses and Circles

You can create ellipses and circles with the same class, `Ellipse2D.Float`, which takes four arguments:

- The x coordinate of the ellipse
- The y coordinate of the ellipse
- Its width
- Its height

The (x,y) coordinates do not indicate a point at the center of the ellipse or circle, as you might expect. Instead, the (x,y) coordinates, width, and height describe an invisible rectangle inside which the ellipse fits. The (x,y) coordinate is the upper-left corner of this rectangle. If it has the same width and height, the ellipse is a circle.

The following statement creates a circle inside the rectangle at the (245,45) coordinate with a height and width of 5 pixels each:

```
Ellipse2D.Float cir = new Ellipse2D.Float(
    245F, 45F, 5F, 5F);
```

Drawing Arcs

Another circular shape you can draw in Java is an *arc*, a partial ellipse or circle. Arcs are created using the `Arc2D.Float` class, which has a constructor method with many of the same arguments. You draw the arc by specifying an ellipse, the portion of the ellipse that should be visible (in degrees), and the place the arc should begin on the ellipse.

To create an arc, specify the following integer arguments to the constructor:

- The x coordinate of the invisible rectangle that the ellipse fits into
- The y coordinate of the rectangle
- The width of the rectangle

- ▶ The height of the rectangle

- ▶ The point on the ellipse where the arc should begin (in degrees from 0 to 359)

- ▶ The size of the arc (also in degrees)

- ▶ The type of arc it is

The arc's starting point and size range from 0 to 359 degrees in a counter-clockwise direction, beginning with 0 degrees at the 3 o'clock position, as shown in Figure 23.1.

The type of arc is specified using class variables: `PIE` for pie graph slices, `CLOSED` if the endpoints are connected with a straight line, and `OPEN` if the endpoints should not be connected.

The following statement draws an open arc at (100,50) that is 120 degrees long, begins at the 30-degree mark, and has a width of 65 and a height of 75:

```
Arc2D.Float smile = new Arc2D.Float(100F, 50F, 65F, 75F,
    30F, 120F, Arc2D.Float.OPEN);
```

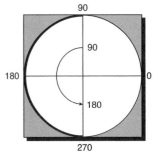

FIGURE 23.1
How arcs are defined in degrees.

Baking a Pie Graph

To draw this hour to a close, you create `PiePanel`, a GUI component that displays a pie graph. This component is a subclass of `JPanel`, a simple Swing container that's useful as a place to draw something.

One way to begin creating a class is to define the way objects of the class are created. Programs that use the `PiePanel` class must undertake the following steps:

- ▶ Create a `PiePanel` object by using the constructor method `PiePanel(int)`. The integer specified as an argument is the number of slices the pie graph contains.

- ▶ Call the object's `addSlice(Color, float)` method to give a slice the designated color and value.

The value of each slice in `PiePanel` is the quantity represented by that slice.

For example, Table 23.1 displays data about the status of student loan repayments in the United States for the first 38 years of the program, according to the Office of Postsecondary Education.

TABLE 23.1   U.S. Student Loan Repayments

Amount repaid by students	$101 billion
Amount loaned to students still in school	$68 billion
Amount loaned to students making payments	$91 billion
Amount loaned to students who defaulted	$25 billion

You could use PiePanel to represent this data in a pie graph with the following statements:

```
PiePanel loans = new PiePanel(4);
loans.addSlice(Color.green, 101F);
loans.addSlice(Color.yellow, 68F);
loans.addSlice(Color.blue, 91F);
loans.addSlice(Color.red, 25F);
```

Figure 23.2 shows the result in an application frame that contains one component: a PiePanel created with the student loan data.

FIGURE 23.2
Displaying student loan data on a pie graph.

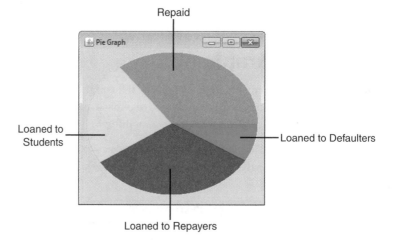

When a PiePanel object is created, the number of slices is specified in the constructor. You need to know three more things to be able to draw each slice:

▶ The color of the slice, represented by a Color object

▶ The value represented by each slice

▶ The total value represented by all slices

A new helper class, `PieSlice`, is used to represent each slice in the pie graph:

```java
import java.awt.*;

class PieSlice {
    Color color = Color.lightGray;
    float size = 0;

    PieSlice(Color pColor, float pSize) {
        color = pColor;
        size = pSize;
    }
}
```

Each slice is constructed by calling `PieSlice(Color, float)`. The combined value of all slices is stored as a private instance variable of the `PiePanel` class, `totalSize`. There also are instance variables for the panel's background color (`background`) and a counter used to keep track of slices (`current`):

```java
private int current = 0;
private float totalSize = 0;
private Color background;
```

Now that you have a `PieSlice` class to work with, you can create an array of `PieSlice` objects with another instance variable:

```java
private PieSlice[] slice;
```

When you create a `PiePanel` object, none of the slices have an assigned a color or size. The only things that you must do in the constructor are define the size of the `slice` array and save the background color of the panel:

```java
public PiePanel(int sliceCount) {
    slice = new PieSlice[sliceCount];
    background = getBackground();
}
```

Use the `addSlice(Color, float)` method to add a slice of the pie to the panel:

```java
public void addSlice(Color sColor, float sSize) {
    if (current <= slice.length) {
        slice[current] = new PieSlice(sColor, sSize);
        totalSize += sSize;
        current++;
    }
}
```

The `current` instance variable is used to put each slice into its own element of the `slice` array. The `length` variable of an array contains the number of elements the array has been defined to hold; as long as `current` is not larger than `slice.length`, you can continue adding slices to the panel.

The `PiePanel` class handles all graphical operations in its `paintComponent()` method, as you might expect. The trickiest thing about this task is drawing the arcs that represent each slice of the pie.

This is handled in the following statements:

```
float start = 0;
for (int i = 0; i < slice.length; i++) {
    float extent = slice[i].size * 360F / totalSize;
    comp2D.setColor(slice[i].color);
    Arc2D.Float drawSlice = new Arc2D.Float(
        xInset, yInset, width, height, start, extent,
        Arc2D.Float.PIE);
    start += extent;
    comp2D.fill(drawSlice);
}
```

The `start` variable keeps track of where to start drawing an arc, and `extent` keeps track of the size of an arc. If you know the total size of all pie slices and the size of a specific slice, you can figure out `extent` by multiplying the arc's size by 360 and dividing that by the total of all slices.

All the arcs are drawn in a `for` loop: After each arc's `extent` is calculated, the arc is created and then `extent` is added to `start`. This causes each slice to begin right next to the last one. A call to the `Graphics2D` method `fill()` draws the arc.

To bring all this together, create a new empty Java file named `PiePanel` and enter into it the full text from Listing 23.1.

LISTING 23.1   The Full Text of `PiePanel.java`

```
 1: import java.awt.*;
 2: import javax.swing.*;
 3: import java.awt.geom.*;
 4:
 5: public class PiePanel extends JPanel {
 6:     private PieSlice[] slice;
 7:     private int current = 0;
 8:     private float totalSize = 0;
 9:     private Color background;
10:
11:     public PiePanel(int sliceCount) {
12:         slice = new PieSlice[sliceCount];
```

LISTING 23.1   Continued

```
13:         background = getBackground();
14:     }
15:
16:     public void addSlice(Color sColor, float sSize) {
17:         if (current <= slice.length) {
18:             slice[current] = new PieSlice(sColor, sSize);
19:             totalSize += sSize;
20:             current++;
21:         }
22:     }
23:
24:     public void paintComponent(Graphics comp) {
25:         super.paintComponent(comp);
26:         Graphics2D comp2D = (Graphics2D) comp;
27:         int width = getSize().width - 10;
28:         int height = getSize().height - 15;
29:         int xInset = 5;
30:         int yInset = 5;
31:         if (width < 5) {
32:             xInset = width;
33:         }
34:         if (height < 5) {
35:             yInset = height;
36:         }
37:         comp2D.setColor(background);
38:         comp2D.fillRect(0, 0, getSize().width, getSize().height);
39:         comp2D.setColor(Color.lightGray);
40:         Ellipse2D.Float pie = new Ellipse2D.Float(
41:             xInset, yInset, width, height);
42:         comp2D.fill(pie);
43:         float start = 0;
44:         for (int i = 0; i < slice.length; i++) {
45:             float extent = slice[i].size * 360F / totalSize;
46:             comp2D.setColor(slice[i].color);
47:             Arc2D.Float drawSlice = new Arc2D.Float(
48:                 xInset, yInset, width, height, start, extent,
49:                 Arc2D.Float.PIE);
50:             start += extent;
51:             comp2D.fill(drawSlice);
52:         }
53:     }
54: }
55:
56: class PieSlice {
57:     Color color = Color.lightGray;
58:     float size = 0;
59:
60:     PieSlice(Color pColor, float pSize) {
61:         color = pColor;
62:         size = pSize;
63:     }
64: }
```

Listing 23.1 defines a `PiePanel` class in lines 1–54 and a `PieSlice` helper class in lines 56–64. The `PiePanel` class can be used as a component in any Java program's GUI. To test `PiePanel`, you need to create a class that uses it.

Listing 23.2 contains an application that uses these panels, `PieFrame`. Create a new empty Java file and enter the source code for this class from the listing.

LISTING 23.2   The Full Text of `PieFrame.java`

```
 1: import javax.swing.*;
 2: import javax.swing.event.*;
 3: import java.awt.*;
 4:
 5: public class PieFrame extends JFrame {
 6:     Color uneasyBeingGreen = new Color(0xCC, 0xCC, 0x99);
 7:     Color zuzusPetals = new Color(0xCC, 0x66, 0xFF);
 8:     Color zootSuit = new Color(0x66, 0x66, 0x99);
 9:     Color sweetHomeAvocado = new Color(0x66, 0x99, 0x66);
10:     Color shrinkingViolet = new Color(0x66, 0x66, 0x99);
11:     Color miamiNice = new Color(0x33, 0xFF, 0xFF);
12:     Color inBetweenGreen = new Color(0x00, 0x99, 0x66);
13:     Color norwegianBlue = new Color(0x33, 0xCC, 0xCC);
14:     Color purpleRain = new Color(0x66, 0x33, 0x99);
15:     Color freckle = new Color(0x99, 0x66, 0x33);
16:
17:     public PieFrame() {
18:         super("Pie Graph");
19:         setLookAndFeel();
20:         setSize(320, 290);
21:         setDefaultCloseOperation(JFrame.EXIT_ON_CLOSE);
22:         setVisible(true);
23:
24:         PiePanel pie = new PiePanel(10);
25:         pie.addSlice(uneasyBeingGreen, 1337);
26:         pie.addSlice(zuzusPetals, 1189);
27:         pie.addSlice(zootSuit, 311);
28:         pie.addSlice(sweetHomeAvocado, 246);
29:         pie.addSlice(shrinkingViolet, 203);
30:         pie.addSlice(miamiNice, 187);
31:         pie.addSlice(inBetweenGreen, 166);
32:         pie.addSlice(norwegianBlue, 159);
33:         pie.addSlice(purpleRain, 139);
34:         pie.addSlice(freckle, 127);
35:         add(pie);
36:     }
37:
38:     private void setLookAndFeel() {
39:         try {
40:             UIManager.setLookAndFeel(
41:                 "com.sun.java.swing.plaf.nimbus.NimbusLookAndFeel"
42:             );
```

LISTING 23.2   Continued

```
43:          } catch (Exception exc) {
44:              // ignore error
45:          }
46:      }
47:
48:      public static void main(String[] arguments) {
49:          PieFrame pf = new PieFrame();
50:      }
51: }
```

The `PieFrame` class is a simple graphical user interface that contains one component, a `PiePanel` object created in line 24. The object's `addSlice()` method is called 10 times in lines 25–35 to add slices to the pie graph.

When you run the application, `PieFrame` displays a pie graph showing the population of the 10 most populated countries (in millions), using figures from a July 2011 U.S. Census International Data Base report. In order, they are China (1.337 billion), India (1.189 billion), United States (311 million), Indonesia (246 million), Brazil (203 million), Pakistan (187 million), Nigeria (166 million), Bangladesh (159 million), Russia (139 million), and Japan (127 million).

Because Java only has a few colors defined in the `Color` class, 10 new ones are created for use here and given descriptive names. The colors are expressed as hexadecimal values—in Java, hexadecimal numbers are preceded by `0x`—but they also could have been specified as decimal values in each `Color()` constructor.

Figure 23.3 shows this application running.

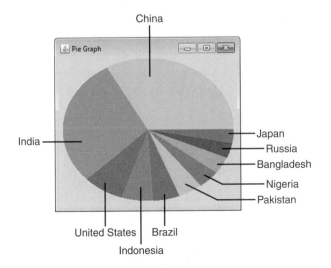

FIGURE 23.3
Displaying population figures in a pie graph.

NOTE

You can find the current U.S. Census world population figures by visiting www.cadenhead.org/census.

Summary

By using fonts, colors and graphics, you can draw more attention to elements of your programs and make them more compelling for users.

Drawing something using the shapes available with Java might seem like more trouble than it's worth. However, graphics depicted with polygons have two advantages over graphics that are loaded from image files:

▶ **Speed**—Even a small graphic, such as an icon, would take longer to load and display than a series of polygons.

▶ **Scaling**—You can change the size of an entire image that uses polygons simply by changing the values to create it. For example, you could add a function to the Sign class that multiplies all (x,y) points in each shape by two before they are created, and it would result in an image twice as large. Polygon images scale much more quickly than image files and produce better results.

Q&A

Q. How can I draw arcs that go clockwise rather than counterclockwise?

A. You can accomplish this by specifying the size of the arc as a negative number. The arc begins at the same point, but goes in the opposite direction in an elliptical path. For example, the following statement draws an open arc at (35,20) that is 90 degrees long, begins at the 0 degree mark, goes clockwise, and has a height of 20 and a width of 15:

```
Arc2D.Float smile = new Arc2D.Float(35F, 20F, 15F, 20F,
    0F, -90F, Arc2D.Float.OPEN);
```

Q. Ellipses and circles don't have corners. What are the (x,y) coordinates specified with the `Ellipses.Float` constructor method?

A. The (x,y) coordinates represent the smallest x value and smallest y value of the oval or circle. If you drew an invisible rectangle around it, the upper-left corner of the rectangle would be the x and y coordinates used as arguments to the method.

Q. How can I use XRender with Java?

A. Java 7 adds support for drawing Java2D graphics with the XRender rendering engine in X11-based environments, typically on Linux. This functionality is off by default and must be turned on using a command-line option: `Dsun.java2d.xrender=true`. XRender enables Java programs to employ the capabilities of modern graphics processing units (GPUs).

In NetBeans, you can set these options by choosing Run, Set Project Configuration, Customize. Use the VM Options field to set this option and click OK.

Q. Why do photographers ask you to say "cheese"?

A. The word cheese forces your mouth into a smile, as do the words "whiskey," "breeze," and "money." Words that end with a long "e" generally cause the sides of your lips to curl upward and your teeth to show.

Another word that photographers sometimes use is "grin." Though it doesn't end in an "e," it contorts the mouth and the meaning makes people smile.

Workshop

Test whether your font and color skills are MAH-ve-lous by answering the following questions.

Quiz

1. Which one of the following is *not* a constant used to select a color?

    A. `Color.cyan`

    B. `Color.teal`

    C. `Color.magenta`

2. When you change the color of something and redraw it on a container, what must you do to make it visible?

    A. Use the `drawColor()` method.

    B. Use the `repaint()` statement.

    C. Do nothing.

3. What do the initials RGB stand for?

    A. Roy G. Biv

    B. Red Green Blue

    C. Lucy in the Sky with Diamonds

Answers

1. **B.** The primary color of the Jacksonville Jaguars, teal, has gone unrepresented in `Color`.

2. **B.** The call to `repaint()` causes the `paintComponent()` method to be called manually.

3. **B.** If C. were the right answer, you could use colors that would only be visible years later during flashbacks.

Activities

To further explore the spectrum of possibilities when using fonts and color in your programs, do the following activities:

▶ Create a version of the `PieFrame` class that takes color values and pie slice values as command-line arguments instead of including them in the source code of the application.

▶ Create an application that draws a stop sign on a panel using colors, shapes, and fonts.

To see Java programs that implement these activities, visit the book's website at www.java24hours.com.

Writing Android Apps

Java's a general-purpose programming language that can run on a wide variety of platforms. One of those platforms has arisen in the past four years to become an enormously successful spark for new Java development.

The Android operating system, which started out on cell phones and has spread to a variety of other devices, exclusively runs programs written in Java.

These programs, called apps, are built on an open-source mobile platform that's completely free for developers to build on. Anyone can write, deploy, and sell Android apps.

During this hour, you learn about how Android came about, what makes it special, and why tens of thousands of programmers are developing on the platform. You also create an app and run it on an Android phone (if you own one) and an emulator (if you don't).

Introduction to Android

Android was launched by Google in 2007, two years after it acquired the technology, as part of industrywide effort to establish a new mobile phone platform that was nonproprietary and open, unlike the technology that drives RIM BlackBerry and Apple iPhone. Some of the biggest names in mobile phones and technology—Google, Intel, Motorola, Nvidia, Samsung, and other companies—formed the Open Handset Alliance to promote the new platform for mutual benefit.

Google released the Android Software Development Kit (SDK), a free set of tools for developing Android apps. The first phone running Android, the T-Mobile G1, came out in June 2008.

WHAT YOU'LL LEARN IN THIS HOUR:

▶ Why Android was created
▶ How to create an Android app
▶ How an Android app is structured
▶ How to run an app on an emulator
▶ How to run an app on an Android phone

This effort started slowly, but since early 2010 it has exploded and become a genuine rival to iPhone and other mobile platforms. All major phone carriers now offer Android phones. There's also a growing market for tablet and e-book readers.

Before Android, mobile application development required expensive programming tools and developer programs. The makers of the phone had control over who'd be allowed to create apps for them and whether the apps could be sold to users.

Android tears down that wall.

The open-source and non-proprietary nature of Android means that anyone can develop, release, and sell apps. The only cost involved is a nominal fee to submit apps to Google's marketplace. Everything else is free.

The place to download the Android SDK and find out more about creating programs for the platform is the Android Developer site at http://developer.android.com. You will consult it often as you write your own apps because it documents every class in Android's Java class library and serves as an extensive online reference.

Writing Android apps is easier if you're using an integrated development environment (IDE) that's equipped to support the Android SDK. The most popular IDE for Android programming is Eclipse, which also is free and open source. An Android Plug-in for Eclipse makes the SDK function seamlessly inside the IDE.

You can use Eclipse to write Android apps, test them in an emulator that acts like an Android phone and even deploy them on an actual device.

For most of its existence, the Java language has been used to write programs that run in one of three places: a desktop computer, a web server, or a web browser.

Android puts Java everywhere. Your programs can be deployed on millions of phones and other mobile devices.

This fulfills the original design goal of Java back when James Gosling invented the language while working at Sun Microsystems in the mid 1990s. Sun wanted a language that could run everywhere on devices such as phones, smart cards, and appliances.

Java's developers set aside those dreams when the language became popular first as a means of running interactive web programs and then as a general-purpose language.

Fifteen years later, the Android platform is hosting as many as a billion Java programs around the world, according to one industry estimate.

Android has the potential to be the most pervasive—and lucrative—area of Java programming for years to come.

It may also be the most fun.

Creating an Android App

Android apps are ordinary Java programs that use an application framework, a core set of classes and files that all apps have in common. The framework embodies a set of rules for how apps must be structured in order to run properly on Android devices.

To get started writing apps, you must install and configure the Android SDK, the Eclipse IDE, and the Android Plug-in for Eclipse.

If this is your first experience with Android programming, you can find out how to acquire and set up these tools in Appendix D, "Setting Up an Android Development Environment."

Go ahead and do that. I'll wait for you here and catch up with some friends on Facebook.

Done? Good.

The first project you undertake is to write a SalutonMondo app, a modest program that displays a single line of text on the screen of an Android device.

1. Run the Eclipse IDE, which looks and acts a lot like NetBeans.

2. Choose File, New, Android Project. The New Android Project Wizard opens, as shown in Figure 24.1.

3. In the Project Name field, enter `SalutonMondo`.

4. In the Contents section, click Create New Project in Workspace.

5. The Use Default Location checkbox determines where the project is stored. If you're happy with the default, keep this selected. Otherwise, deselect the checkbox, click the Browse button, and choose the folder where the project is stored.

6. Every Android project requires a build target. The target represents the oldest version of Android that can run your app. Because each new Android release has enhanced features, your target choice determines which features you can use.

> **CAUTION**
>
> This hour is the longest in the book because there's a lot to cover when getting your start as an Android app developer and future millionaire. It would have been split over two hours if my publisher had not vetoed the prospective title *Sams Teach Yourself Java in 25 Hours.*

FIGURE 24.1
Creating a new Android project in
Eclipse.

For a simple app like this one, an early target is OK. Choose
Android 2.2.

7. In the Application name field, give the app the name `Saluton
Mondo!`. This name will be displayed on Android devices.

8. The Package name field should contain the name of the Java package
to which the classes of this app belong. Enter
`org.cadenhead.android`.

9. The Create Activity checkbox indicates whether the new app will be
created with an Activity class. An activity is a task the app can
accomplish. Keep this checkbox selected and enter `SalutonActivity`
in the adjacent text field.

10. Click Finish. The new app is created and a SalutonMondo item
appears in the Package Explorer pane.

Exploring a New Android Project

A new Android project consists of around 20 files and folders that always
are organized the same way in an Android app. There might be more files

you add depending on the capabilities of the app, but these starting files and folders always must be present.

Figure 24.2 shows the Eclipse Package Explorer after a new Android project has been created.

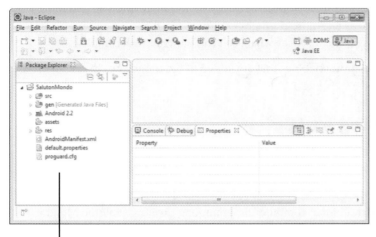

FIGURE 24.2
Viewing the parts of an Android project.

Package Explorer

You can use the folder to explore the file and folder structure of the project. The new SalutonMondo app starts out with the following components:

▶ /src folder—The root folder for the app's Java source code.

▶ /src/org.cadenhead.android/SalutonActivity.java—The class for the activity that launches by default when the app is run.

▶ /gen folder—The folder for generated Java source code you do not edit manually.

▶ /gen/org.cadenhead.android/R.java—The automatically generated resource management source code for the app. (Never edit this!)

▶ /assets—The folder for file resources that will not be compiled into the app.

▶ /res—The folder for application resources such as strings, numbers, layout files, graphics and animation. There are subfolders for specific resource types: layout, values, drawable-hdpi, drawable-ldpi, and drawable-mdpi. These folders contain five resource files: three versions of icon.png, main.xml and strings.xml.

▶ AndroidManifest.xml—The app's primary configuration file.

▶ `default.properties`—A build file generated by the Android Plug-in that you should not edit.

▶ `proguard.cfg`—A configuration file for ProGuard, a tool that optimizes an app and makes the source code harder for others to decompile.

These files and folders form the application framework. The first thing you undertake as an Android programmer is to learn how to modify the framework so you can discover what each component can accomplish.

There are additional files that are added to the framework to suit specific purposes.

Creating an App

Although you haven't done anything to it yet, you could successfully run the new Android project. The framework functions as a working app.

Because there's no fun in that, you customize the SalutonMondo app to offer the traditional computer programming greeting "Saluton Mondo!"

In Hour 2, "Writing Your First Program," you displayed the text "Saluton Mondo!" as a string by calling the method `System.out.println()`.

Android apps display strings that have been stored first in a resource file called `strings.xml`. You can find this file in the `/res/values` folder.

Use the Package Explorer to navigate to this folder. Double-click `strings.xml`. A Resources editor opens, as shown in Figure 24.3.

FIGURE 24.3
Editing an Android app's string resources.

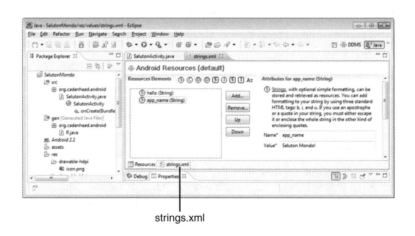

strings.xml

Strings and other resources are given a name and a value, just like a variable in Java. There are two string resources listed in the Resources elements pane: `hello` and `app_name`.

The names of resources follow three rules:

- ▶ They must be all lowercase.
- ▶ They must have no spaces.
- ▶ They must use only the underscore character ("_") as punctuation.

Click a string in the Resources elements pane. Name and Value text fields appear along with some guidance on how to edit strings (which also is shown in Figure 24.3).

The `app_name` string resource was something you chose when running the New Android Project Wizard. The name should match what you gave it earlier, but you can make changes at any time by editing this string.

The `hello` string contains text to display on the app's main (and only) screen when it is run. Click the name of this string to bring it up for editing.

In the Value field, enter `Saluton Mondo!`.

Resources are stored in XML files. The Resources editor is a simple XML editor. You also can directly edit the XML itself. Click the `strings.xml` tab at the bottom of the editor to load this file for direct editing. (Refer to Figure 24.3 where this tab is identified.)

Here's what `strings.xml` looks like at the moment:

Output ▼

```xml
<?xml version="1.0" encoding="utf-8"?>
<resources>
    <string name="hello">Saluton Mondo!</string>
    <string name="app_name">Saluton Mondo!</string>
</resources>
```

This editor allows everything in the XML file to be edited, even the markup tags. The `string` element contains a `name` attribute that identifies the name of the resource. The value is enclosed within the tag as character data.

To go back to the Resources editor, click the Resources tab. Click the Save button in the Eclipse toolbar to save your change to the file `strings.xml`.

With that modification, you're almost ready to run the app.

CAUTION

Although you can edit XML directly, don't. There's usually no need to do it when creating resources for an Android app. The exception is when the Eclipse editor doesn't support something you want to do in defining a resource. This isn't the case with strings, so it's better to stick to the Resources editor. You're more likely to make errors editing the XML files directly.

Setting Up an Android Emulator

Before you can build an Android app, you must set its debugging environment. This can be handled within Eclipse. You must set up an Android Virtual Device (AVD) that can run the app on your desktop as an emulator. You also must create the project's debug configuration. When you're done, you can build the app and run it in the emulator.

To configure an Android Virtual Device, first click the green Android icon with a down arrow in the Eclipse toolbar, which is shown in Figure 24.4.

FIGURE 24.4
Configuring an Android Virtual Device.

Android SDK and AVD Manager

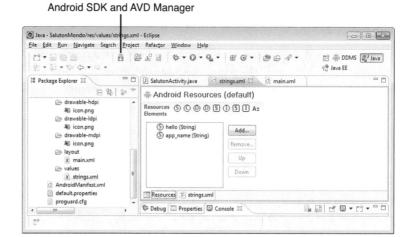

This launches the Android SDK and AVD Manager, one of the tools in the Android SDK. Click the Virtual Devices item in the left pane. The emulators that you've created are listed to the right. The manager is shown in Figure 24.5.

To add a new emulator, click New and follow these steps:

1. In the Name field, give it the name SimpleAVD.

2. In the Target field, you must choose a target version of Android from the drop-down menu. Choose Android 2.2 - API Level 8.

3. In the Size field, choose a size for the fake SD card. Enter 1024 and choose MiB from the associated drop-down for an SD card that's 1024MB in size. You must have this much available space on your computer, so choose smaller if you'd prefer not to take up that much space. The minimum size is 9MB.

FIGURE 24.5
Creating a new Android emulator.

4. Click Create AVD. The new emulator is created, which might take a little while (no longer than a minute, generally).

You can create as many emulators as you need. They can be customized for different versions of Android and different kinds of displays.

Close the Android SDK and AVD Manager to return to the main Eclipse interface.

Creating a Debug Configuration

The last thing required before you can launch the SalutonMondo app is to create a debug configuration in Eclipse. Follow these steps:

1. Choose Run, Debug Configurations. The Debug Configurations window opens.

2. In the left pane, double-click the Android Application item (shown in Figure 24.6). A new entry called New_configuration is created as its subitem. The right pane displays some configuration options for the new item.

FIGURE 24.6
Creating an Android debug
configuration.

Android Application item

3. In the right pane, in the Name field, change it to SalutonDebug.

4. Click the Browse button. The Project Selection dialog opens.

5. Choose the project SalutonMondo and click OK.

6. Click the Target tab.

7. Under Deployment Target Selection Mode, choose Automatic (if it isn't already chosen). A table enables you to select a target AVD.

8. In the table, select the checkbox for the SimpleAVD emulator.

9. Click Apply to save your changes and then click Close.

Running the App

Now that you have an Android emulator and a debug configuration, you can run your first app. Click SalutonMondo, the top item in the Package Explorer, and then click the bug icon in the Eclipse toolbar.

The Android emulator loads in its own window. This can take a minute or more, so wait patiently as the fake phone boots up. (The emulator is so slow to load it gives you time to ponder this Chinese proverb: "The oxen are slow but the earth is patient.")

The emulator displays "Saluton Mondo!" as the text and title bar of the app, as shown in Figure 24.7. Controls enable the emulator to be used like a phone, but with a mouse instead of your finger. Click the back button to close the app and see how the Android device is emulated.

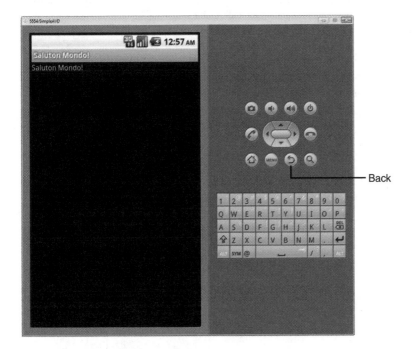

Back

FIGURE 24.7
Running an app in the Android emulator.

An emulator can do many of the things a real device can do, including connect to the Internet if the computer has an active connection. It also can receive fake phone calls and SMS messages.

Because it's not a fully functional device, the apps that you develop must be tested on actual Android phones and tablets.

If you can connect an Android phone (or other device) to your computer using a USB cord, you should be able to run the app if the phone is set in debugging mode. Apps developed with the Android SDK can be deployed only on a phone in this mode.

On the phone, enter this mode by choosing Home, Settings, Applications, Development. The Development settings are displayed. Choose the USB debugging option.

Next, in Eclipse, follow these steps:

1. Choose Run, Debug Configurations. The Debug Configurations window opens.

2. Click the Target tab in the right pane to bring it to the front.

3. Change Deployment Target Selection Mode from Automatic to Manual.

4. Click Apply and Close.

Connect your Android phone with the USB cord. An Android bug icon should appear on the bar at the top of the screen. If you drag this bar down, you should see the message "USB Debugging Connected."

Back in Eclipse, click the bug icon in the toolbar. The Android Device Chooser dialog opens (see Figure 24.8).

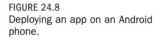

FIGURE 24.8
Deploying an app on an Android phone.

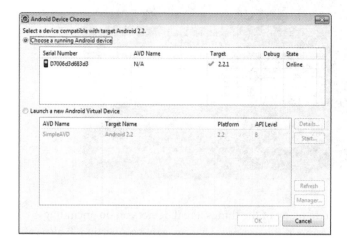

If the Android phone has been detected, it appears in the top table in Figure 24.5 under the Choose a Running Device option.

Select this option, click the device, and click OK. The app runs on the phone as it did on the emulator.

Like the first program you wrote in Java back in Hour 2, the first app you created on Android is exceptionally unexceptional. The next project is more ambitious.

Designing a Real App

Android apps can exploit all the device's functionality, such as SMS messaging, location-based services, and touch input. In this book's final programming project, you create a real app called Take Me To Your Leader.

This app takes advantage of an Android phone's capabilities to make a phone call, visit a website, and load a location in Google Maps. The app puts you in touch with the White House via phone, Web, and maps. (If the president of the United States is not your leader, the app can be customized.)

To get started, you create a new project in Eclipse by performing these steps:

1. Click File, New, Android Project. The New Android Project Wizard opens.

2. In the Project Name field, enter **Leader**.

3. Make sure Create New Project in Workspace is selected.

4. Choose the Build Target Android 2.2.

5. In the Application Name field, enter **Take Me To Your Leader**.

6. In the Package Name field, enter **org.cadenhead.android**.

7. Make sure Create Activity is selected, and enter **LeaderActivity** in the adjacent text field. The wizard should resemble Figure 24.9.

8. Click Finish.

FIGURE 24.9
Creating a new Android project.

TIP

This project covers a lot of ground. As you work through it, you'll find it handy to keep a browser open to the Android Developer site's reference section at http://developer. android.com/reference. You can search for the Java classes in the Android class library and the filenames of the files in the project to learn more.

The project appears in the Eclipse Package Explorer, as does the SalutonMondo project. To avoid confusion, you should close SalutonMondo before proceeding. Right-click SalutonMondo in the Package Explorer, and then choose Close Project from the pop-up menu.

Organizing Resources

Creating an Android app requires Java programming, but a lot of the work is done in the Eclipse interface. When you are fully versed in the capabilities of the Android SDK, you can accomplish a great deal without writing a single line of Java code.

One thing you do without programming is create resources that will be used by the app. Every new Android project starts out with several folders where resources are placed. To see these folders, expand the Leader folder in the Package Explorer, and then expand the /res folder and all of its subfolders (as shown in Figure 24.10).

FIGURE 24.10
Examining an app's resource folders.

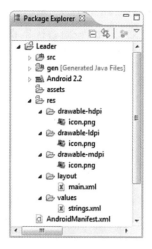

Resources consist of graphics in the PNG, JPG, or GIF format, strings stored in a file called strings.xml, user interface layout files in XML format, and other files you can create. Two you add often to projects are colors.xml for colors used in the app and dimens.xml for dimensional measurements that set text size and other things that are displayed.

The /res folder of a new project contains folders called drawable-hdpi, drawable-mdpi, and drawable-lpdi that have three different versions of icon.png, the app's icon. The icon is the small graphic used to launch the app.

The three versions of icon.png are the same graphic sized for high-resolution, medium-resolution, and low-resolution displays. You won't be using these icons, so it's OK to delete them: Click one of the icon.png files in Package Explorer, and then press the Delete key. You'll be asked to confirm each deletion.

Deleting these files causes two red X's to appear in Package Explorer: One over AndroidManifest.xml and another over the top-level Leader item (which are identified in Figure 24.11). These X's indicate that the app now has errors that will prevent it from being compiled and run.

The errors cropped up because the app now lacks an icon. A new graphics file, appicon.png, will be added to the project and designated as its icon in the file AndroidManifest.xml, the app's main configuration file.

This book's website contains appicon.png and four other graphics files needed by this app: browser.png, maps.png, phone.png, and whitehouse.png. Visit www.java24hours.com and go to the Hour 24 page for this edition of the book. Download all five files and save them in a temporary folder on your computer.

Android's support for multiple resolutions is handy, but it's not necessary here. Instead of using the existing drawable folders, a new one will be created by following these steps:

1. Click the /res folder in Package Explorer to select it.

2. Choose File, New, Folder. The New Folder dialog opens.

3. Enter **drawable** in the Folder Name field.

4. Click Finish.

A new folder will be created inside /res called drawable. All the graphics needed by the app can be stored here without consideration of their resolution.

FIGURE 24.11
Detecting and fixing errors in the app.

Resources are identified in an app using an ID formed from their filename with the extension removed. `appicon.png` has the ID `appicon`, `browser.png` has the ID `browser`, and so on. No two resources can have the same ID (with the exception of the same graphic being stored at different resolutions in the three `drawable-*dpi` folders, because they count as a single resource).

If two resources have the same name without the extension, such as `appicon.png` and `appicon.gif`, Eclipse will flag the error and the app won't compile.

Resources also must have names that contain only lowercase letters, numbers, underscores (_), and periods (.). The files in this project follow these rules.

Files can be added to resources using drag and drop. Open the temporary folder containing the five files, select them, and drag them to the `drawable` folder in Package Explorer.

Now that the project has a new icon, you can set it as the app's icon and get rid of the errors noted in Package Explorer. This will be handled by editing `AndroidManifest.xml`.

Configuring the App's Manifest File

The primary configuration tool in an Android app is a file called `AndroidManifest.xml` in the main app folder. All XML files utilized by an app can be edited manually or by using the built-in editor in Eclipse. The latter is easier and less error prone. Unless you're extremely comfortable editing XML, you should stick to the editor until you've gained more experience as an Android programmer.

To choose the proper icon for the app, do the following:

1. Double-click `AndroidManifest.xml` in Package Explorer. The file opens for editing in the main Eclipse window using the built-in editor.

2. Several tabs run along the bottom edge of the editor. Click the Application tab to see settings related to the app (see Figure 24.12).

FIGURE 24.12
Editing the app's
`AndroidManifest.xml` file.

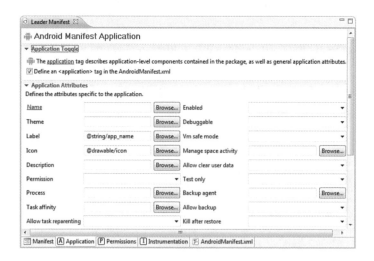

3. The Icon field identifies the app's icon, which currently has the incorrect value @drawable/icon. Click the Browse button next to this field. A Resource Chooser dialog appears listing the five "drawable" resources contained in the app.

4. Choose appicon and click OK. The Icon field now has the correct value.

5. Save the file: Click the Save button in the main Eclipse toolbar or choose File, Save.

The red X's disappear from the Package Explorer, indicating that the app now has a properly designated icon.

Designing a User Interface

An app's graphical user interface consists of layouts, which are containers that hold widgets such as text fields, buttons, graphics, and custom widgets of your own design. Each screen displayed to a user can have one layout or multiple layouts within each other. There are layouts to stack components vertically or horizontally, organize them in a table, and other arrangements.

An app can be as simple as a single screen or contain multiple screens. A game could be organized into these screens:

▶ A splash screen that displays as the game is loading

▶ A main menu screen with buttons to view the other screens

▶ A help screen explaining how to play

▶ A scores screen that lists the highest player scores

▶ A credits screen naming the game's developers

▶ A game screen for actual play

The Leader app consists of a single screen, which holds buttons for contacting the president of the United States or a leader to be named later.

All of an app's screens are kept in the /res/layout folder. A new project has a main.xml file in this folder that's already designated as the screen to display when the app loads.

To begin editing this screen's layout, double-click main.xml in Package Explorer. The screen opens in the main Eclipse window, as shown in Figure 24.13.

FIGURE 24.13
Editing the app's
AndroidManifest.xml file.

The editing window includes a Palette pane with several folders that can be expanded. The Form Widgets subpane, which is likely to be expanded, displays some simple widgets that can be dragged and dropped onto the screen at right.

Follow these steps to add three graphical buttons to the screen:

1. Delete the textview widget that displays the "Hello World" text. Click this widget on the screen and press Delete.

2. Double-click the Images & Media folder in the Palette pane. The subpane expands.

3. Drag an ImageButton widget from the Palette to the screen. A narrow blue box appears on the screen and an error message appears below the screen. The error is flagged because the button lacks an image— don't worry about it.

4. Drag two more ImageButton widgets to the screen. They will be stacked vertically.

5. An Outline pane lists the widgets on the screen. Select the imageButton1 item. The properties of the button open in the Properties pane (see Figure 24.14).

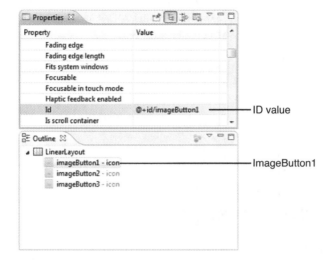

ID value

ImageButton1

FIGURE 24.14
Customizing a widget's properties.

6. Scroll down the Properties pane until you see an ID property. Its value currently is set to @+id/imageButton1. Change this to @+id/phonebutton.

7. Scroll down to the Src property, which currently equals drawable/icon. Click this value. An ellipse (...) button appears.

8. Click the ... button. A Reference Chooser dialog opens.

9. Expand the Drawable heading to see a list of the app's graphics, which are the resources you added earlier. Choose phone and click OK. The button now has a graphic of a phone.

10. In the On Click property, enter the value processClicks. (This is explained in the next section.)

11. Repeat steps 5–10 for imageButton2, giving it the ID @+id/webbutton and the Src drawable/browser.

12. Repeat steps 5–10 for imageButton3, giving it the ID @+id/mapbutton and the Src drawable/maps.

13. Click the Set Horizontal Orientation button above the screen (refer to Figure 24.13). The buttons now are lined up side by side.

14. Click the LinearLayout item in the Outline. The properties for the screen appear in the Properties pane.

15. Click the value for Background, and then click the ... button. The Reference Chooser opens.

16. Expand Drawable, choose `whitehouse`, and click OK. A graphic of the White House becomes the screen's background.

17. Click the Save button.

The finished screen appears in Figure 24.15.

Writing Java Code

At this point you've done the bulk of the work on the new app, but you haven't written a single line of Java code. App development is easier when you utilize as many capabilities of the Android SDK as possible without resorting to programming.

Apps are organized into Activities, which represent things an app can do. Each Activity is defined by its own Java class. When you created this app, you specified that an Activity named `LeaderActivity` should be created. A class matching this name runs automatically when the app is loaded.

The source code for `LeaderActivity.java` can be found in Package Explorer in the `/src/org.cadenhead.android` folder. Double-click this file to edit it.

When you start, the class has the code in Listing 24.1.

LISTING 24.1   The Starting Text of `LeaderActivity.java`

```
 1: package org.cadenhead.android;
 2:
 3: import android.app.Activity;
 4: import android.os.Bundle;
 5:
 6: public class LeaderActivity extends Activity {
 7:     /** Called when the activity is first created. */
 8:     @Override
 9:     public void onCreate(Bundle savedInstanceState) {
10:         super.onCreate(savedInstanceState);
11:         setContentView(R.layout.main);
12:     }
13: }
```

Like all Activities, the `LeaderActivity` class is a subclass of `Activity` in the `android.app` package, which contains the behavior necessary to display a screen, collect user input, save user preferences, and so on.

The `onCreate()` method defined in lines 9–12 is called when the class is loaded. The first thing the method does is use `super()` to call the same method in its superclass. Next, it calls `setContentView()`, a method that selects the screen that will be displayed. The argument to this method is an instance variable, `R.layout.main`, that refers to the file `main.xml` in `/res/layout`. As you may recall, the ID of a resource is its filename without the extension.

The first thing you must do in the `LeaderActivity` class is give it a class variable. Add the following statement right below the class definition:

```
public static final String TAG = "Leader";
```

This variable serves as an identifier for the class, which you use to log events that occur as it runs. Android classes can log their activities to let you know what's happening in the app. Here's one of the log statements you will add later:

```
Log.i(TAG, "Making call");
```

This statement displays a log message tagged with the name "Leader."

The `Log` class in the `android.util` package displays messages in the log. This class has five different methods to log messages, each of which indicates what type of message it is, such as a warning, debugging message, or error. The `i()` method is for info messages—information that explains what's going on in the app.

NOTE

You can open the `R.java` file for editing in the `/res/gen/ org.cadenhead.android` folder to learn more about why the main resource is referred to as `R.layout.main`. The R class is generated automatically by the Android SDK to enable resources to be referenced by their IDs. You never should edit this class yourself.

The first argument to Log.i() identifies the app and the second contains the message.

When you designed the app's user interface earlier, you set the On Click property of each button to processClicks. This indicated that a method called processClicks() would be called when a user clicked a widget on the screen. Now it's time to implement that method. Add these statements to LeaderActivity below the onCreate() method:

```
public void processClicks(View display) {
    Intent action;
    int id = display.getId();
}
```

This method is called with one argument, a View object from the android.view package. A View is a visual display of some kind in an app. In this case, it's the screen containing the Dialer, Browser, and Maps buttons.

The View object's getId() method returns the ID of the button that was clicked: phonebutton, webbutton, or mapbutton.

This ID is stored in the id variable so it can be used in a switch statement to take action based on the click:

```
switch (id) {
    case (R.id.phonebutton):
        // ...
        break;
    case (R.id.webbutton):
        // ...
        break;
    case (R.id.mapbutton):
        // ...
        break;
    default:
        break;
}
```

This code will take one of three actions, using the integer of each ID as the conditional in the switch. The first statement in the processClicks() method creates a variable to hold an Intent object, a class in Android's android.content package:

```
Intent action;
```

Intents in Android are how Activities tell another Activity what to do. They're also the way an app communicates with the Android device.

Here are the three Intents employed in this method:

```
action = new Intent(Intent.ACTION_DIAL, Uri.parse("tel:202-456-1111"));

action = new Intent(Intent.ACTION_VIEW,
➥ Uri.parse("http://whitehouse.gov"));

action = new Intent(Intent.ACTION_VIEW, Uri.parse("geo:0,0?q=White House,
➥ Washington, DC"));
```

The Intent() constructor takes two arguments:

▸ The action to take, represented by one of its class variables

▸ The data associated with the action

These three Intents tell the Android device to set up an outgoing phone call to the White House public phone line at (202) 456-1111, visit the website http://whitehouse.gov, and load Google Maps with the partial address "White House, Washington, DC," respectively.

After you have created an Intent, the following statement makes it do something:

```
startActivity(action);
```

The full text of the LeaderActivity class is in Listing 24.2. Add the import statements in lines 3–8 and the processClicks() method to what you already have entered. Make sure your code matches the entire listing.

LISTING 24.2   The Full Text of LeaderActivity.java

```
 1: package org.cadenhead.android;
 2:
 3: import android.app.Activity;
 4: import android.content.Intent;
 5: import android.net.Uri;
 6: import android.os.Bundle;
 7: import android.util.Log;
 8: import android.view.View;
 9:
10: public class LeaderActivity extends Activity {
11:     public static final String TAG = "Leader";
12:
13:     /** Called when the activity is first created. */
14:     @Override
15:     public void onCreate(Bundle savedInstanceState) {
16:         super.onCreate(savedInstanceState);
17:         setContentView(R.layout.main);
18:     }
19:
```

LISTING 24.2   Continued

```
20:    public void processClicks(View display) {
21:        Intent action;
22:        int id = display.getId();
23:        switch (id) {
24:            case (R.id.phonebutton):
25:                Log.i(TAG, "Making call");
26:                action = new Intent(Intent.ACTION_DIAL,
27:                    Uri.parse("tel:202-456-1111"));
28:                startActivity(action);
29:                break;
30:            case (R.id.webbutton):
31:                Log.i(TAG, "Loading browser");
32:                action = new Intent(Intent.ACTION_VIEW,
33:                    Uri.parse("http://whitehouse.gov"));
34:                startActivity(action);
35:                break;
36:            case (R.id.mapbutton):
37:                Log.i(TAG, "Loading map");
38:                action = new Intent(Intent.ACTION_VIEW,
39:                    Uri.parse("geo:0,0?q=White House, Washington, DC"));
40:                startActivity(action);
41:                break;
42:            default:
43:                break;
44:        }
45:    }
46: }
```

Save the file when you're done. It should compile successfully (something Eclipse does automatically)—if not, the familiar red X's appear in the Package Explorer, identifying the files in the project where the errors were found.

When there are no errors, you're almost ready to run the app.

You must create a new debug configuration for the project first:

1. Click the arrow next to the Debug button in the main Eclipse toolbar, then choose Debug Configurations. The Debug Configurations dialog opens.

2. Double-click Android Application in the left pane. A new configuration called New_configuration (1) is created.

3. Enter **LeaderDebug** as the Name.

4. Click the Browse button, choose the project Leader, and click OK.

5. Click the Target tab to bring it to the front.

6. With Automatic selected as the Deployment Target Selection Mode, select the SimpleAVD Android virtual device.

7. Change Deployment Target Selection Mode to Manual, click Apply, and then click Close.

A new debug configuration called LeaderDebug is created.

To run the app, click the arrow next to the Debug button and choose LeaderDebug (if it is present). If not, choose Debug Configurations, choose LeaderDebug, and click Debug. The Android Device Chooser opens. Select Launch a New Android Virtual Device, select SimpleAVD, and click OK.

The emulator loads over the next few minutes, then automatically runs the app.

An emulator does not emulate everything an Android device can do. The Leader app's Dialer and Browser buttons should work properly, but you might encounter problems with Maps.

The app also can be run on an Android phone, if you have one working with the Android SDK and the phone has been set to debugging mode. Click the arrow next to Debug and choose LeaderDebug, which definitely should be present this time. Select Choose a Running Android Device, select your phone in the list, and then click OK.

Figure 24.16 shows the app running on my phone. When the phone is shifted from portrait mode to landscape mode, the app shifts accordingly. (The figure also shows that I have 141 new voicemail messages. I probably should check those.)

FIGURE 24.16
Take me to your leader!

The Leader app also has been added to the phone's applications with its own "Take Me to Your Leader" icon. It will stay on the phone even after you disconnect the USB cable.

Congratulations! The world now has one billion and one Android apps.

Summary

The goal of *Sams Teach Yourself Java in 24 Hours* has been to help you become comfortable with the concepts of programming and confident in your ability to write your own applications, whether they run on a desktop computer, web page, web server, or even a phone. Java has an approach that is somewhat difficult to master. (Feel free to scratch out the word "somewhat" in the previous sentence if it's a gross misstatement of the truth.)

As you build experience in Java, you're building experience that grows increasingly relevant, because concepts such as object-oriented programming, virtual machines, and secure environments are on the leading edge of software development.

If you haven't already, you should check out the appendixes for additional useful information.

At the conclusion of this hour, you can explore Java in several different places. Programmers are discussing the language on the weblogs at http://weblogs.java.net. Numerous Java job openings are displayed in the database of employment websites such as http://www.careerbuilder.com. There's also a website for this book at http://www.java24hours.com where you can send email to the author and read answers to reader questions, clarifications to the book, and (gulp) corrections.

One way to continue building your skills as a Java programmer is to read *Sams Teach Yourself Java in 21 Days*. I wrote that book also, and it expands on the subjects covered here and introduces new ones, such as JDBC, Java servlets, and network programming.

There's also more coverage of Android.

If you didn't skip ahead and have just completed all 24 hours, kudos. Please use your newfound programming skills to get a good job and rebuild the world economy.

Q&A

Q. Why is Eclipse used to create Android apps instead of NetBeans?

A. You can use NetBeans to develop apps, but it's a more cumbersome and less well-supported IDE for Android programming. Eclipse has been designated by Google as the preferred Android IDE. The official documentation and tutorials on the Android Developer site at http://developer.android.com all use Eclipse.

Most programming books for Android also employ Eclipse. Although there's a learning curve required to switch from NetBeans to Eclipse when you dive into Android, after you master the basics of writing, debugging, and deploying an app, you should find Eclipse easier to use because it's so much better supported by programmers and technical writers.

Q. How does ProGuard make it harder for an app's source code to be decompiled?

A. Java class files are susceptible to being reverse engineered, which is the process of taking executable code and figuring out the source code that was used to create it. Because the designers of Android apps might not want other developers to copy their source code in their own apps, ProGuard is available in every Android project you create.

ProGuard optimizes an app by removing unused code from its class files when they're compiled. ProGuard also obfuscates code by changing the names of classes, fields, and methods to something meaningless and obscure. That way, even if someone decompiles the Java code, the source code is a lot harder to figure out.

The obfuscation feature only is applied when an app is built in release mode. Doing it earlier than that would make debugging much more difficult.

Q. Why do so many movies have the same exact sound of a man screaming in anguish?

A. That sound's the Wilhelm scream, a sound effect that was heard first in the 1951 movie *Distant Drums*. It turns up most often when somebody falls from a great height, is shot by a gun, or knocked back by an explosion. Two famous uses are in the original *Star Wars*, when a stormtrooper is shot by Luke Skywalker and falls off a ledge, and in the animated movie *Toy Story* when Sheriff Woody knocks Buzz Lightyear out the window.

The sound was popularized by movie sound designer Ben Burtt, who found it in a Warner Brothers stock library when developing sound for *Star Wars* and included it in every Steven Spielberg and George Lucas movie he worked on. It has since become a tradition among sound designers and can be heard in more than 140 movies.

The voice actor who screamed is believed to be Sheb Wooley, an actor and singer who recorded the 1958 novelty song "Purple People Eater."

The name Wilhelm comes from the third movie to use the sound effect. In the 1953 film *The Charge at Feather River*, Private Wilhelm yells in anguish as he's shot by an Indian's arrow.

Workshop

If you would like to dial up the knowledge you've just acquired in Android development, answer the following questions.

Quiz

1. Which of the following companies was not part of the Open Handset Initiative, the group that championed Android?

    A. Google

    B. Apple

    C. Motorola

2. What tool makes it harder for developers to snoop on a Java program's source code?

    A. A decompiler

    B. A recompiler

    C. An obfuscator

3. Which of the following tasks can an Android emulator not perform?

    A. Receiving an SMS message

    B. Connecting to the Internet

    C. Making a phone call

Answers

1. **B.** Apple, because Android was created in part as an open source, non-proprietary alternative to the Apple iPhone.

2. **C.** Trips off the tongue, doesn't it? Say obfuscator five times fast.

3. **C.** Emulators can't do everything an actual device can do, so they're only part of the testing process for apps.

Activities

To make your Android knowledge go for longer distance, undertake the following activities:

▶ Change the text of the SalutonMondo app to "Hello, Android" and run the app in the emulator and on an Android device (if one is available to you).

▶ Create a new version of Take Me To Your Leader for a different world leader, customizing the phone, Web, and map destinations.

To see Java programs that implement these activities, visit the book's website at www.java24hours.com.

Using the NetBeans Integrated Development Environment

Although it's possible to create Java programs with nothing more than the Java Development Kit and a text editor, the experience is considerably less masochistic when you use an integrated development environment (IDE).

The first 23 hours of this book employ NetBeans, a free IDE offered by Oracle for Java programmers. NetBeans is a program that makes it easier to organize, write, compile, and test Java software. It includes a project and file manager, graphical user interface designer, and many other tools. One killer feature is a code editor that automatically detects Java syntax errors as you type.

Now in version 7.0, NetBeans has become a favorite of professional Java developers, offering functionality and performance that would be worth the money at 10 times the price. It's also one of the easiest IDEs for Java novices to use.

In this appendix, you learn enough about NetBeans to install the software and put it to use in all of the projects in this book.

Installing NetBeans

From inauspicious beginnings, the NetBeans IDE has grown to become one of the leading programming tools for Java developers. James Gosling, the creator of the Java language, gave it the ultimate vote of confidence in his Foreword to the book *NetBeans Field Guide*: "I use NetBeans for all my Java development." I've become a convert as well.

NetBeans supports all facets of Java programming for the three editions of the language—Java Standard Edition (JSE), Java Enterprise Edition (JEE), and Java Mobile Edition (JME). It also supports web application development, web services, and JavaBeans.

You can download the software, available for Windows, MacOS, and Linux, from www.netbeans.org. NetBeans is available for download bundled with the Java Development Kit, which is the option to choose if you don't already have the kit on your computer.

If you'd like to ensure that you're downloading the same version of NetBeans used in the preparation of this book, visit the book's website at www.java24hours.com. Click the cover of this book to open the site for this edition, and then look for the Download JDK and Download NetBeans 7.0 links. You'll be steered to the proper file.

Creating a New Project

The JDK and NetBeans are downloaded as installation wizards that set up the software on your system. You can install the software in any folder and menu group you like, but it's best to stick with the default setup options unless you have a good reason to do otherwise.

When you run NetBeans for the first time after installation, you see a start page that displays links to news and programming tutorials (see Figure A.1). You can read these within the IDE using NetBeans' built-in web browser.

FIGURE A.1
The NetBeans user interface.

New Project

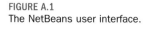

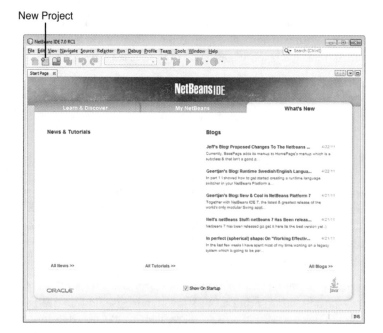

A NetBeans project consists of a set of related Java classes, files used by those classes, and Java class libraries. Each project has its own folder, which you can explore and modify outside of NetBeans using text editors and other programming tools.

To begin a new project, click the New Project button shown in Figure A.1 or choose the File, New Project menu command. The New Project Wizard opens, as shown in Figure A.2.

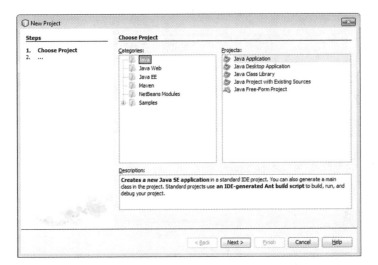

FIGURE A.2
The New Project Wizard.

NetBeans can create several different types of Java projects, but during this book you can focus on just one: Java Application.

For your first project (and most of the projects in this book), choose the project type Java Application and click Next. The wizard asks you to choose a name and location for the project.

The Project Location text field identifies the root folder of the programming projects you create with NetBeans. On Windows, this is a subfolder of My Documents called NetBeansProjects. All projects you create are stored inside this folder, each in its own subfolder.

In the Project Name text field, enter **Java24**. The Create Main Class text box changes in response to the input, recommending java24.Java24 as the name of the main Java class in the project. Change this to **Spartacus** and click Finish, accepting all other defaults. NetBeans creates the project and its first class.

Creating a New Java Class

When NetBeans creates a new project, it sets up all the necessary files and folders and creates the main class. Figure A.3 shows the first class in your project, Spartacus.java, open in the source editor.

FIGURE A.3
The NetBeans source editor.

Save All Files

Project Pane —————

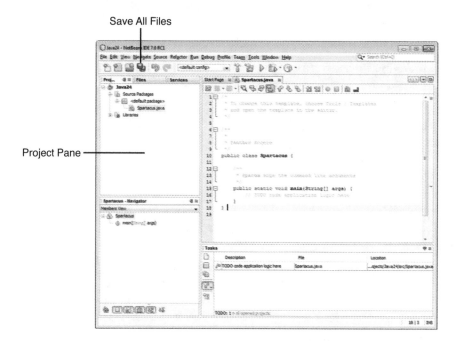

Spartacus.java is a bare-bones Java class that consists only of a main() method. All the light gray lines in the class are comments that exist to explain the purpose and function of the class. Comments are ignored when the class is run.

To make the new class do something, add the following line of code on a new line right below the comment // TODO code application logic here:

System.out.println("I am Spartacus!");

The method System.out.println() displays a string of text, in this case the sentence "I am Spartacus!"

Make sure to enter this exactly as it appears. As you type, the source editor figures out what you're doing and pops up helpful information related to the System class, the out instance variable, and the println() method. You'll love this stuff later, but for now try your best to ignore it.

After you make sure you typed the line correctly and ended it with a semi-colon, click the Save All Files toolbar button to save the class.

Java classes must be compiled into executable bytecode before you can run them. NetBeans tries to compile classes automatically. You also can manu-ally compile this class in two ways:

▶ Choose the menu command Run, Compile File.

▶ Right-click `Spartacus.java` in the Project pane to open a pop-up menu, and choose Compile File.

If NetBeans doesn't allow you to choose either of these options, that means it already has compiled the class automatically.

If the class does not compile successfully, a red exclamation point appears next to the filename `Spartacus.java` in the Project pane. To fix the error, compare what you've typed in the text editor to the full source code of `Spartacus.java` in Listing A.1 and save the file again.

LISTING A.1   The Java Class `Spartacus.java`

```
 1: /*
 2:  * To change this template, choose Tools ¦ Templates
 3:  * and open the template in the editor.
 4:  */
 5:
 6: /**
 7:  *
 8:  * @author User
 9:  */
10: public class Spartacus {
11:
12:     /**
13:      * @param args the command line arguments
14:      */
15:     public static void main(String[] args) {
16:         // TODO code application logic here
17:         System.out.println("I am Spartacus!");
18:
19:     }
20:
21: }
```

The class is defined in lines 10–21. Lines 1–9 are comments included by NetBeans in every new class

Running the Application

After you've created the Java class `Spartacus.java` and compiled it successfully, you can run it within NetBeans in two ways:

▶ Choose Run, Run File from the menu.

▶ Right-click `Spartacus.java` in the Projects pane, and choose Run File.

When you run a Java class, its `main()` method is called by the compiler. The string "I am Spartacus!" appears in the Output pane, as shown in Figure A.4.

FIGURE A.4
Output of the Spartacus application.

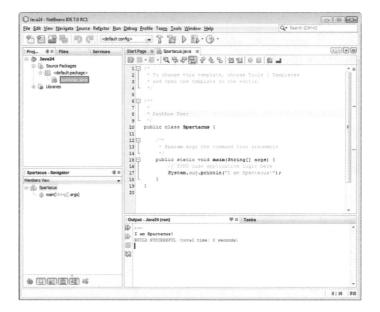

A Java class must have a `main()` method to be run. If you attempt to run a class that lacks one, NetBeans responds with an error.

Fixing Errors

Now that the Spartacus application has been written, compiled, and run, it's time to break something to get some experience with how NetBeans responds when things go terribly wrong.

Like any programmer, you'll have plenty of practice screwing things up on your own, but pay attention here anyway.

Return to Spartacus.java in the source editor, and take the semicolon off the end of the line that calls System.out.println() (line 17 in Listing A.1). Even before you save the file, NetBeans spots the error and displays a red alert icon to the left of the line (see Figure A.5).

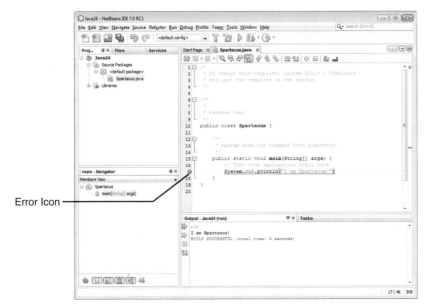

Error Icon

FIGURE A.5
Flagging errors in the source editor.

Hover over the alert icon to see a dialog appear that describes the error NetBeans thinks it has spotted.

The NetBeans source editor can identify most of the common programming errors and typos that it encounters as you write a Java program. It stops the file from being compiled until the errors have been removed.

Put the semicolon back at the end of the line. The error icon disappears, and you can save and run the class again.

These basic features are all you need to create and compile the Java programs in this book.

NetBeans is capable of a lot more than the features described here, but you should focus on learning Java before diving too deeply into the IDE. Use NetBeans as if it were just a simple project manager and text editor. Write classes, flag errors, and make sure you can compile and run each project successfully.

When you're ready to learn more about NetBeans, Oracle offers training and documentation resources at www.netbeans.org/kb.

Where to Go from Here: Java Resources

After you have finished this book, you might be wondering where you can turn to improve your Java programming skills. This appendix lists some books, websites, Internet discussion groups, and other resources you can use to expand your Java knowledge.

Other Books to Consider

Sams Publishing and other publishers offer several useful books on Java programming, including some that follow up on the material covered in this book. Use these ISBN numbers at bookstores if they don't currently carry the book that you're looking for:

▶ *Sams Teach Yourself Java in 21 Days*, by Rogers Cadenhead (me! me! me!), ISBN: 0-672-33574-3. Though some of the material in the first half of this book is redundant, it covers Java in more depth and adds a lot of advanced topics. If you're ready to make another 504-hour commitment to learning Java, this should be a suitable book.

▶ *The Java EE 6 Tutorial: Basic Concepts*, Fourth Edition, by Eric Jendrock and others, ISBN 0-13708-185-5. This book introduces the Java Enterprise Edition (JEE), an extended form of the Java class library for use in large businesses in large-scale computing environments.

▶ *Java Phrasebook*, by Timothy R. Fisher. ISBN 0-67232-907-7. A collection of more than 100 snippets of code for use in your own Java projects, created by a professional programmer and Java Developer's Journal contributor.

▶ *Agile Java Development with Spring, Hibernate and Eclipse* by Anil Hemrajani. A book for Java Enterprise Edition that shows how to use the Spring framework, Hibernate library, and Eclipse IDE to reduce the complexity of enterprise application programming.

Chapters and other material from many Sams Publishing Java books have been made freely available on www.informit.com, a website for information technology professionals produced in collaboration with Sams.

The Sams Publishing website, www.informit.com/sams, is a good place to see what's coming from Sams Publishing and other imprints of the Pearson Technology Group.

Oracle's Official Java Site

The Java software division of Oracle maintains three websites of interest to programmers and users of its language.

The Oracle Technology Network for Java Developers, which is published at http://www.oracle.com/technetwork/java, is the first place to visit when looking for Java-related information. New versions of the Java Development Kit and other programming resources are available for download, along with documentation for the entire Java class library. There's also a bug database, a user group directory, and support forums.

Java.net at www.java.net is a large community of Java programmers. You can start your own weblog focused on the language, create a new open-source project and host it for free on the site, and collaborate with other programmers.

Java.com at www.java.com promotes the benefits of the language to consumers and nonprogrammers. You can download the Java runtime environment from the site, which enables users to run programs created with Java on their computers. There's also a gallery showing examples of where Java is being used today.

Java Class Documentation

Perhaps the most useful part of Oracle's Java site is the documentation for every class, variable, and method in the Java class library. Thousands of pages are available online at no cost to you to show you how to use the classes in your programs.

To visit the class documentation for Java 7, go to http://download.oracle.com/javase/7/docs/api.

Other Java Websites

Because so much of the Java phenomenon was originally inspired by its use on web pages, a large number of websites focus on Java and Java programming.

This Book's Official Site

This book's official website is www.java24hours.com and is described fully in Appendix C, "This Book's Website."

Café au Lait

Elliotte Rusty Harold, the author of several excellent books on Java programming, offers Café au Lait, a long-running weblog covering Java news, product releases, and other sites of interest to programmers. The site is a terrific resource for people interested in Java and is published at www.cafeaulait.org. Harold also offers a list of frequently asked questions related to Java. Updates have been infrequent since he began an overhaul of the site, but it may have been relaunched by the time of this writing.

Workbench

I also publish a weblog, Workbench, which covers Java, Internet technology, computer books, and similar topics along with other subjects. You can find it at http://workbench.cadenhead.org.

Java 7 Developer Blog

Java developers Ben Evans and Martijn Verburg have been following the progress of Java 7 on their Java 7 Developer Blog, which is online at www.java7developer.com. There are code examples that demonstrate new features of the current language release, tips for using them effectively, and discussion of features expected to be in Java 8.

Other Java Weblogs

Hundreds of other weblogs cover Java programming, either as their primary focus or part of more diverse subject matter. The search engine IceRocket provides a tagged list of the latest weblogs to write about Java at www.icerocket.com/tag/java.

InformIT

The tech reference site InformIT, available at www.informit.com, is a comprehensive resource supported by the publisher of this book. The site devotes sections to more than a dozen subjects related to software development and the Internet. InformIT's Java section includes how-to articles and a beginner's reference.

Stack Overflow

The online community Stack Overflow is a place where programmers can ask questions and rate the answers provided by other users. The site is tagged, so you can narrow your search to the language or topic that's of interest. To see Java-related questions, visit http://stackoverflow.com/questions/tagged/java.

Java Review Service

The Java Review Service reviews new programs, components, and tools that are published on the Web, recognizing some as Top 1%, Top 5%, or Top 25%. Resources also are categorized by topic with a description of each resource and links to download the source code, if it is available. To visit, direct your web browser to www.jars.com.

JavaWorld Magazine

A magazine that has been around since the inception of the language, *JavaWorld*, publishes frequent tutorial articles along with Java development news and other features. There's also video and audio podcasts. Visit www.javaworld.com.

Developer.com's Java Directory

Because Java is an object-oriented language, it's easy to use resources created by other developers in your own programs. Before you start a Java project of any significance, you should scan the Web for resources you might be able to use in your program.

A good place to start is Developer.com's Java directory. This site catalogs Java programs, programming resources, and other information at www.developer.com/java.

Twitter

For a more interactive place to seek guidance from Java programmers, try Twitter, the popular microblog service used by millions of people to send short messages to their friends and others who follow them.

The #java hashtag identifies messages related to Java—though some might reference the island of Java or coffee because hashtags are informal and user-created.

To search Twitter for the most recent messages about Java, load http://search.twitter.com in a web browser and search for #java.

Job Opportunities

If you're one of those folks learning Java as a part of your plan to become a captain of industry, several of the resources listed in this appendix have a section devoted to job opportunities. Check out some of the Java-related job openings that might be available.

The job posting search engine indeed has a section devoted to Java jobs. Visit www.indeed.com/q-Java-jobs.html to see the latest help-wanted ads for programmers proficient in the language. Another good job site for Java programmers is Dice at www.dice.com.

Although it isn't specifically a Java employment resource, the CareerBuilder website enables you to search the job classifieds of more than two dozen job databases, including newspaper classifieds and many other sources. You can search more than 100,000 job postings using keywords such as Java, Internet, or snake charmer. Go to www.careerbuilder.com.

This Book's Website

As much as I'd like to think otherwise, there are undoubtedly some things you're not clear about after completing the 24 hours of this book.

Programming is a specialized technical field that throws strange concepts and jargon at you, such as "instantiation," "ternary operators," and "big- and little-endian byte order."

If you're unclear about any of the topics covered in the book, or if I was unclear about a topic (sigh), visit the book's website at www.java24hours.com for assistance (see Figure C.1).

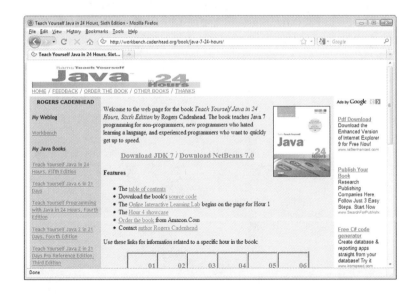

FIGURE C.1
The website for this book.

The website offers the following:

▸ Error corrections and clarifications—When errors are brought to my attention, they are described on the site with the corrected text and any other material that could help.

▸ Answers to reader questions—If readers have questions that aren't covered in this book's Q&A sections, many are presented on the site.

▸ The source code, class files, and resources required for all programs you create during the 24 hours of this book.

▸ Sample Java programs—Working versions of some programs featured in this book are available on the site.

▸ Solutions, including source code, for activities suggested at the end of each hour.

▸ Updated links to the sites mentioned in this book: If sites mentioned in the book have changed addresses and I know about the new link, I'll offer it on the website.

You also can send me email by visiting the book's site. Click the Feedback link, and you are taken to a page where you can send email directly from the Web.

Feel free to voice all opinions positive, negative, indifferent, undecided, enraged, enthused, peeved, amused, irked, intrigued, bored, captivated, enchanted, disenchanted, flummoxed, and flabbergasted.

—Rogers Cadenhead

APPENDIX D
Setting Up an Android Development Environment

Although Android apps are written in Java, they require more than just standard Java programming tools. Apps require the Java Development Kit, the Android Software Development Kit (SDK), an integrated development environment tailored to Android programming, and drivers for Android devices.

Eclipse is the most popular and best-supported integrated development environment (IDE) for Android.

In this appendix, you set up all of these tools and make sure they can work together to run an Android app. Each of the tools is free and can be downloaded over the Internet.

Getting Started

You can accomplish Android programming on the following operating systems:

▶ Windows XP or later

▶ Mac OS X 10.5.8 or later (x86)

▶ Linux

You need to have around 600MB of disk space to install the Android SDK and another 1.2GB for the Eclipse IDE.

At this point you already should have the Java Development Kit installed because it was used throughout the hours of the book in conjunction with NetBeans to run Java programs. Android requires JDK 5.0 or later.

If you still need the JDK for some reason, you can download it from http://oracle.com/technetwork/java/javase.

NOTE

Eclipse also is used in popular tutorials for Android programming such as *Sams Teach Yourself Android Application Development in 24 Hours*, Second Edition, by Lauren Darcey and Shane Conder (ISBN 0-672-33569-7). You can move from this book straight into that one because the tools being set up in this appendix are used in that book as well. I've read the book and recommend it highly as a follow-up to this one.

Installing Eclipse

Though other IDEs such as NetBeans offer Android development support, Eclipse has emerged as the most common choice for writing apps for Android. Android's developers have designated Eclipse as the preferred environment and employ it throughout their official documentation and tutorials.

Eclipse, like NetBeans, provides a graphical user interface for writing Java programs. You can use it to create any kind of Java program (and it supports other programming languages as well).

Android requires Eclipse 3.5 or later.

To download Eclipse, visit http://eclipse.org/downloads.

Several different versions of the IDE are available. Pick the Eclipse IDE for Java EE Developers. Java EE is the Java Enterprise Edition, and this version of Eclipse includes two things you use on Android projects: Eclipse's Java Development Tools (JDT) plug-in and the Web Tools Platform (WTP).

Eclipse is packaged as a ZIP archive file. There's no installation program to guide you through the process of setting it up on your computer. The ZIP archive contains a top-level `eclipse` folder that holds all of the files you need to run Eclipse.

Unzip this to the folder where you store programs. On my Windows system, I put it in the `Program Files (x86)` folder.

After unzipping the files, go to the `eclipse` folder you just created and look for the executable Eclipse application. Create a shortcut to this application and put it in your menu or somewhere else where you run programs, such as the desktop or taskbar.

Before launching Eclipse, you should install the Android SDK.

Installing Android SDK

The Android SDK is a free set of tools used to create, debug, and run Android applications. The SDK is used by Eclipse as you're working on Android apps.

You can download the SDK from the official Android website at http://developer.android.com/sdk. It's available for Windows, Mac OS, and Linux.

The Windows version is available as an installation wizard that walks you through the process of setting it up. The others, at the time of this writing, are a ZIP archive (Mac OS) or a TGZ archive (Linux).

Either with the installation wizard or a program that handles archives, put Android in a folder where you store programs—presumably the same parent folder where Eclipse's folder was placed. On my computer, I put it in `Program Files (x86)`.

The SDK includes an SDK and AVD Manager that will be used to update and enhance the SDK after it has been installed.

The manager, which is run from a menu command in Eclipse, makes it easy to keep the SDK current with each new release of the Android.

After you've installed the SDK, you're ready to run Eclipse for the first time.

Installing the Android Plug-in for Eclipse

The Eclipse IDE supports numerous programming languages and technologies, but all of them are not supported right away. The IDE is enhanced with plug-ins that provide the functionality you need.

Eclipse needs a plug-in to integrate the IDE with the Android SDK. The plug-in adds menu commands to the IDE interface related to Android and makes it possible to create and manage Android apps.

Follow these steps:

1. Launch Eclipse by using the shortcut you created or opening the folder where it was installed and running the executable application. The program loads with several windows and a menu bar and toolbar running across the top.

2. Select the menu command Help, Install New Software. The Install Wizard opens, which enables you to find and install plug-ins for Eclipse. The plug-ins are downloaded from software repositories, but Eclipse must know the location of a repository before it can find plug-ins there.

3. Click the Add button. The Add Repository dialog opens.

4. Leave the Name field blank. In the Location field, enter the web address `http://dl-ssl.google.com/android/eclipse/` and click OK. A Developer Tools item should appear in the Install window, as shown in Figure D.1.

5. Expand this item by clicking the arrow next to it. You see several subitems for Android-related tools you can add to Eclipse, as shown in Figure D.1.

FIGURE D.1
Adding new plug-ins to Eclipse.

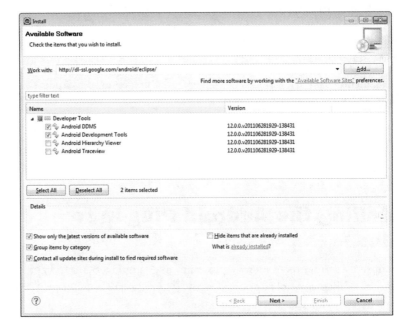

6. Select the checkboxes for Android DDMS and Android Development Tools. (You also can add the other tools such as the Android Hierarchy Viewer, but you won't see them at the start of your Android programming.)

7. Click Next to review the licensing agreement and check whether anything else needs to be installed. When you reach the end of the wizard, click Finish.

After the plug-in has been installed, close Eclipse and run it again.

Your preferences in Eclipse must be checked to make sure the IDE can find the Android SDK.

To check this, undertake the following:

1. Choose the menu command Window, Preferences. The Preferences dialog opens with a list of categories running along the left side.

2. Click Android to see the general Android preferences.

3. Make sure the SDK Location field contains the folder where the Android SDK was installed. If it doesn't, click Browse to navigate to that folder and choose it with a file folder dialog.

4. After the SDK has been located, you see a table with a list of SDK targets, as depicted in Figure D.2.

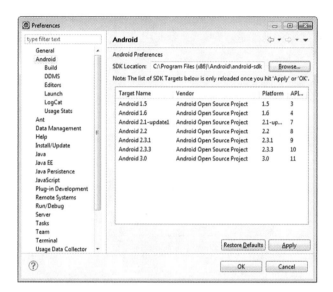

FIGURE D.2
Setting Android preferences in Eclipse.

These targets are the versions of Android you can create apps for with the SDK. Android apps must designate the earliest version of Android they are created to work on.

Click OK to close the dialog and save your preferences.

With the Android plug-in installed and the SDK located properly, you should find new menu commands in Eclipse. One of them is Window, Android SDK, and AVD Manager.

If this command is absent, close Eclipse and restart it.

You can use the manager to keep the SDK up to date. Choose Window, Android SDK, and AVD Manager. The manager opens.

Click Installed Packages in the left pane to see which SDK components are installed on your computer.

Click Available Packages to see what else is available that hasn't been installed yet.

Check a box for one of the packages. Eclipse checks the contents of that package and presents check boxes for the specific things you need to install, as shown in Figure D.3.

FIGURE D.3
Installing new packages for the Android SDK.

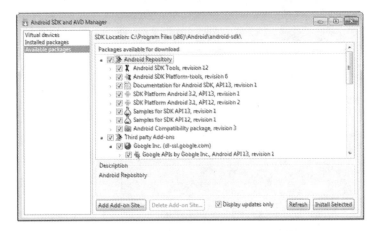

When you have checked the boxes for packages you want and have unchecked the ones you don't, click Install Selected.

You should periodically check for new updates. Android is being developed at a furious pace as new phones and other devices hit the market and the SDK must support them.

Setting Up Your Phone

The Android SDK includes an emulator that acts like an Android phone and can run the apps you create. This comes in handy as you're writing an app because you can get it working in a test environment, but at some point you need to see how it works on an actual Android phone (or other device).

You can deploy apps you write with the SDK on an Android device over your computer's USB connection. You can use the same cord you use to transfer files to and from the device.

Before connecting the cord, you must enable USB debugging on the phone by following these steps:

1. On the phone's Home screen, choose Menu, Settings. The Settings app opens.

2. Choose Applications, Development and check the USB debugging box.

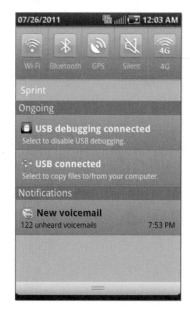

Other devices might have this option elsewhere in the settings. It is called something like USB connection mode, USB debugging, or the like. The Android site at http://developer.android.com has documentation for how to set this for different Android devices.

Connect the USB cord to your computer and the other end to your phone. A small bug-like Android icon should appear along the top edge of the device alongside the time and icons for connection bars and the battery.

Drag the top bar down. You should see the USB Debugging Connected and USB Connected messages (see Figure D.4).

FIGURE D.4
Using an Android phone in USB debugging mode.

This sets up your phone, but your computer also might require configuration to be able to connect to the device. If you have never connected to the phone over a USB cord, check your phone's documentation for how to do this. You might need to install a driver from a CD that came with the phone or the manufacturer's website.

On Windows, the Android SDK and AVD Manager run from within Eclipse, and you can use them to download the USB Driver Package, a collection of drivers for various phones and other devices, and other packages related to your device. Choose Window, Android SDK, and AVD Manager to see what's available.

During Hour 24, you use the Android development tools to create and run an Android app. If everything's set up correctly, it should run properly on both the emulator and an Android phone.

INDEX

NUMERICS

SYMBOLS

A

Sams **Teach Yourself**

When you only have time
for the answers™

Whatever your need and whatever your time frame, there's a Sams **Teach Yourself** book for you. With a Sams **Teach Yourself** book as your guide, you can quickly get up to speed on just about any new product or technology—in the absolute shortest period of time possible. Guaranteed.

Learning how to do new things with your computer shouldn't be tedious or time-consuming. Sams **Teach Yourself** makes learning anything quick, easy, and even a little bit fun.

C++ in 24 Hours

Jesse Liberty
Rogers Cadenhead
ISBN-13: 978-0-672-33331-6

Visual Basic 2010 in 24 Hours Complete Starter Kit

James Foxall
ISBN-13: 978-0-672-33113-8

Visual C# 2010 in 24 Hours Complete Starter Kit

Scott Dorman
ISBN-13: 978-0-672-33101-5

Android Application Development in 24 Hours

Lauren Darcey
Shane Conder
ISBN-13: 978-0-672-33569-3

iPhone Application Development in 24 Hours

John Ray
ISBN-13: 978-0-672-33576-1

FREE Online Edition

Your purchase of **Sams Teach Yourself Java in 24 Hours (Covering Java 7 and Android)** includes access to a free online edition for 45 days through the Safari Books Online subscription service. Nearly every Sams book is available online through Safari Books Online, along with more than 5,000 other technical books and videos from publishers such as Addison-Wesley Professional, Cisco Press, Exam Cram, IBM Press, O'Reilly, Prentice Hall, and Que.

SAFARI BOOKS ONLINE allows you to search for a specific answer, cut and paste code, download chapters, and stay current with emerging technologies.

Activate your FREE Online Edition at www.informit.com/safarifree

> **STEP 1:** Enter the coupon code: LXRAOVH.

> **STEP 2:** New Safari users, complete the brief registration form.
> Safari subscribers, just log in.

If you have difficulty registering on Safari or accessing the online edition, please e-mail customer-service@safaribooksonline.com